November 2014

Further Praise for *Inside the House of Money*
from Hedge Fund Investors

"Drobny has done a great job of capturing the inner workings of macro trading by interviewing some of the most interesting people in the field today. This book is a treat and a must-read if you want to understand how the market's best manage their portfolios."

> —Mark Taborsky, Managing Director,
> Absolute Return and Fixed Income,
> Stanford Management Company

"*Inside the House of Money* provides a unique insight into the hedge fund business. For those who think hedge funds are mysterious, here they will find them transparent. Readers will be fascinated to see that there are so many ways to make money from an idea."

> —Bernard Sabrier, Chairman, Unigestion

"With its behind-the-scenes perspective and macro focus, this book is an entertaining, educational read, and also fills a substantial gap in hedge fund literature."

> —Jim Berens, Cofounder and Managing Director,
> Pacific Alternative Asset Management
> Company (PAAMCO)

"An exciting, fast-paced insider's look at the elite, often mysterious world of high finance. This book is the real deal. An absolute must-read for every endowment, foundation, or pension fund officer considering investing with hedge funds."

> —Michael Barry, Chief Investment Officer,
> University of Maryland Endowment

INSIDE

THE

HOUSE

OF

MONEY

Top Hedge Fund Traders on Profiting in the Global Markets

STEVEN DROBNY

Foreword by Joseph G. Nicholas

WILEY

John Wiley & Sons, Inc.

Published by John Wiley & Sons, Inc., Hoboken, New Jersey
Published simultaneously in Canada

For general information on our other products and services or for technical support, please contact our Customer Care Department within the United States at (800) 762-2974, outside the United States at (317) 572-3993 or fax (317) 572-4002.

Wiley also publishes its books in a variety of electronic formats. Some content that appears in print may not be available in electronic books. For more information about Wiley products, visit our web site at www.wiley.com.

Library of Congress Cataloging-in-Publication Data:

Drobny, Steven.
    Inside the house of money : top hedge fund traders on profiting in the global markets / by Steven Drobny.
       p.   cm.
    Includes bibliographical references.
    ISBN-13: 978-0-471-79447-9 (cloth)
    ISBN-10: 0-471-79447-3 (cloth)
    1. Hedge funds   2. Mutual funds.   3. Investment advisors.   4. Portfolio management.   5. Investments.   I. Title.
    HG4530.D74 2006
    332.64'524—dc22

                                                              2005035952

Printed in the United States of America.

10   9   8   7   6   5   4   3   2   1

The social objective of skilled investment should be to defeat the dark forces of time and ignorance which envelop our future.

—*John Maynard Keynes*

Once we realize that imperfect understanding is the human condition, there is no shame in being wrong, only in failing to correct our mistakes.

—*George Soros*

After a certain high level of technical skill is achieved, science and art tend to coalesce in esthetics, plasticity, and form. The greatest scientists are always artists as well.

—*Albert Einstein*

CONTENTS

FOREWORD

I first met Steven Drobny several years ago at an exclusive hedge fund conference run by Drobny Global Advisors, an independent global macro research and advisory firm that he runs with his business partner, Dr. Andres Drobny (no relation). Although hedge fund managers have a reputation for being reluctant to discuss their market views and trading strategies, several dozen of the top managers sat in the same room, presented favorite trades, and engaged in lively debate about world markets.

What I found most interesting about having all these managers gathered in one place was that a different dimension of global macro investing was revealed. Global macro is a vast strategy comprising many substrategies, styles, and specialties. Each global macro hedge fund manager approaches the world of trading opportunities in a unique way, playing to his or her particular strengths. Each represents a facet of global macro, but only as a group does a picture of the whole of global macro take shape.

This book is unique in that it lets readers into the room. Because it is done in interview format, it captures an element of frank debate. And because it offers a broad selection of the top managers within global macro, the debate is multidimensional.

Readers will quickly find that no two managers are alike. There are classically educated ones and others who left school at an early age, ones who have been trading for themselves their entire careers and others who rose through the ranks of traditional banks, ones who sit on the pulse of the markets in major financial centers and others who prefer to remain far away.

For curious investors, traders, and money managers, this book provides an inside look at how the best fund managers approach world markets and offers subtle insights into how these managers approach their craft. For anyone in the business of investing, it will lead to a higher understanding of global market dynamics.

For the lay reader, this book offers a rare glimpse into the somewhat closed world of hedge funds, where high intensity and enormous stakes are part of everyday life. Instead of indulging the glamorous image of hedge fund managers often presented by the media, this book, through its first-person accounts, illuminates a far different world of thoughtful, careful, yet smart and creative professionals working hard to increase their investors' worth wherever in the world the opportunity presents itself.

Joseph G. Nicholas
Founder and Chairman of HFR Group
Chicago
January 2006

PREFACE

Hedge funds are everywhere today. The term *hedge fund* used to conjure images of speculators hunting for absolute returns in any market in the world, using any instrument or style to capture their prey. The managers of the original multibillion-dollar mega-funds, such as George Soros or Julian Robertson, became well-known figures because of their speculative prowess. Yet they were also accused of such modern ills as attacks on developed world central banks and capital flight in the third world.

After the stock market crash of 2000, hedge funds came into their own by proving to be a superior asset management vehicle. As most global investors were suffering year after year of negative returns, hedge funds performed. This encouraged a wave of institutional money to flow into such alternative investment vehicles. At the same time, given the superior flexibility and attractive compensation structure of hedge funds, the most talented financial minds migrated over in what became a mass exodus from The City and Wall Street.

As hedge funds have matured, they have become more of a business. The tremendous inflow of capital has altered the freewheeling image of more than a decade ago. This shift has spawned a more formalized industry where managers often implement rather narrow, specific strategies and where investors in hedge funds no longer tolerate down years or even down months of performance. Competition has smoothed returns, both on the upside and the downside, and lower returns have led to questions about hedge fund fees.

Amidst this evolution and change in the hedge fund business, one strategy has remained true to its original mandate of absolute return investing, seeking outsized returns from investments anywhere in the world, in any asset class and in any instrument: global macro.

Global macro investing is still a relatively unknown and misunderstood area of money management but increasingly of interest. Given that my firm, Drobny Global Advisors, advises global macro hedge funds on market strategy and counts most of the top funds as clients, I am often asked the question, "What is global macro?"

The classic definition—a discretionary investment style that leverages long and short positions in any asset class (equities, fixed income, currencies, and commodities), in any instrument (cash or derivatives), in any market around the world with the goal of profiting from macroeconomic trends—often fails to satisfy. What I think people are really asking is, "How does one define what the top global macro money managers actually do?"

That's a trickier question. Global macro is the most difficult of the hedge fund strategies to define, simply because there is no definition. Just as the term *hedge fund* can be used to describe a wide variety of investing styles, so too *global macro* does not mean just one thing. Global macro has no mandate, is not easily broken down into numbers or formulas, and style drift is built into the strategy as managers often move in and out of various investing disciplines depending on market conditions. Even professional hedge fund investors struggle at times to decipher what global macro managers actually do.

To help my inquisitors, I searched for books and research papers on the topic to recommend but found very little of value. This is surprising given the tremendous growth of assets and sophistication in the hedge fund business over the past few years and the fact that the public still associate hedge funds with the doyen of global macro, George Soros.

Another reason the lack of literature on global macro is odd is that global macro variables influence all investment strategies. When a mutual fund increases its cash position, an endowment allocates to real estate, or an equity long/short hedge fund goes net long stocks, they are all making implicit global macro calls—even if they are not aware of it. Their investment decisions are subject to changes in the world economy, the U.S. dollar, global equities, global interest rates, global growth, geopolitical issues, energy prices, and a multitude of variables of which they may never have heard. As such, an understanding of the global macro picture would seem of the utmost importance to the wider investment community.

This book attempts to fill the gap in the literature. With the dearth of quality information out there about global macro, the next logical step was to speak directly to the smartest global macro managers I knew. With the benefit of the access afforded through my business, I was able to draw on a host of resources to do just that.

The original plan for these discussions with practitioners was simply to discover what global macro means to them, but the conversations proved to be much deeper. I learned how the best minds in the business think about risk, portfolio construction, history, politics, central bankers, globalization, trading, competition, investors, hiring, the evolution of the hedge fund business, and a variety of other details. As a result, a more involved research project developed.

After these initial discussions, I set out to speak with a broader selection of today's top global macro hedge fund managers. In search of the widest possible variety of views, I interviewed managers who have different product specialties, diverse backgrounds, and varied mandates. I chose to focus on fundamental discretionary managers rather than those who depend solely on technical patterns or computer-driven trading models, because fundamental discretionary managers rely on their own judgment above and beyond any analytical tools they may employ.

As it turns out, there is no simple way to define what the top global macro managers actually do. Rather, global macro is an approach to markets in the way that science is an approach to the unknown. As in science, many different approaches can be used to tackle a question and, while many fail, several wildly different paths can lead to success. It is in the course of the development and testing of market hypotheses where the art or the genius lies.

Although global macro funds tend to be idiosyncratic, I found that all global macro managers begin with a broad top-down approach to the world before drilling down into the fine details. It is in the process of drilling down where they differentiate themselves, ending in a wide variety of specialties. In a sense, global macro is evolving into global micro, whereby today's managers derive their investment edge through having the latitude to express their micro expertise in various specialties and markets.

I found other similarities among the managers in that they all love what they do, are incredibly hardworking, and are extremely smart. Yet despite their intelligence and strong opinions, they all seemed open-minded and flexible when it came to being challenged by the market or their colleagues. This flexibility and willingness to admit that they could be wrong is, in a sense, how good hedge fund managers limit their downside risk and cut off the left side of the return distribution. When it comes down to it, no matter the specific style of the manager, the goal of all global macro hedge fund managers is to produce superior risk-adjusted absolute returns for their investors and themselves.

In the end, this book does not answer the question, "What is global macro?" Instead, it offers an inside look at how some of today's best and the brightest practitioners think about their area of expertise. Hopefully, this book will simultaneously help to demystify what today's global macro managers actually do and show why there are so few who truly excel in this endeavor. If you learn as much from reading these interviews as I did conducting them, I will consider this research project a success.

I begin with a word from Joseph G. Nicholas, founder and chairman of HFR Group, who offers a professional investor's perspective of global macro. Nicholas has been investing in global macro hedge funds since the 1980s and now manages over $4 billion in hedge fund assets via HFR Asset Management. He founded the leading hedge fund data firm, Hedge Fund Research, in 1992 and has since authored several books on hedge funds and hedge fund investing.

Next, I briefly highlight some of the key historical events in global macro to offer background and perspective which should prove helpful while reading the interviews. I attempt to show the evolution of global macro from its origins with John Maynard Keynes to George Soros, and then on to the future where increased competition and specialization are leading today's global macro manager into the realm of global micro.

Finally, we go "inside the house of money" via a collection of 13 interviews with top global macro practitioners, each of whom offers a unique perspective on global markets. The interviews were conducted all over the world between October 2004 and July 2005.

CHAPTER 1

INTRODUCTION TO GLOBAL MACRO HEDGE FUNDS

By Joseph G. Nicholas
Founder and Chairman of HFR Group

The global macro approach to investing attempts to generate outsized positive returns by making leveraged bets on price movements in equity, currency, interest rate, and commodity markets. The *macro* part of the name derives from managers' attempts to use macroeconomic principles to identify dislocations in asset prices, while the *global* part suggests that such dislocations are sought anywhere in the world.

The global macro hedge fund strategy has the widest mandate of all hedge fund strategies whereby managers have the ability to take positions in any market or instrument. Managers usually look to take positions that have limited downside risk and potentially large rewards, opting for either a concentrated risk-taking approach or a more diversified portfolio style of money management.

Global macro trades are classified as either outright *directional*, where a manager bets on discrete price movements, such as long U.S. dollar index or short Japanese bonds, or *relative value*, where two similar assets are paired on the long and short sides to exploit a perceived relative mispricing, such as long emerging European equities versus short U.S. equities, or long 29-year German Bunds versus short 30-year German Bunds. A macro trader's approach to finding profitable trades is classified as either *discretionary*, meaning managers' subjective opinions of market conditions lead them to the trade, or *systematic*, meaning a quantitative or rule-based approach is taken. Profits are derived from correctly anticipating price trends and capturing spread moves.

Generally, macro traders look for unusual price fluctuations that can be referred to as far-from-equilibrium conditions. If prices are believed to fall on a bell curve, it is only when prices move more than one standard deviation away from the mean that macro traders deem that market to present an opportunity. This usually happens when market participants' perceptions differ widely from the actual state of underlying economic fundamentals, at which point a persistent price trend or spread move can develop. By correctly identifying when and where the market has swung furthest from equilibrium, a macro trader can profit by investing in that situation and then getting out once the imbalance has been corrected. Traditionally, timing is everything for macro traders. Because macro traders can produce significantly large gains or losses due to their use of leverage, they are often portrayed in the media as pure speculators.

Many macro traders would argue that global macroeconomic issues and variables influence all investing strategies. In that sense, macro traders can utilize their wide mandate to their advantage by moving from market to market and opportunity to opportunity in order to generate the outsized returns expected from their investor base. Some global macro managers believe that profits can and should be derived from other, seemingly unrelated investment approaches such as equity long/short, investing in distressed securities, and various arbitrage strategies. Macro traders recognize that other investment styles can be profitable in some macro environments but not others. While many specialist strategies present liquidity issues for other, more limited investing styles in charge of substantial assets, macro managers can take advantage of these occasional opportunities by seamlessly moving capital into a variety of different investment styles when warranted. The famous global macro manager George Soros once said, "I don't play the game by a particular set of rules; I look for changes in the rules of the game."

SUMMARY

Global macro traders are not limited to particular markets or products but are instead free of certain constraints that limit other hedge fund strategies. This allows for efficient allocation of risk capital globally to opportunities where the risk versus reward trade-off is particularly compelling. Whereas significant assets under management can prove an issue for some more focused investing styles, it is not a particular hindrance to global macro hedge funds given their flexibility and the depth and liquidity in the markets they trade. Although macro traders are often considered risky speculators due to the large swings in gains and losses that can occur from their leveraged directional bets, when viewed as a group, global macro hedge fund managers have produced superior risk-adjusted returns over time.

From January 1990 to December 2005, global macro hedge funds have posted an average annualized return of 15.62 percent, with an annualized standard deviation of 8.25 percent. Macro funds returned over

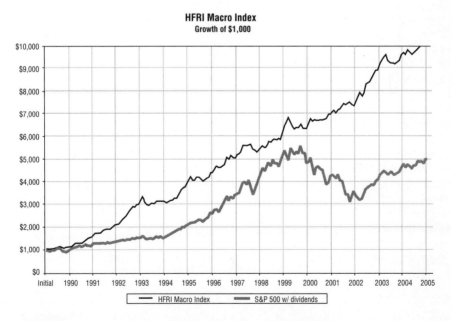

FIGURE 1.1 Comparison of HFRI Macro Index with S&P 500
Source: HFR.

500 basis points more than the return generated by the S&P 500 index for the same period with more than 600 basis points less volatility. Global macro hedge funds also exhibit a low correlation to the general equity market. Since 1990, macro funds have returned a positive performance in 15 out of 16 years, with only 1994 posting a loss of 4.31 percent. (*See Figure 1.1.*)

In light of the correlation, volatility, and return characteristics, global macro hedge fund strategies are a welcome addition to any portfolio.

CHAPTER 2

THE HISTORY OF GLOBAL MACRO HEDGE FUNDS

The path to today's style of global macro investing was paved by John Maynard Keynes a century ago. For an economist, Keynes was a renaissance man. Not only was he the father of modern macroeconomic theory but he also advised world governments, was involved in the Bloomsbury intellectual circle, and helped design the architecture of today's global macroeconomic infrastructure by way of the World Bank and International Monetary Fund. At the same time, he was also a successful investor, using his own macroeconomic principles as an edge to extract profit from the markets. Some say he was the first of the modern global macro money managers.

In the words of Keynes' biographer Robert Skidelsky, "[Keynes] was an economist; he was an investor; he was a patron of the arts and a lover of ballet. He was a speculator. He was also confidant of prime ministers. He had a civil service career. So he lived a very full life in all those ways."

Keynes speculated with his personal account, invested on behalf of various investment and insurance trusts and even ran a college endowment, each of which had different goals, time horizons, and product mandates. Upon his death, he left a substantial personal fortune primarily a result of his financial market activities.

Evidence of Keynes' investing acumen can be found in the returns of the King's College Cambridge endowment, the College Chest, for which he had total discretion as the First Bursar. A publicly available track record shows he returned an average of 13.2 percent per annum from 1928 to 1945, a time when the broad UK equity index lost an average of 0.5 percent per annum.

(*See Figure 2.1.*) This was quite a feat considering the 1929 stock market crash, the Great Depression, and World War II occurred over that time frame.

But, like all great investors, Keynes first had to learn some difficult lessons. He was not immune to blowups in spite of his superior intellect and understanding of global markets. In the early 1900s, he successfully speculated in global currencies on margin before switching to the commodity markets. Then, during the commodity slump of 1929, his personal account was completely wiped out by a margin call. After the 1929 setback, his greatest successes came from investing globally in equities but he continued to speculate in bonds and commodities.

Skidelsky adds, "His investment philosophy . . . changed in line with his evolving economic theories. He learned a lot of his theory from his experience as an investor and this theory in turn modified his practice as an investor."

Keynes' distaste of floating currencies (ironically his original vehicle of choice for speculating) eventually led him to participate in the construction of a global fixed currency regime at Bretton Woods in 1945. The post-World War II economic landscape, coupled with the ensuing Cold War–induced peace and the relative stability fostered by Bretton Woods, led to a boom in

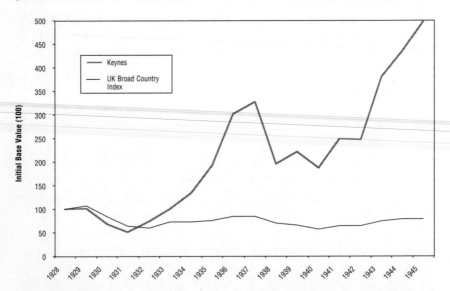

FIGURE 2.1   King's College Cambridge Chest Fund and the UK Broad Country Equity Index
Source: Motley Fool.

THE HISTORY OF GLOBAL MACRO HEDGE FUNDS

developed-country equity markets starting in 1945 and lasting until the early 1970s. During that time, there were few better opportunities in the global markets than buying and holding stocks. It wasn't until the breakdown of the Bretton Woods Agreement in 1971, and the subsequent decline in the U.S. dollar, that the investment universe again offered the opportunities that spawned the next generation of global macro managers.

POLITICIANS AND SPECULATORS

Recent history is riddled with examples of politicians attempting to place blame on speculators for shortcomings in their own policies, and the breakdown of Bretton Woods was no exception. When the currency regime unraveled, President Nixon attempted to lay blame on speculators for "waging an all-out war on the dollar." In truth, his own inflationary policies are more often cited as the underlying problem, with speculators a mere symptom of the problem.

As Andres Drobny (Drobny Global Advisors) describes it in his interview:

> Speculators definitely don't [drive markets]. There's an old debate in economics as to whether speculators are deviation "dampeners" or deviation "amplifiers." Milton Friedman, the eternal optimist, argued that if people see an anomaly, they'll pick on it and limit how far that anomaly goes. I think both are right at different times. Sometimes speculators add to volatility; other times they dampen it. The important point is, they don't influence the trend. Underlying pressures combined with policy decisions drive market events.

THE NEXT GENERATION OF GLOBAL MACRO MANAGERS

The next round of global macro managers emerged out of the breakdown of the Bretton Woods fixed currency regime, which untethered the world's markets. With currencies freely floating, a new dimension was added to the investment decision landscape. Exchange rate volatility was introduced while new tradable products were rapidly being developed. Prior to the breakdown of Bretton Woods, most active trading was done in the liquid equity and physical commodity markets. As such, two different streams of global macro hedge fund managers emerged out of these two worlds in parallel.

The Equity Stream

One stream of global macro hedge fund managers emerged out of the international equity trading and investing world.

Until 1971, the existing hedge funds were primarily focused on equities and modeled after the very first hedge fund started by Alfred Winslow Jones in 1949. Jones's original structure is roughly the same as most hedge funds today: It was domiciled offshore, largely unregulated, had less than 100 investors, was capitalized with a significant amount of the manager's money, and charged a performance fee of 20 percent. (Allegedly, the now standard 20 percent performance fee was modeled by Jones upon the example of another class of traders who demanded a profit sharing arrangement that provided the proper incentive for taking risk: Fifteenth-century Venetian merchants would receive 20 percent of the profits from their patrons upon returning from a successful voyage.)

The A.W. Jones & Co. trading strategy was designed to mitigate global macro influences on his stock picking. Jones would run an equally weighted "hedged" book of longs and shorts in an attempt to eliminate the effects of movements by the broader market (i.e., stock market beta). Once currencies became freely floating, though, a new element of risk was added to the equation for international equities. Whereas managers using the Jones model sought to neutralize global macro–induced moves, the global macro managers who emerged from the international equity arena sought to take advantage of these new opportunities. Foreign exchange risk was treated as a whole new tradable asset class, especially in the context of foreign equities where currency exposure became a major factor in performance attribution.

Managers from this stream such as George Soros, Jim Rogers, Michael Steinhardt, and eventually Julian Robertson (Tiger Management) were all too willing to use currency movements as an additional opportunity set to be capitalized upon. They were already successful global long/short equity investors whose experience in global markets made the shift to currencies and foreign bonds seamless in the post–Bretton Woods world. In the early days of this new paradigm, these managers saw little in the way of competition. Over time, though, as their superior returns attracted larger amounts of capital, the funds were increasingly forced to trade deeper, more liquid markets and thus move beyond their core competence of stock picking. At the same time, competition intensified.

The Commodity Stream

The other stream of global macro managers developed out of the physical commodity and futures trading world that was centered in the trading pits of Chicago. It developed independently although simultaneously with the equity stream.

The biggest global macro names to emerge from the commodity world, however, did not come from the Chicago epicenter but instead learned their craft from the most forward thinking of commodity and futures trading firms: Commodities Corporation of Princeton, New Jersey.

The founder of Commodities Corporation (CC), Helmut Weymar, is said by many to be the father of the commodity stream of global macro. Weymar, an M.I.T. PhD and former star cocoa trader for Nabisco, founded CC along with his mentor and legendary trader Amos Hostetter, wheat speculator Frank Vannerson, and his former professor, Nobel Prize winner Paul Samuelson, with the goal of providing an ideal environment where traders could take risk without worrying about administration and other distractions. The management of CC had a solid understanding of risk taking and offered an incredibly open framework in which traders thrived. CC incubated or served as an important early source of funding for some of the best known global macro managers of all time, including Bruce Kovner (Caxton), Paul Tudor Jones (Tudor Investment Corporation), Louis Bacon (Moore Capital), Michael Marcus, Grenville Craig, Ed Seykota, Glen Olink, Morry Markowitz, and Willem Kooyker (Blenheim Capital), to name a few.

Commodities Corporation was originally set up to take advantage of tradable physical commodities, and traders were siloed such that each focused exclusively on one commodity market. As world trade opened up in the 1970s and 1980s, global macroeconomic influences started to play a larger and more important role in determining the price movements in the commodity markets. Being accustomed to the sometimes extreme volatility, and having the knowledge of the macroeconomic influences on their specific markets, the firm easily moved into trading currency and financial futures as those markets developed. For CC traders, as long as there was volatility, they were indifferent to the underlying asset.

Commodities Corporation traders involved in all products became known as "generalists." While CC founder Hostetter had been trading stocks, bonds, and commodities since the 1930s, the first successful generalists to emerge at CC were plywood and cotton trader Michael Marcus and

his young assistant Bruce Kovner. Kovner especially pushed CC toward a
more global macro style of trading, which meant trading all products, anytime, anywhere. He also started another trend in the organization, namely,
leaving the firm to set up his own fund. Started with the blessing and initial
capital from CC, Kovner's fund, Caxton, is now one of the largest hedge
fund management groups in the world as measured by assets under management. Likewise, several other CC alumni are managing some of the largest
hedge fund complexes today. Many credit their success to lessons learned at
CC about risk management, leverage, and trading. As a testament to its success, Commodities Corporation was purchased by Goldman Sachs in 1997
after evolving into more of a fund of hedge funds investment vehicle, with
many allocations still out to original CC traders.

MAJOR GLOBAL MACRO MARKET EVENTS

For the purposes of this book, we are going to use the experiences of the
global macro pioneers, such as Soros, Robertson, and Tudor Jones to discuss some of the important episodes in the global macro arena over the
past few decades, mainly because macro markets were dominated by these
managers until 2000.

What is interesting about these episodic moments in global macro history is not what happened to the macro trading community, but rather
that the lessons learned from these events served as the education for today's generation of global macro managers.

Today's managers, many of whom are alumni of the original global
macro fund managers, earned their stripes during the ensuing crises and
events. While Keynes had his 1929 event to learn about the positive and
negative effects of trading on leverage, which he subsequently incorpo-
rated into his trading style and translated into future success, today's managers had the 1987 stock market crash, the sterling crisis of 1992, the bond
market rout of 1994, the Asia crisis of 1997, the Russia/LTCM crisis of
1998, and finally the dot-com bust of 2000. (*See Figure 2.2.*) The ways that
today's managers look at markets, control risk, and manage their businesses
include lessons learned through these important events.

The Stock Market Crash of 1987

Although the U.S. stock market crash of October 1987 is now a mere blip
on long-term stock market charts (*see Figure 2.3*), as indexes fully recov-

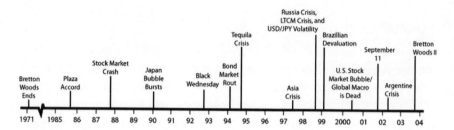

FIGURE 2.2   Major Global Macro Market Events since 1971
Source: DGA.

ered only two years later, the intensity of Black Monday for traders who lived through it has certainly left its mark. Most notably, the notions of liquidity risk and fat tails were introduced to the wider investment community without mercy. Entire portfolios and money management businesses were obliterated on that day as margin calls went unfunded. Indeed, even so-called "portfolio insurance" hedges didn't work as the futures and options markets became unhinged from the cash market.

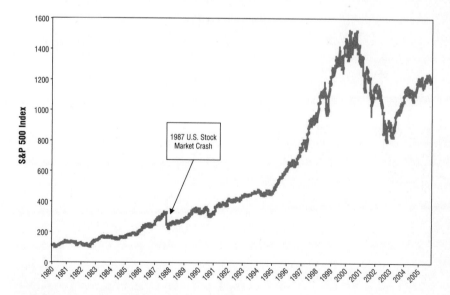

FIGURE 2.3   S&P 500 Index, 1980–2005
Source: Bloomberg.

FAT TAILS

"Fat tails" are anomalies in normal distributions, whereby observed outcomes differ from those suggested by the distribution. In other words, extreme occurrences can be more frequent than otherwise theoretically expected. Because markets are governed by human behavior, under- and overreactions to various data and indicators and the herding instincts of participants sometimes push prices to extremes, explaining the prevalence of such extreme but infrequent events in reality.

Yra Harris (Praxis Trading) explains in his interview later in this book what he saw that day on the floor of the Chicago Mercantile Exchange:

It was eerie and scary because you just didn't know the extent of everything. People were clearly hurting badly but you just didn't know how badly. I've traded through a lot of devaluations and debacles but I've never seen as many people pulled off the floor by clearinghouses as I did that day. The pit was practically empty, which actually turned into a great opportunity to trade the S&Ps. I went into the S&P pit and starting making markets because nobody else was. Spreads were so unbelievably wide that it was pretty easy to make money just scalping around. Honestly, I couldn't help it.

Global macro managers from the equity stream, including George Soros, got hurt in the 1987 crash. Just prior to the crash, *Fortune* magazine ran a cover story entitled, "Are Stocks Too High?" in which Soros disagreed with the notion. Days later, Soros lost $300 million as stocks collapsed (yet Soros Fund Management still ended the year up 14 percent). Meanwhile, Tiger Management posted its first down year (−1.4 percent) only one year after an *Institutional Investor* article, noting Tiger's 43 percent average annual returns since inception in 1980, sparked the next wave of hedge fund launches.

For global macro traders from the commodities stream, however, the 1987 crash served as a windfall event. Paul Tudor Jones in particular was elevated to star status when he famously caught the short side of the stock market and the long side of the bond market by identifying similarities between technical trading patterns in 1987 and the great crash of 1929. (*See Figure 2.4.*) Jones's Tudor Investment Corporation returned 62 percent for the month in October 1987 and 200 percent for the year.

The year 1987 also marked the introduction of a new Federal Reserve chairman in Alan Greenspan. Greenspan came into office in August 1987 and his first act a few weeks later was to raise the discount rate by 50 basis points. This unexpected tightening created volatility and uncertainty in the markets as traders adjusted to the style of a new Fed chairman. Some argue that Greenspan's rate hike was actually the cause of the subsequent equity market meltdown a month-and-a-half later. Immediately after the stock market crash, Greenspan flooded the market with liquidity, initiating a process that came to be known as the "Greenspan put." The Greenspan put is an implicit option that the Fed writes anytime equity markets stumble, in hopes of bailing out investors.

Former Federal Reserve chairman William McChesney Martin famously observed that the job of a central banker is to "take away the punch bowl just when the party is getting started." Alan Greenspan, on the other hand, seemed to interpret his role as needing to intervene only as the partygoers are stumbling home. As he has claimed, bubbles can only be clearly observed in hindsight, such that the role of a central banker is to

FIGURE 2.4   Dow Jones Industrial Average: The Late 1920s versus the Late 1980s
Source: Bloomberg.

soften the impact of the bubble's bursting rather than to take away the fuel for the party.

Black Wednesday 1992

The term *global macro* first entered the general public's vocabulary on Black Wednesday, or September 16, 1992. Black Wednesday, as the sterling crisis is called, was the day the British government was forced to withdraw the pound sterling from the European Exchange Rate Mechanism (ERM)—a mere two years after joining—sending the currency into a free fall. The popular press credited global macro hedge fund manager George Soros with forcing the pound out of the ERM. As Scott Bessent (Bessent Capital), head of the London office of Soros Fund Management at the time, noted, "Interestingly, no one had ever heard of George Soros before this. I remember going to play tennis with him at his London house on the Saturday after it happened. It was as if he were a rock star with cameramen and paparazzi waiting out front."

The ERM was introduced in 1979 with the goals of reducing exchange rate variability and achieving monetary stability within Europe in preparation for the Economic and Monetary Union (EMU) and ultimately the introduction of a single currency, the euro, which culminated in 1999. The process was seen as politically driven, attempting to tie Germany's fate to the rest of Europe and economically anchor the rest of Europe to the Bundesbank's successful low interest rate, low inflation policies.

The United Kingdom tardily joined the ERM in 1990 at a central parity rate of 2.95 deutsche marks to the pound, which many believed to be too strong. To comply with ERM rules, the UK government was required to keep the pound in a trading band within 6 percent of the parity rate. An arguably artificially strong currency in the United Kingdom soon led the country into a recession. Meanwhile, Germany was suffering inflationary effects from the integration of East and West Germany, which led to high interest rates. Despite a recession, the United Kingdom was forced to keep interest rates artificially high, in line with German rates, in order to maintain the currency regime. In September 1992, as the sterling/mark exchange rate approached the lower end of the trading band, traders increasingly sold pounds against deutsche marks, forcing the Bank of England to intervene and buy an unlimited amount of pounds in accordance with ERM rules. Fears of a larger currency devaluation sent British companies scrambling to hedge their currency exposure by selling pounds, further compounding pressures on the system.

In an effort to discourage speculation, UK Chancellor Norman Lamont raised interest rates from 10 percent to 12 percent, making the pound more expensive to borrow and more attractive to lend. However, this action only served to embolden traders and further frighten hedgers, all of whom continued selling pounds. Official threats to raise rates to 15 percent fell on deaf ears. Traders knew that continually raising interest rates to defend a currency during a recession is an unsustainable policy. Finally, on the evening of September 16, 1992, Great Britain humbly announced that it would no longer defend the trading band and withdrew the pound from the ERM system. The pound fell approximately 15 percent against the deutsche mark over the next few weeks, providing a windfall for speculators and a loss to the UK Treasury (i.e., British taxpayers) estimated to be in excess of £3 billion. (*See Figure 2.5.*)

It was reported at the time that Soros Fund Management made between $1 billion and $2 billion by shorting the pound, earning George Soros the moniker "the man who broke the Bank of England." But he was

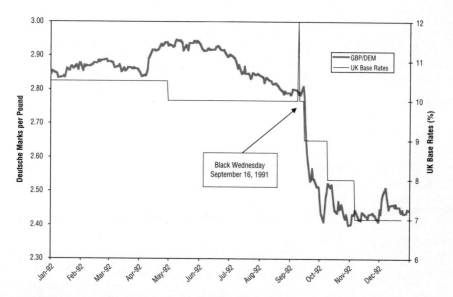

FIGURE 2.5 Sterling/Mark and UK Base Rates, 1992
Source: Bloomberg.

certainly not alone in betting against the pound. While he may have borne a disproportionate amount of the criticism because of his significant gains, the government's own policies are believed by many to have been the root cause of the problem, the speculators merely a symptomatic presence.

The pound eventually traded as low as 2.16 deutsche marks in 1995 but then rose as high as 3.44 in 2000 as the British economy recovered from recession and Germany suffered from the negative effects of euro integration. (*See Figure 2.6.*) Some credit today's strength in the British economy with the interest rate and currency flexibility afforded by its position outside of the euro system. This is especially striking when the United Kingdom's economic growth over the last decade is compared to the growth rates of formerly strong euro area countries such as Germany and France.

Yra Harris amusingly claims in his interview that Great Britain should erect a statue of George Soros in Trafalgar Square as an expression of gratitude for taking the pound out of the ERM. Bessent adds, "A lot of credit should go to the UK officials . . . they knew to fold their hand quickly. UK Chancellor Norman Lamont and Prime Minister John Major suffered short-term humiliation for long-term good. I mean, look at the muddle France and Germany are still in."

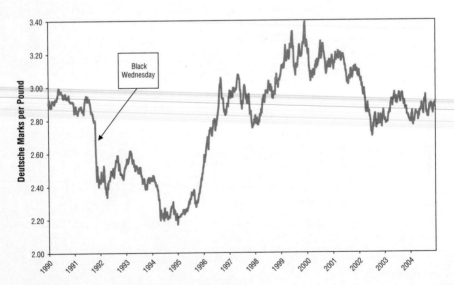

FIGURE 2.6   Sterling/Mark, 1990–2005
Source: Bloomberg.

Following the sterling crisis, the next systemic event for the global macro community was the bond market rout of 1994, but this time, the outcome was not profitable.

Bond Market Rout of 1994

As the euro project gathered political steam throughout the late 1980s and early 1990s, convergence trades—trades profiting from the convergence of various currencies and bonds toward a single currency and interest rate—became the dominant theme in European foreign exchange and fixed income markets. The early 1990s especially witnessed several strong years in the European fixed income and currency markets. Global macro traders at banks and hedge funds jumped on the trend along with relative value traders and trend followers, who were all heavily long European bonds. Leveraged positions were predominantly taken in the bonds and currencies of the weaker, high interest rate eurozone countries which, after the United Kingdom opted out of the ERM, were Italy and Spain.

Then, in February 1994, Fed Chairman Greenspan surprised the markets by raising overnight U.S. interest rates from 3 percent to 3.25 percent, beginning a series of hikes that served to abruptly end the early 1990s' period of easy money. Given the sizeable leveraged positions that had built up in the falling interest rate environment pre-1994, especially in the budding derivatives market, this unforeseen reversal of trend led to a generalized market sell-off. The 10-year U.S. government bond yield moved from 5.87 percent to 7.11 percent three months after the first hike, and most other markets also suffered trend reversals and declines. Likewise, the European bond trade that had worked so well until this point began to unravel. The sell-off was further compounded as margins were called, leveraged positions unwound, and continued price declines created a vicious cycle of forced selling. (*See Figure 2.7.*)

Corporations on the receiving end of Wall Street's derivative prowess, such as Procter & Gamble and Gibson Greetings, suffered major losses as their hedges went against them; Orange County, California, the wealthiest county in the United States at the time, declared bankruptcy as interest rate derivative structures imploded; and several well-known global macro funds either closed or went into hiding. Indeed, 1994 was the only down year for the HFR global macro index, which lost 4.3 percent (see Chapter 1).

FIGURE 2.7 Yields: U.S. 10-Year Treasury, UK 10-Year Gilt, and German 10-Year Bund, 1993–1994
Source: Bloomberg.

Asia Crisis 1997

For most of the 1990s many Southeast Asian countries had currency regimes that were linked to the U.S. dollar (USD) through trading bands that were set and managed by the local central banks. For the first half of the 1990s the USD was falling, improving the competitiveness of the Southeast Asian countries. Then, in 1995, the USD started to appreciate on a trade-weighted basis and especially against the yen, where it appreciated by more than 50 percent from April 1995 to January 1997. Due to their link to the USD, the Southeast Asian currencies appreciated in kind, slowly eroding their competitive advantage. (*See Figure 2.8.*)

The USD link allowed local Southeast Asian borrowers to access cheaper funds offshore as U.S. interest rates were below local rates and their currencies were essentially pegged. They also borrowed a lot from Japan where interest rates were less than 1 percent and, post-1995, the Japanese clearly had a policy to weaken their currency. Given their confidence in the stable currency regime, Southeast Asians deemed such cross-currency borrowing as largely riskless. But expanding current account

FIGURE 2.8   Japanese Yen, 1990–1998
Source: Bloomberg.

deficits, along with a rising competitive environment, most notably from China, and a strengthening USD, created pressures in the managed exchange rate system. Towards the middle of 1997, the Japanese banks were forced to increase their asset bases and were thus less inclined to roll over short-term debts. This drying up of liquidity for the Southeast Asian borrowers, coupled with a sudden rally in the yen in May 1997, brought to light some of the strains in the system.

As the risks became increasingly apparent, locals began to hedge their foreign exchange exposure, which meant heavy selling of local Southeast Asian currencies. As pressures on the system built, it became more difficult and more expensive for the local central banks to defend their currency regimes when their exchange rates approached the lower ends of the trading bands.

By July 1997, the Central Bank of Thailand saw its foreign currency reserve position dwindle in a futile effort to defend their currency regime and was left with little choice but to abandon the trading band. Without central bank support, the Thai baht immediately fell by 23 percent against the USD. (*See Figure 2.9.*) Lenders to Southeast Asian countries panicked en masse, withdrawing capital from the region or hedging their currency risk, which further depressed the Asian currencies. At the same time, locals

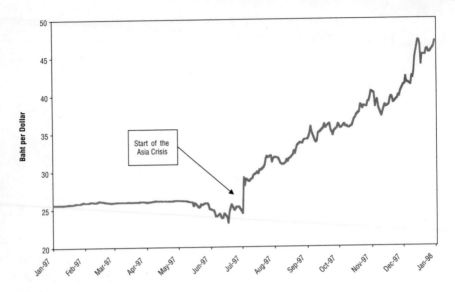

FIGURE 2.9   Thai Baht, 1997
Source: Bloomberg.

borrowing in U.S. dollars and yen but getting paid in local currency rushed to hedge their worsening foreign exchange position. This led to a systemic sell-off across all Southeast Asian currencies, stock markets, and other assets linked to the former "Asian Tigers," creating a contagion-like effect. Foreign investors rushed to pull their capital from the region without regard to specific country situations. The Thai baht eventually lost more than 50 percent of its value with other Southeast Asian currencies and stock markets sharing a similar fate. It was like a classic run on the bank, but in this case it was small economies and an entire region.

Many economists and institutions at the time blamed the Asia crisis on the openness of the global capital markets and the herd mentality of speculators. Malaysia's prime minister, Dr. Mahathir Mohamad, publicly blamed George Soros for the economic ills that Malaysia suffered following the crisis and even considered currency speculation a crime. He shut down his country's economy to so-called hot money by instituting draconian capital controls and fixing the Malaysian ringgit to the USD at 3.80. (*See Figure 2.10.*) As Scott Bessent recalls, it "was slightly worrying [because] it was the first time that someone had actually stopped paying lip service and actually shut down an economic system."

While Soros Fund Management returned 11.4 percent for the month

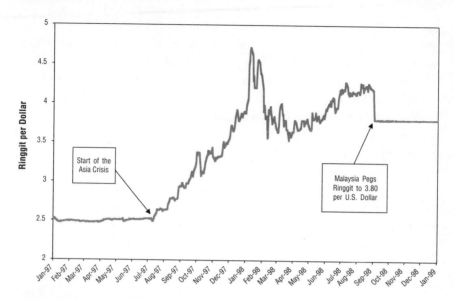

FIGURE 2.10   Malaysian Ringgit, 1997–1998
Source: Bloomberg.

of July 1997 largely from shorting the Thai baht, if profiting from the collapse of the Southeast Asian market deserves blame, then Julian Robertson should have received the lion's share of attention. His Tiger Management made $7 billion in profit after catching Asia crisis trades across currency, commodity, and equity markets. Going into July 1997, the fund's returns were approximately flat for the year on an asset base of $10 billion but after a strong finish, Tiger completed the year up 70 percent.

To say that speculators caused the Asia crisis, though, would be oversimplifying the situation. More likely the local borrowers, who built up excessive foreign exchange exposures prior to 1997 when the system was still largely stable, were also largely to blame. As such, the Southeast Asian governments merit responsibility for running ill-conceived policies that allowed excessive foreign currency borrowing to build up in the first place.

Russia Crisis 1998

The Russia crisis, according to some, was essentially a continuation of the Asia crisis as the Asian "economic flu" made its way around the globe, causing investors to retrench and reduce exposure to riskier investments such as emerging markets. Prior to 1998, Russia was the darling of the investment community as the large, commodity-rich economy emerged out from under the Iron Curtain. But as foreign investors retrenched and pulled their capital from Russia, the deteriorating situation was compounded again by locals moving money offshore and by less-than-perfect government financial management.

As capital started to flee Russia, successive changing of finance ministers, increases in interest rates to incredibly high levels, and various proposals of international bailout packages were all attempted by the Russian government before it finally capitulated. On August 17, 1998, the government of the Russian Federation and the Central Bank of Russia announced a currency devaluation and a moratorium on 281 billion rubles of government debt. The ruble fell from 6 to the U.S. dollar to 20 (and eventually to over 30 in 2002), while the bonds became almost worthless. The Russian stock market index (RTSI$) collapsed from a high of 570 to 36 during the lead-up to the crisis. (*See Figure 2.11.*) At the same time, many Russian financial institutions immediately became insolvent. This caused ripples through the world financial system, as many institutions had exposure to Russia that was thought to be hedged through derivative contracts with local Russian banks. Rather than being hedged, these positions

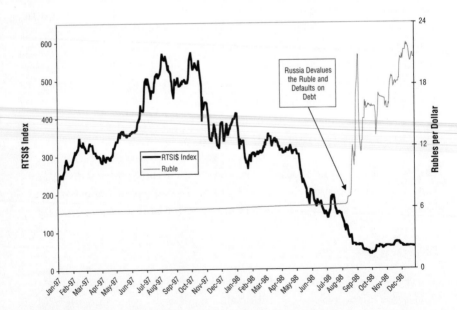

FIGURE 2.11   Russian Ruble and Russia Equity Index (RTSI$), 1997–1998
Source: Bloomberg.

became the subject of counterparty credit risk when the Russian banks became insolvent, leaving only the losing side of the trade.

The devaluation of the Russian ruble and simultaneous default of the country's sovereign debt caught many macro managers poorly positioned. It also marked the beginning of the end for the great global macro hedge funds, with 1998 denoting the peak in assets for Soros and Tiger (approximately $22 billion and $25 billion, respectively). George Soros made headlines again by losing between $1 billion and $2 billion on a single day (but yet again managed to finish positive for the year, returning 12 percent to investors) while Julian Robertson also took an estimated $1 billion hit in Russia. Tiger's woes were compounded with large losses in other markets, notably yen carry trades. (*See Figure 2.12.*)

As with most major crises, the Russian event created anomalies in other seemingly unrelated world markets. In this case, as investors dramatically reduced overall exposure to risky assets, they moved their capital into on-the-run U.S. government bonds in what was called "a flight to quality." As a result, spreads between the benchmark U.S. government bonds and all other risk assets widened dramatically, leading the world to its next financial crisis: Long Term Capital Management.

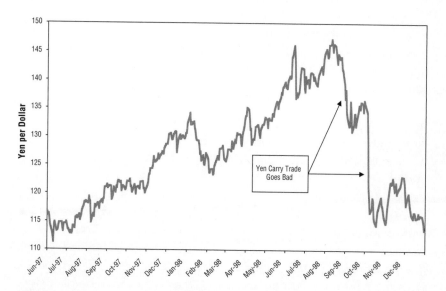

FIGURE 2.12 The Dollar/Yen Carry Trade, 1997–1998
Source: Bloomberg.

Long Term Capital Management 1998

Although Long Term Capital Management (LTCM) was not a global macro fund, it is worth mentioning for several reasons. For one, the arbitrage-focused fund drifted into global macro trades and its subsequent unwind had ramifications for global macro markets. Two, it offers insights into what can go wrong at a hedge fund, as well as shed light on such important issues as liquidity, risk management, and correlations. And three, almost every interviewee in this book mentions LTCM.

LTCM was started in 1994 by infamous Salomon Brothers proprietary trader John Meriwether, who hired an all-star cast of financial minds including former Fed vice chairman David Mullins and Nobel Prize winners Robert Merton and Myron Scholes (pioneers in option pricing theory and methodology). LTCM started with $1.3 billion in assets from a who's who list of investors and initially focused on fixed income arbitrage opportunities (which had become more attractive as spreads widened after the bond market rout of 1994). The original core strategy was to bet on the convergence of the spread between "off-the-run" and "on-the-run" bonds, as well as other relative value and arbitrage opportunities, primarily in fixed income. Due to the small spread in these arbitrage trades, the fund was leveraged many times in order to generate the 40-plus percent annual returns it posted for the first few years of its existence.

LTCM's success at exploiting these arbitrages caused assets under management to grow at the same time that the opportunities were disappearing. LTCM was forced to increase leverage to maintain returns as well as allocate risk capital to markets and trades that were beyond its original scope of expertise. Going into 1998, LTCM had $5 billion in assets with notional outstanding positions estimated at well over $1 trillion. At the same time, risk arbitrage trades (bets on mergers and acquisitions), directional positions, and emerging market bets became a larger portion of portfolio risk.

As the summer of 1998 approached, global markets became increasingly unsettled due to a combination of the fallout from the Asia crisis and the hint of trouble in Russia. To exacerbate matters, Salomon Brothers, Meriwether's former employer, decided to exit the arbitrage business, closing out similar positions and causing a widening of spreads in LTCM's trades. Russia's eventual devaluation and default then led to a large-scale reduction in risk appetite and a global flight to quality. Long-term fundamental values were deemed irrelevant by investors, causing a further widening of the spreads on LTCM's arbitrage and relative value trades. (*See Figure 2.13.*) LTCM's losses escalated to worrisome levels.

Given the leverage and size of LTCM's positions, liquidation was all but impossible. At the same time, LTCM's counterparties knew they were in trouble and at risk of imploding, leading them to hedge their own counterparty risk, further compounding LTCM's mark-to-market woes. To mitigate default—and, some would argue, the potential collapse of the world financial system—the Federal Reserve Bank of New York called a meeting with LTCM's creditors and implemented a bailout package. It was yet another iteration of the Greenspan put.

LTCM was at the forefront of investing at the time and offers insight into some of the failings of risk management systems. Risk management systems based on historical prices are one way to look at risk but are in no way faultless. Financial market history is filled with theoretically low probability or fat tail events. In LTCM's case, its risk systems calculated roughly a 1-in-6-billion chance of a major blowup. Ironically, however, one correlation the brilliant minds of LTCM neglected to consider was the correlation coefficient of positions that were linked for no other reason than the fact

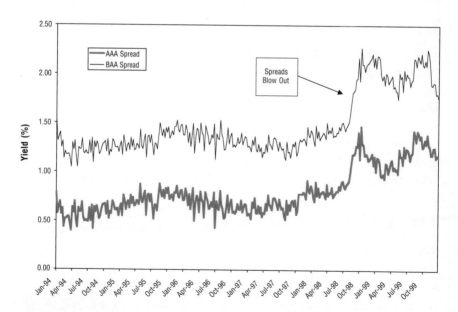

FIGURE 2.13   Corporate Spreads to Treasuries, 1994–1999
Source: Bloomberg.

GREENSPAN ON LTCM

How much dependence should be placed on financial modeling, which, for all its sophistication, can get too far ahead of human judgment? This decade is strewn with examples of bright people who thought they had built a better mousetrap that could consistently extract an abnormal return from financial markets. Some succeed for a time. But while there may occasionally be misconfigurations among market prices that allow abnormal returns, they do not persist. Indeed, efforts to take advantage of such misalignments force prices into better alignment and are soon emulated by competitors, further narrowing, or eliminating, any gaps. No matter how skillful the trading scheme, over the long haul, abnormal returns are sustained only through abnormal exposure to risk.

Source: Testimony of Chairman Alan Greenspan before the Committee on Banking and Financial Services, U.S. House of Representatives, on *Private-Sector Refinancing of the Large Hedge Fund, Long Term Capital Management,* October 1, 1998.

that they were in LTCM's portfolio. In other words, their models didn't provide for the LTCM liquidity premium.

LTCM was a reminder of the notion that there is no such thing as a risk-free arbitrage. Because the arbitrage positions they were exploiting were small, the fund had to be leveraged many times to produce meaningful returns. This put them at risk to their lenders' financing fees as well as general market liquidity. The problem with liquidity is that it is never there when really needed.

Dot-Com Bust 2000

Chairman Greenspan issued his famous "irrational exuberance" speech on December 6, 1996, warning of the perceived overvaluation of the U.S. stock market. Over the next three years, the stock market did nothing but go up, minus a hiccup during the Russia/LTCM episode, which Greenspan quickly corrected by cutting interest rates by 75 basis points. The rate cuts included a famous intrameeting cut normally reserved for emergencies, despite the fact that the U.S. unemployment rate was 4.5 percent (so much for taking away the punch bowl). Meanwhile, from the famous speech through to March 2000, the broader S&P 500 index doubled while the technology stock–laden NASDAQ quadrupled. (*See Figure 2.14.*)

As such, the returns being produced by global macro hedge funds were no longer as interesting to investors as the 50 to 100 percent or more annual returns being posted by some technology mutual funds. At the same time, the two largest global macro fund managers struggled with the new momentum-driven paradigm. Robertson and Soros both became vocal naysayers of the tech stock–driven rally. It was widely perceived that dot-com and tech stocks were in a bubble but, as shares rallied ceaselessly, it was all but impossible for many investors to jump on the bandwagon. Indeed, Soros Fund Management flipped its position in late 1999, going from short to long high tech stocks, and in the process converted a 19 percent loss into a 35 percent gain for the year.

Julian Robertson, on the other hand, chose to maintain his core theme of long "old economy" versus short "new economy," which led to further losses in 1999 and 2000 as old economy stocks continued to decline and growth rallied. Eventually, Robertson was forced to close Tiger

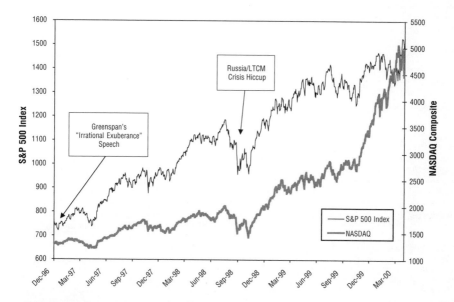

FIGURE 2.14 Boom! 1996–2000
Source: Bloomberg.

Management as investor redemptions piled up and assets under management sank from $25 billion to $6 billion. Upon shuttering his fund, Robertson remarked in his final investor letter, "As you have heard me say on many occasions, the key to Tiger's success over the years has been a steady commitment to buying the best stocks and shorting the worst. In a rational environment, this strategy functions well. But in an irrational market, where earnings and price considerations take a back seat to mouse clicks and momentum, such logic, as we have learned, does not count for much." Ironically, Tiger's final month in operation, March 2000, coincided with the absolute top of the tech stock bubble, after which Robertson's investment thesis would have proven a winner. (*See Figure 2.15.*)

Meanwhile, Soros's long tech stocks position that had been rewarded so handsomely in late 1999 and early 2000 turned viciously against him after March of that year. Down 22 percent by April 2000, Soros announced plans to change the nature of his Quantum Fund to a lower-risk vehicle dubbed Quantum Endowment. Soros remarked at the time, "We have come to realize that a large hedge fund like Quantum Fund is no longer the best way to manage money. Markets have become extremely unstable and historical measures of value at risk no longer apply."

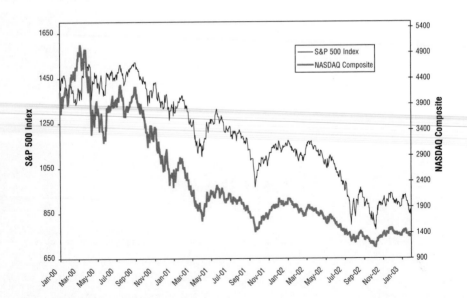

FIGURE 2.15   Bust! 2000–2003
Source: Bloomberg.

> "Our large macro bet days are over."
>
> —George Soros, April 2000

GLOBAL MACRO IS DEAD

As 1999 rolled into 2000, many other global macro funds also closed down, prompting the popular press and Wall Street pundits to declare global macro "dead." While 2000 may have marked the end of the $20 billion–plus global macro mega-funds, it was premature to cite the end of a strategy that profits from global misalignments and macroeconomic trends.

When the stock market bubble finally did burst in March 2000, the Greenspan put was written once again as interest rates were reduced from 6.5 percent to 1 percent—levels not seen since the 1950s. It was in this new paradigm that the up-and-coming crop of global macro managers made their names. They caught not only the interest rate move, but also other parts of the classic macro view at the time: long bonds, short stocks, and eventually short the U.S. dollar.

Instead of ushering in the end of global macro, the year 2000 in fact marked the beginning of another great run for global macro funds. Macro funds were once again among the top performers in the investment world, producing strong positive returns at a time when the average global investor was suffering from the fallout of one of the greatest investment bubbles seen since the Nifty Fifty in the early 1970s.

A FINAL WORD ON SOROS

For whatever reason, the popular press and historical accounts like to talk about the fees charged or the absolute dollar gains and losses of hedge funds rather than the net percentage returned to investors. For Soros Fund Management, it was $1 billion on Black Wednesday, $2 billion in Russia, and $3 billion when the tech bubble burst. Very rarely does one read about the percentage returns for Soros Fund Management, which were extraordinary. Through all of Soros's ordeals, wins, and losses, he posted a positive annual return for every single year from inception in 1969 until 1999. In Quantum Fund's final letter to shareholders, dated April 28, 2000, George Soros noted, "During its 31½ year history, Quantum provided its shareholders with an annual return in excess of 30 percent. An investment of $100,000 in the fund at its inception would be worth approximately $420 million today."

CHAPTER 3

The Future of Global Macro Hedge Funds

The restructuring of Soros Fund Management and the winding down of Tiger Management marked the end of the global macro giant era. Gone are the days when a few strong personalities dominate a small, concentrated number of funds and markets. The increase in information flow, competition, influx of assets, and development of new markets has added tremendous complexity and scope to the global macro landscape today. The strategy that started with Keynes and made famous by Soros has become a broadly diversified collection of many different managers and styles.

One of the main reasons for the trend away from the big mega-funds is the issue of diseconomies of scale encountered by hedge funds when a large asset base is accumulated. When a fund gets too big—and many would put Soros and Tiger during the late 1990s into this camp—meaningful positions can only be taken in the most liquid instruments and deepest markets, thus limiting scope and diversification options.

As Christian Siva-Jothy (SemperMacro) notes in his interview later in this book, Soros and Tiger used to be able to drive macro markets, so one had to pay attention to their activities. That is no longer the case for any one fund today. Along the same lines, Marko Dimitrijević (Everest Capital) observes that emerging markets, which used to be controlled by a few guys sitting in New York or London, have developed and more players, including local investing institutions, have deepened the field.

Today, the global macro arena is populated with alumni of Soros, Tiger, and other big players from the early days of the strategy, as well as those from the global macro–oriented proprietary trading desks at Bankers Trust, Goldman Sachs, and Credit Suisse First Boston, who compete with a varied and diverse field. While there are no longer global macro hedge funds managing over $20 billion in assets, the capital controlled by macro fund managers today, in aggregate, is several times what it was 15 years ago (estimated by HFR at $116 billion in 2005 versus $39 billion in 1990). At the same time, the size and choice in global macro markets has expanded significantly with the growth in central bank assets and the development of various derivative instruments and emerging markets.

FROM GLOBAL MACRO TO GLOBAL MICRO

The days of breaking central banks or levering up to produce annual returns north of 100 percent seem to be over. The influx of capital to hedge funds by traditional investing institutions, including pension funds with public money under management, has decreased the appetite for risk in general. At the same time, many managers today are increasingly complaining about the increased difficulty of profiting in the markets and the shortage of opportunities. Whether global macro markets have become more challenging or whether they have merely changed is a current topic of debate.

Some argue that the outsized returns available to global macro funds over the past few decades were solely the result of central bank and policy errors, such as trying to fix nominal exchange rates (sterling crisis, Asia crisis) and micromanaging economies (politically driven interest rate policy, bubble management). Yet it seems as though policy makers have come up the curve and learned from past mistakes. The introduction of financial market professionals, such as Robert Rubin, to government policy decision-making positions seems to have calmed markets and smoothed volatility, limiting the glaring anomalies for funds to exploit.

Others question whether the triumph of central banks over inflation and the managing of financial market expectations via increased transparency have in turn created a paradox of perfection. As some battles have been won (inflation and exchange rate volatility), bigger problems may have been created (global trade imbalances and asset bubbles).

Whether better policy has changed the game, few question that increased competition has forced specialization. Many of today's global macro managers have investment styles that are more aptly described as global micro.

Soros Fund Management and Tiger Management were the pioneers of the global micro investing style. As Scott Bessent explains, George Soros and his chief investment officer (CIO) Stanley Druckenmiller have long held the belief that deciphering what is happening at the micro level provides valuable insights for the macro picture. Likewise, as Dwight Anderson (Ospraie Management) discusses, before Tiger got into a position, they would do mountains of primary, on-the-ground micro research in order to confirm a hypothesis. But although Soros and Tiger may have sown the seeds for today's global micro style, their largest moves (on both the upside and downside) often came from big sweeping bets on currencies, equity indexes, interest rates, and other classic macro instruments. In actual practice, they operated in what Dr. Sushil Wadhwani (Wadhwani Asset Management), in his interview, calls "the narrow end of global macro."

Other global macro funds formerly on this "narrow end," such as Tudor and Caxton, have evolved to a more global micro style of investing with significant assets. They achieve the necessary specialization and diversification by hiring and allocating capital to internal teams with specific skills, who then work independently. As Paul Tudor Jones explains it, having many diversified traders internally "lets Tudor traders practice patience" so that "if you don't see anything, you don't trade. You take risk only when you see an opportunity." In 2004, a little more than half of the risk at Tudor was managed by Jones and other in-house macro traders. Global equities accounted for a third of the risk with the remainder allocated to other strategies, such as distressed and risk arbitrage.

At Caxton, as assets have grown from $7.6 million in 1983 to over $12 billion today, the firm has evolved from a single portfolio manager global macro fund into a multistrategy hedge fund complex with around 30 teams trading a broadly diversified mix of strategies. Over time, Caxton CIO and founder Bruce Kovner has gone from being the sole risk taker to becoming just one of many traders, while, at the same time, his role has shifted to that of business leader, overall risk manager, and motivator of traders and employees.

Jim Leitner (Falcon Management), in his interview, describes his vision for global macro as:

> . . . the willingness to opportunistically look at every idea that comes along, from micro situations to country-specific situations, across every asset category and every country in the world. It's the combination of a broad top-down country analysis with a bottom-up micro analysis of companies. In many cases, after we

make our country decisions, we then drill down and analyze the companies in the sectors that should do well in light of our macro view. . . . Macro themes expressed in a micro style. Global macro only means that you start at the top and work your way down.

Leitner is at the forefront of the evolution from global macro to global micro. For a detailed explanation of some of the financial theory and mathematics driving this evolution, see Appendix A for the presentation by Dr. Lee R. Thomas III (Allianz Global Investors) entitled "Why Global Macro Is the Way to Go." Appendix B offers a note to investors considering global macro hedge funds for their portfolios.

Meanwhile, in today's uncertain world, global imbalances are becoming more pronounced while political, geopolitical, and social instability seem to be evolving more rapidly than traditional investing institutions can manage. The following chapters present the thinking of some of the best minds in the investment world about how they interpret these events and try to profit from them, using what remains the most open and flexible mandate in the investment world: global macro.

CHAPTER 4

THE FAMILY OFFICE MANAGER

Jim Leitner
Falcon Management
Wyckoff, New Jersey

The sign reads both "Falcon Management" and "Aikido Spirit" outside the sprawling suburban New Jersey house that Jim Leitner calls base for his family office when he is not on the ground scouring for investments in India, the Ivory Coast, or some other far-flung location. Leitner manages mostly his own money and has been doing so for years. As a result, his approach to global macro markets is different from most other fund managers in that he is not long an implicit put option. In other words, if his portfolio blows up, instead of losing his job or his investors, he goes on welfare. But his office environment would imply that he is far from the welfare scenario.

His new office is a noticeable step up from his old locale, one stark room in a strip mall behind a dirty, run-down gas station, where I first met him during the summer of 1999. I was in the Hedge Fund Group at Deutsche Bank in London and eagerly trying to pitch trade ideas to fund managers. Leitner had been doing quite a bit of business in Turkey and had been planning a trip there with Merrill Lynch to kick the tires. He loves doing research on the ground, and Turkey, with one-year interest rates greater than 100 percent and inflation around 60 percent, screamed of opportunity for macro managers with a strong enough stomach to weather the potential volatility and risk.

The central bank governor of Turkey had been embarking on a plan to reduce inflation and Leitner wanted to see how it might impact his investments. As usual, he was way ahead of the curve and was already heavily invested in Turkish equities and one-year currency forwards.

When the central bank governor committed suicide in August 1999, Merrill cancelled the trip. I took the opportunity to make one on Deutsche Bank's tab, taking Leitner and a group of other hedge funds around to meet the new central bank governor, other public officials, banks, and companies. During one meeting in Istanbul with a prominent local banker who was discussing net foreign exposure to the Turkish lira, Leitner leaned over and whispered to me, "Is he saying my little family office owns 10 percent of the market?"

The aikido studio in his office might shed some light on his trading style: disciplined and patient, fluid, respecting the power of the market to crush any individual, and always seeking more knowledge. Leitner's quick and friendly "Hey, buddy," every time I called him was a welcome reprieve from the majority of traders and money managers who prefer listening to their own voices. Leitner takes information from any source and is always appreciative. In fact, taking care of people who in turn take care of him is one of his many edges.

Although he does not have the household name that a George Soros or a Julian Robertson has, he is very well-known and respected in the trading world. Leitner came up through the bucket shops in New York, brokering bank products while completing his studies. He rose through the ranks to become the primary risk taker for Bankers Trust and has managed money for many other well-known hedge fund managers. He calculates that he has harvested about $2 billion from the markets over his career. Since founding Falcon Management in 1997, he has returned approximately 30 percent on a compound annual basis.

Leitner uses an option-based strategy whenever possible to manage his fund and is not afraid to sit on long-dated out-of-the money options and just wait until they eventually pay off. He epitomizes global macro in that he will truly invest in any asset in any market in the world and is known for wild out-of-consensus trades, like being long inflation-linked housing bonds in Iceland or being a primary equity partner in a Ghanaian brewery.

After we completed this interview, Leitner asked me to join him for lunch with a gentleman who was coming to see him. We went upstairs to enjoy a fine Italian meal in the dining room of his office-converted home while listening to cries from the aikido studio in another part of the house. His guest explained to me that he was launching a global macro hedge fund.

Curious, I asked, "If you are launching your own fund, why come to see Jim, who is ostensibly your competition?"

The guest replied, "Because Jim is the Pope of global macro and I came by to seek his blessing."

How did you get started in the business?

I was in graduate school at Columbia University, studying international finance and Russian studies. I needed money so I answered a *Wall Street Journal* ad that said, "Money broker trainee wanted."

I sent a letter saying, "I don't know what a money broker does, but I'll be the best trainee you ever hire. I am a student and can only work a half day, but in a half day I'll do the job that would take everybody else a full day." Eventually, a letter from Dominion Securities Tradition turned up inviting me for an interview.

As luck would have it, the guy who interviewed me was German. I grew up in Germany and Turkey, and in the latter had attended a German school, so we did the interview in German. He liked me and said, "What I need is a monkey to run this big board with all the information that's going on around the world."

They had a little amphitheater where all the brokers looked down at a big board that had to be up-to-date at all times with customer orders that came blaring in from loudspeakers connected to offices in Lausanne, Singapore, and London.

I said to the guy, "I can only work a half day." He said, "That's perfect because at noon, London and Lausanne close, while Singapore is only open for a couple of hours in the morning. How about you work from 6 A.M. till noon?"

After working there for a short while, I said to the guy, "This is easy and so much fun. I want to be a broker and I can do it at the same time I am the monkey filling out the board." They gave me a phone and I started calling small banks in the Midwest.

What products were you dealing with?

I was a broker for interbank deposits for the Nassau and Grand Cayman branches. At the time, all the banks were running these offshore Eurodollar businesses and there was a real active deposit market between banks.

As a new broker, I had all the little teeny banks that no one wanted, but they ended up being very active because no one had ever cared about them before. When I started, I called them up and said, "I am a student and can only work until noon, so I hope you don't mind only getting coverage until then," but they were all excited because they were getting coverage for the first time and felt like they were supporting this poor grad student.

I did this full-time for two years after graduating when I decided I wanted to be on the other end of the phone. I called JP Morgan and said, "Next time you guys want to hire a trainee on the Morgan Nassau desk, please consider me." Two weeks later I was working there and took a huge pay cut to do it. My salary went from $70,000 down to $17,000 but I figured it was worth it to keep learning. I also went to law school at night.

The Eurodollar market that I was trading was growing, but what really started taking off then were the euro currency markets. Any domestic currency that was being handled offshore became a euro currency, and I became somewhat of an expert in euroswiss francs, eurodeutsche marks, and europesetas.

After a while, I figured I'd learned everything I could on the Morgan Nassau desk, so I walked over to the head of foreign exchange and said, "I'll write all your tickets and bring you coffee if I can sit next to you, be your trainee, and learn currency trading." He said, "Done," so I became his foreign exchange trainee.

Next I became the currency forward trader, which was a little bit related to the deposit market because it had to do with interest rates. It was slightly more complex than just buying and selling spot currency. Then they started throwing the esoteric currencies at me to trade. In those days, a Spanish peseta trade was esoteric because no one knew how to price it, what relationship to use, what cross to look at to value it, and so on.

A few years later, I was hired by Bank of America to run forwards, exotics, and all currency trading outside of the four major currencies (deutsche mark, sterling, yen and Swiss franc). For me, it was a great job because I was trading all of these things and making a lot more money than the guys trading spot and the major currencies.

Back then, you could make a lot of money on market imperfections if you had better information and a lot of friends. I was able to dominate trading in two markets, the Venezuelan bolivar and Mexican peso, in terms of being the largest market maker and knowing exactly what the bid/offer spreads could be. I could shut other market makers out. Because we dealt with all the corporates and funds that traded in these two currency markets, I knew more people and had more information than anybody else. It was a great time and a great learning experience. However, in other currencies the profits were totally driven by the desks' ability to take risk, to understand the liquidity of different currency markets, and to analyze currency moves directionally.

I left there to join Shearson Lehman as a pure proprietary trader, but quickly realized that they didn't like taking risk. At one point, I was up $3 million and had a drawdown to $2.2 million, which they weren't happy with. I felt I was still up $2.2 million, yet they looked at it as if I had just lost $800,000 of their money.

When Bankers Trust called saying they were stepping up risk taking, I jumped at the chance. The next five years, from 1986 to 1991, at Bankers were just phenomenal, blow-away years. Bankers became the most dominant trading firm in currency markets during that time.

Was it the firm, the traders, or the market environment that made those years so great?

Bankers had a management culture that was willing to take risks and had a sense of how to measure it. They had a system called "RAROC," risk-adjusted return on capital, which was really the first version of value at risk (VAR). Management was good at encouraging people who did well to continue to do well—the thought was, if you're doing well and it's not random, then here's more rope.

When I started, they set an annual budget of $12 million for the forwards and exotics desk. I asked how they set that budget and they said, "You have six people working for you and no one's ever made more than a million. If they each make two million, that'll be a phenomenal success." We made $12 million by February 20.

They quickly realized that I was good at making money and that I really enjoyed finding fantastic risk/reward trades, thinking about the relationships between currencies and finding things that were mispriced, so they gave me a lot more rope.

Markets were so much easier in those days. The industry was still in its infancy and mispricings occurred much more frequently. There were so many more currencies to trade. Back then, nobody could keep 4 currencies straight, much less 20. But I had a facility to see relationships and could sense when things were out of whack.

Do you think you have an innate skill where you can "just tell" when prices are out of line?

I don't have an innate skill. It comes from being extremely interested in markets and looking at everything all the time. After doing it for years, I've developed a mental database of where things should be, such that when something makes an irregular move, it shows up on my radar screen. I used to have so much fun playing around in the market and knowing that I knew my markets better than other people.

Also, the central banks were so much more active back then, especially in Europe. It was a no-brainer because they were keeping everything in ranges and leaving orders at fixings. The central banks would all set the value of their currencies every day and each one wanted to have their own daily fixing. There was one in the Netherlands, one in Paris, one in Germany, and so on.

Logically, the French franc versus the Dutch guilder should be the same whether it's being fixed in Paris or in the Netherlands because it's the same thing. But it wouldn't be the same because it would be traded differently due to the different orders. Meanwhile, I knew who had big orders and where, because I spoke to all the banks and customers. I would leave orders in one center and unwind them in another center at official fixings and make money. It was just a great period of time.

That first year at Bankers, my group made $65 million on an annual budget of $12 million. Management said, "If you can do that with six guys sitting around in New York, I wonder what you can do in London?" They sent me to London to run trading for everything liquid in Europe, which is how I learned about bond trading. Because bond trading fit in with my forward trading experience and with the stuff I did on the Nassau desk, it wasn't totally new but was rather a deeper market and longer-term in nature than the currency markets.

I soon realized that I didn't enjoy managing people—I preferred managing risk. A year after getting to London, I told the bank that I only wanted to be the major risk taker in Europe, without management responsibility. They thought it was a bad career move but they agreed and brought a guy over to run the businesses while I ran risk. I was only responsible for my own profit and loss (P&L), although I still had a small team of traders and was linked into the overall risk management of the European branches.

Around that time, another trader at Bankers blew himself up and the firm had to restate earnings by $80 million. I wasn't involved with him but I knew about him because he was a bit wild. We were always helping him buy or sell a billion of this currency or that currency. The importance of his implosion was that it led me to believe that Bankers needed to get away from proprietary trading as such an important revenue source. Because we were an FDIC-insured institution, I also believed that regulators would someday restrict our ability to take risks. I proposed that the bank start a customer fund as a way of mitigating risk and creating a new, stable revenue source.

They gave me the go-ahead to try it, so I asked four clients for $20 million, which they gave me. I started the fund in 1989 with $80 million and it was run as a diversified high yield versus low yield currency fund. In other words, we extracted risk premia from the market in an intelligent way where the key was to get out when you started seeing signs of a pending devaluation.

The first year, we were up around 45 percent and assets grew to $800 million. The second year was up 35 percent. I don't remember how big the fund got but I realized at that point that I no longer needed the bank. Once I realized that, it made it impossible to commute to work every day, so I quit and started Falcon, which started with four managed accounts.

At what point along the way did you know with certainty that you were a good trader?

I knew I had skill at making money from the days when I was running the Bank of America trading room in New York. Except for the bolivar and the peso, there weren't any customers, so I was solely responsible for the results.

At Bankers, I came to realize that I was absolutely unemotional about numbers. Losses did not have an effect on me because I viewed them as purely probability-driven, which meant sometimes you came up with a loss. Bad days, bad weeks, bad months never impacted the way I approached markets the next day. To this day, my wife never knows if I've had a bad day or a good day in the markets.

Is being too emotional a failing you've seen in other traders?

Oh yeah, for sure. Another thing that I realize about myself that I don't see in other traders is that I'm really humble about my ignorance. I truly feel that I'm ignorant despite having made enormous amounts of money. I calculated the other day that I have taken over $2 billion out of the market for my investors and employers so far. That seems like a lot of money and yes, I am relatively wealthy and happy to be independent, but there's never a day when I feel a lot smarter than everybody else. All I know is every day there's the possibility that I will find a better trade than someone else by looking and searching. But I still feel ignorant.

Many traders I've met over the years approach the market as if they're smarter than other people until somebody or something proves them wrong. I have found this approach eventually leads to disaster when the market proves them wrong.

What do you look for when hiring traders?

That's a really hard question because I've never been able to identify good traders *ex ante*. It's difficult identifying someone who is a good trader versus someone who is a good analyst because the two don't always mesh. There are some people who are really good thinkers but can't make money and there are other people who aren't the greatest thinkers but who end up making tons of money trading. How much of that is random versus a better approach or better risk management is not clear to me.

At Bankers, we tried to identify trading talent but we never could despite experimenting with new, innovative ideas. We'd hire chess champions and backgammon champions because we thought that trading was akin to applied game theory, but none of those people really worked out. In the end, the two talents weren't the same. Not for lack of trying, but we were never able to identify where trading talent comes from.

What advice would you give to a young trader who would like to be in your shoes in 20 years' time?

They should be open to the entire spectrum of market experiences. I never locked myself down to investing in one style or in one country because the greatest trade in the world could be happening somewhere else. My advice would be to make sure that you do not become too much of an expert in one area. Even if you see an area that is inefficient today, it's likely that it won't be inefficient tomorrow. Expertise is overrated.

There's a book called *The Wisdom of Crowds* (by James Suroweicki) that contains a lot of examples where the average results of a group were much better estimators than expert opinions. We wrongly tend to look at other people as experts. If you ask currency experts where an exchange rate is going, they are just as likely to be wrong as some average guy on the street.

One also needs to learn to fight certain human biases such as buying into stories. The thing that gets fundamental discretionary traders involved in trades is stories because we can grasp onto them. But, in general, it's good to step away from the story and take it back to the numbers. Trading off a story is too amorphous. We need to quantify things and understand why things are cheap or expensive by using some hard measure of what cheap or expensive means. Then there has to be a combination of story and value. A story is still required because a story will appeal to other people and appeal is what drives markets. If there's no story and something's cheap, it might just stay cheap forever. But if there's a story involved, make sure that you first look at the numbers before you get involved to be sure there is some quantitative backing to the idea.

Where do you source your stories?

I read a tremendous amount of books and papers, I subscribe to research services, and I read *The Economist* religiously. If somebody asked me how to get involved in global macro investing, I would say start with a subscription to *The Economist*, read it every week, and think about what you learned this week that you didn't know the week before.

If you read about an oil discovery, start thinking about how to develop it into a trade. The idea is to do as much research as you can just reading and thinking about anything in the world before reaching out to your network. Developing a network by going out and meeting groups of intelligent people is also very important.

Another thing that's important is not to be afraid to be ignorant or ask questions. Learn to love to listen to people and when you hear something interesting, follow up on it. Don't just think, "Well that's an interesting idea," only to find out a year later that the company you could have bought shares in is now up five hundredfold. You never want to say coulda, woulda, shoulda. When I find a really compelling idea that I don't know much about, I put a tiny amount of money into it and treat it like a cheap option.

Could you do what you do if all you had was The Economist?

I think I could. If I only read *The Economist*, my portfolio right now would be long Asian equities for the next 10 years.

The world has become divided into a producer center, which is Asia, and a consumer center, which is the United States. Asia has better demographics and people there are willing to work 60-hour weeks at much cheaper rates. Americans, on the other hand, are only willing to work 40 to 45 hours a week but are willing to leverage themselves to the hilt to buy more things. There's also an amorphous area in the middle called Europe, which is neither an aggressive consumer nor an aggressive producer, and demographically it's all screwed up.

As an investor, I want to be invested in the producer as opposed to the consumer. I also want to be focused on buying value stocks instead of growth stocks, so I would go through and pick all of the value stocks in Asia that I could find.

I'd be buying Thai property developers because Thailand has a twin surplus and is expanding nicely. I'd be long Indian stocks out the wazoo. I'd be long Korea. I'd be long Hong Kong. I would not be buying Chinese stocks because I'm not comfortable with the rule of law there, but I really believe China's doing something special so I'm investing in the people that supply China.

What's the biggest threat to your Asia 10-year view?

One risk is that oil prices remain high and lead to another Asia crisis. They would have to stay high for a considerable period of time, which would give ample time to get out. If oil gets to 80 dollars a barrel and stays there for a while such that inflation starts picking up, I'll get out.

Another risk is that the global financial system becomes less global. If trade flows suddenly start shrinking and protectionism starts gaining momentum, I'll get out. Protectionism is a beggar-thy-neighbor policy that doesn't work because global wealth declines.

Nuclear war between India and Pakistan would also be a problem for my Asia view although, in the long run, you should be buying things when they get destroyed. As terrible as nuclear war sounds, demographics will win out over the next 30 years.

Are disaster and tragedy always a buying opportunity?

Yeah, look at Russia or Botswana or Turkey. For example, when Turkey had a massive earthquake in 1999, we bought shares of glass manufacturers because we knew everybody was going to have to replace their windows. It was a no-brainer. Turkish stocks were going down across the board but we bought all the shares of glass manufacturers we could.

The opportunity is a result of people panicking based on news. News is random and it might not look good but it's not exactly easy to analyze how it's all going to work out at that moment. Changing your position because of news is usually not a great idea.

That's one of the reasons why I love options. Options take away that whole aspect of having to worry about precise risk management. It's like paying for someone else to be your risk manager. Meanwhile, I know I am long XYZ for the next six months. Even if the option goes down a lot in the beginning to the point that the option is worth nothing, I will still own it and you never know what can happen.

I once owned a one-year option on the euro swap rate that became worthless soon after I bought it. Then, with two weeks to go to expiry, the swap rate came back my way and blew through my strike. After being worthless for 11 months, I ended up selling it for five times what I paid for it.

Has your usage of options increased since you shifted to managing your own money?

I've used options much more since I became a family office but that's partly due to the fact that the options market has grown up a lot over the last decade. When I started trading currencies, options didn't even exist. Today you can get options on anything and the bid/offer spreads are peanuts. In general, I like using options as a risk reduction tool for managing my own money. It allows me to sleep comfortably at night.

Speaking of disasters, how did the World Trade Center attacks affect your portfolio?

I honestly don't remember how they affected my portfolio. I could have been up or down but if I had to guess, I'd say we probably made a little bit of money only because we're net buyers of options. On average, when there is a bad event, volatility goes up because everybody gets nervous and pays up for insurance.

One thing the September 11 attacks did for me was reconfirm that tail risk should not be allowed in your portfolio because things happen that you can't imagine.

I'll give you an example that shows how serious I am about cutting off tail risk. After the stock market bubble burst in 2000 and the Fed started cutting rates, I thought there was a chance the United States could be headed toward a Japan-like deflation situation. I bought butterfly option structures on front-end interest rates whereby I bought one call struck at 2 percent yield and sold two times as many calls struck at 1 percent yield, such that we'd make money if interest rates went anywhere from 2 percent to zero. The option structure was very cheap and our biggest payout came if rates stopped at 1 percent.

Meanwhile, we insisted that the banks sell us an option struck at zero percent, such that we were protected if interest rates went below zero. The banks asked us why in the world we would want the zero percent option back, and my answer was, "I don't know. Maybe if someone lights up a nuke in New York, interest rates will be negative 25 percent and, with my luck, that would be the day my option matures." They all laughed at us.

I actually had a big argument with another hedge fund manager who later told me that he was on the other side of that trade selling me the zero strike options via the bank because I was overpaying for volatility. I just had to laugh. I said to him, "Volatility has nothing to do with it. Volatility is a stupid concept. We all know that it probably will not happen and that probability is very, very high, but Long Term Capital also thought there was a 1 in 6 billion chance that their portfolio could blow up."

Implied volatility is based on historical volatility, but who cares about historicals? They're irrelevant. The point is, things can happen for the first time that aren't in your distribution so they can't be priced. If it's never happened before, how can you hedge yourself? The only way to hedge the unknown is to cut off tail risk completely.

What was your favorite trade of all time?

The trade I remember the most only made a small amount of money but it was the first time I took on a large position based on my belief that I understood the market better than the market.

The trade was for the price of overnight Swiss franc interest rates, one day in advance. I had the sense that Swiss franc interest rates the next day were going to be very, very high so I went out and borrowed billions of Swiss francs for one day forward. The next day I found out that I'd made one tick because I borrowed at a rollover rate of 2.5 pips and got out at 1.5 pips.

There was very little money involved, but my wife still remembers me just jumping up and down in the middle of the night screaming "I did it! I did it!" It was the first time I felt that I'd seen something that I understood and actually did something about it. I felt the power of doing something and knowing that the money made was due to my wits versus customer flows or bank positions. It was the most phenomenal feeling of control and creativity all coming together.

Can you tell me about your most profitable trade ever?

The most profitable trade wasn't a trade but an approach to markets and a realization that, over time, positive carry works. Applying this concept to higher yielding currencies versus lower yielding currencies was my most profitable trade ever. I got to the point in this trade where I was running portfolios of about $6 billion and I remember central banks being shocked at the size of currency positions I was willing to buy and hold over the course of years.

FORWARD RATE BIAS

The empirical tendency of forward exchange rates is to overestimate changes in spot exchange rates. According to the theory of uncovered interest arbitrage, forward exchange rates are unbiased predictors of future spot exchange rates, implying that a forward contract's expected return equals 0 percent. It is an empirical fact, however, that during the modern floating rate era, the forward exchange rates of the major currencies have predicted larger subsequent changes in the spot rates than have occurred. Forward contracts that have sold at discounts have produced positive returns on average, while forward contracts that have sold at premia have produced negative returns on average.

Source: www.riskinstitute.ch.

One thing that I'm really good at is cribbing ideas. I actually didn't spot this forward rate bias first. There was a guy at Bankers Trust who spotted it from a portfolio standpoint and wrote a little piece on it. I noticed that it worked in individual currency pairs but I never really thought of it in a portfolio context. Anyway, this guy wanted to build it into a trade but was just too nervous to actually do it.

I asked him, "Why don't you just go put the trade on?"

He said, "No, because sometimes you're going to get devalued on and then you're going to lose money."

I said, "You've got to be joking."

The next week, I put on the first billion of the trade and when it started working I did more and more and more. It became such an obvious thing that no one else was doing at the time. I started running large carry portfolios in 1986 and wasn't devalued on once while at Bankers Trust. I was always able to sidestep currency devaluations because there were always clear signals by central banks that they were pending and then I just didn't get involved. Devaluations are such a digital process that it doesn't make sense to stand in front of the truck and try to pick up that last nickel before getting run down. You might as well wait, let the truck go by, then get back on the street and continue picking up nickels.

I do admit that I was devalued on once after I left Bankers Trust. Finland devalued when I was working for myself and I got caught long. I was partially asleep and a bit cocky because it had never happened to me before. The trading gods had to remind me to be humble.

Having missed all the major currency devaluations other than Finland over the past few decades, have you ever been sideswiped by the market?

I was sideswiped during the October 1987 stock market crash but it wasn't a huge deal. I lost $9 million in one day, but going into it I had already been up $10 million for the month. I only ended up making $1 million that month.

I've had other experimental trades that have blown up and were scary but never for a lot of money. For example, I tried applying the high yield versus low yield concept to Asia. In order to create yield, I bought stocks in Hong Kong and shorted the Hang Seng futures against them, which generated a very high yield on Hong Kong dollars with little stock market exposure. When the Asian stock markets blew up in October 1997, the Hang Seng futures market actually shut down. Suddenly, I was reminded about credit risk. I was long all these Hong Kong stocks and wasn't sure if my hedge was in place because there were rumors that the futures exchange had gone bust.

How did you manage through the Russia devaluation and Long Term Capital unwind?

As it turned out, 1998 was my best year ever—I was up 90-something percent for the year. Going into the turmoil in the fall, I was long a lot of volatility. I owned so many Eurodollar futures options that I made a killing when the Fed started cutting interest rates. I'd invested $6 million in option premium between June and July of that year, which turned into $48 million by September. (*See Figure 4.1.*)

I didn't know exactly what was going to happen but I thought the world looked wicked. Volatility was priced so low, implying nothing was going to happen, so I bought one-year options in several markets because I wasn't sure about timing. I didn't expect two major events to happen in the same month, but when they did, we cleaned up.

While LTCM was unwinding, there were all sorts of rumors of hedge fund blowups across the Street. I received a phone call from JP Morgan's credit department. They called me to tell me that we should continue

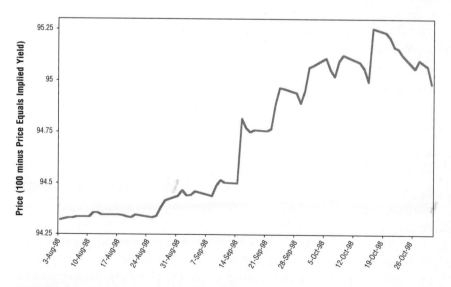

FIGURE 4.1   Eurodollar Futures, Fall 1998
Source: Bloomberg.

trading like we always did because they knew we would never blow up. They said they were worried about a lot of hedge funds but not us because we were always long volatility. They ended the call saying, "This is probably going to be a great month for you," and it was. It was very gratifying, and a really nice phone call to get.

Do you think we're in a similar state now where volatility is priced too low in light of the imbalances that are building up?

Yes, but you also have to see some kind of a trigger because you don't want to spend a lot of premium and time decay waiting for something to happen. In 1998, for some reason, I had a sense that something bad was building up. Maybe it was the 1997 blow-up in Asia that made me nervous, that something else was lurking out there. Right now, there are all kinds of bad things lurking but I'm just not sure when we're going to fall on the knife.

One of the things that makes me nervous today is how cheap credit risk has become. The whole credit default swaps (CDS) market has grown tremendously and derivatives have become ubiquitous. People are using derivatives with very little understanding of the kinds of risk they are taking on. I don't think the Bob Citrons of the world really thought about what they could lose if things went wrong.

Human biases tend to force people to focus exclusively on the good side of trades, which can be very dangerous. We are in an environment today where yields are very low and people are reaching for yield. One way to do this is via derivatives, where you can extract a little extra yield by selling optionality in a direction you don't think the market is going to go. The problem is, something can always happen, and markets often go where they are least expected to go.

Do you always focus on what can go wrong with a trade?

I'm very risk-neutral and focus on both sides. What I was saying is that humans in general are biased to look for confirmatory evidence. When someone is bullish oil, they tend to pick out the pro-oil arguments in whatever they read. Very few people train themselves to look for disconfirming evidence. Psychologists have done tests about how humans approach problem solving and found that we are somehow preprogrammed to look for confirmation and not for disconfirmation.

What I try to do in my trades is look for disconfirming evidence. It's a

BOB CITRON

In December 1994, the investment pool of Orange County, California, suffered a loss of over $1.6 billion, the largest loss ever recorded by a local government investment portfolio. It led to the subsequent bankruptcy of the county. Bob Citron, the county treasurer, was the man ultimately responsible for the $7.5 billion municipal funds portfolio, which financed county schools, certain city and special district projects, and the general workings of the county itself. Citron made heavy investments in reverse repurchase agreements and inverse floaters, the latter an interest rate derivative instrument that pays lower coupons as interest rates rise and higher coupons as interest rates fall. The instrument is thus extremely sensitive to interest rate movements. Citron's highly leveraged strategy—leverage enhanced through the reverse repurchase agreements—was based on speculation that interest rates would either stay flat or come down. In essence, he borrowed long and loaned out short, as long rates had remained consistently higher than short rates prior to this period. In 1994, however, the Fed began a series of interest rate hikes, leading to a spike in short term rates and a flattening of the yield curve. For someone invested in inverse floaters, this was a disaster scenario compounded by a vicious circle of collateral needs to satisfy the reverse repurchase agreements.

very difficult practice and I have to continually train myself to ask why I believe something is going to go down, not why it should go up.

What does global macro mean to you?

Global macro is the willingness to opportunistically look at every idea that comes along, from micro situations to country-specific situations, across every asset category and every country in the world. It's the combination of a broad top-down country analysis with a bottom-up micro analysis of companies. In many cases, after we make our country decisions, we then drill down and analyze the companies in the sectors that should do well in light of our macro view.

Take the former Yugoslavia, for example. We find it an interesting region from an investment standpoint because we believe Europe wants to show that they can rebuild countries even if they aren't good at sending troops. Also, Bosnia is a Muslim country, and with the question of Turkey joining the European Union looming, the Europeans are keen to show that they have nothing against Muslims, just a problem with Turkey. So we like the former Yugoslavia because money is pouring in behind a political agenda to rebuild the place. The problem is, you can't trade the Yugoslav currency and there isn't a Yugoslav bond market, so we have to get involved in equities. There isn't a Yugoslav equity index, so we have to get to the micro fiber of the companies to help decide which ones we should buy. The macro reason we like Yugoslavia is because it is being rebuilt, so we're buying Serbian construction stocks and infrastructure stocks like telecom and energy, as well as various companies in Bosnia. It's a macro theme expressed in a micro style.

Global macro only means that you start at the top and work your way down. A simple way to start is to differentiate between good countries and bad countries. We classify twin surplus countries as good and twin deficit countries as bad. When we find good countries, we then dig in and ask, "What can we do in this country? Why are things changing for the better?" When we find bad countries we ask, "Which sectors of this country are bad? How is that going to express itself? Is the currency going to go down? Is the stock market going to go down?"

When we find a twin surplus or good country, it doesn't mean that we then have to be long the currency and long the stocks necessarily. Every market could be a good buy or sell at any particular point. Take the United States, for example. It's a twin deficit country. We might be short dollars today but that doesn't mean that we have to be short the equity market.

Global macro means that we start out by saying that we're trying to find the right countries or the right asset categories to invest in. Once we've identified that, we still dig as deep as the micromanager who is specifically the equity guy in that country. Take India—we love India. There are a lot of things I can do in India. I can buy the currency, I can invest in Indian bonds, or I can invest in Indian equities. The most upside is going to come from the equities, so it then becomes my job to go out and find the best equity guy in India to help me figure out which stocks to buy. Just because I'm a macro guy doesn't mean I don't look at micro strategies.

How has global macro changed since you started?

First, more and more money has been directed toward it as a strategy. Number two, the market has become a lot more quantitative and analytical. When we all started in the 1970s and 1980s, it was all about gut feeling. It was a lot of fun then, but we've become a lot more scientific about it, like so many other things in today's world.

Currently, I am spending a lot of time pondering the difference between real money and hedge funds, asking why they are different from each other. We all play in the same pool, so why should a hedge fund have different returns from a good real money manager?

When you look at the statistics, you find different return distributions and noncorrelations between hedge funds and real money managers. This is attractive in a portfolio sense from a diversification standpoint. Given that I manage mostly my own money, I'm looking to create optimal performance over the long term, so moving out the efficient frontier is of strong interest to me.

I observe three main differences between hedge funds and real money funds. The first is *risk management*. Risk management is crucial. The smart real money accounts like Harvard Management Company or the Yale Endowment Fund rely on diversification as their essential risk management tool. They do not have stop-losses, nor do they believe in micromanaging their portfolio. They start out by setting their asset allocation mix and then, through rebalancing, they actually increase the risk.

We can illustrate this with a simple case study. Say they start out with an asset allocation mix of 50 percent equities and 50 percent bonds, and equities go down 20 percent. They now have approximately 45 percent of their portfolio in equities and 55 percent in bonds. To keep their asset allocation mix stable, they'll go out and sell some bonds and buy some equities to get back to 50 percent in each. If the stock market drops another 20 percent, they'll do the same thing again. Eventually, if the stock market keeps falling

REAL MONEY

Real money is another term for a "long-only" traditional asset manager who typically owns (long) instruments and does not short. The term *real money* means money is managed on an unleveraged basis, as opposed to hedge funds, which manage money using borrowed funds. Examples would be a corporate pension fund, a university endowment, a mutual fund, or a public pension fund.

like it did in Russia or in the NASDAQ, they end up taking on significantly more risk over time.

This differs from the hedge fund approach, which would just cut risk at a certain point. There are times when a hedge fund manager recognizes that the cost of being involved could be substantially larger than the cost of not being involved, in which case they are in cash. Meanwhile, the real money manager philosophy is, "If I'm not invested, I'm not earning risk premia, and over the long term I want to earn risk premia." This difference in approach probably accounts for most of the difference between hedge fund and real money manager performance.

The second difference is *leverage*. Real money managers do not take on leverage and their portfolio is limited by the capital they have under management. If an endowment or pension fund allocates money to a hedge fund and that hedge fund manager is six times leveraged, then the real money manager does have some leverage but isn't risking any more capital beyond what is allocated to the hedge fund. It's similar to spending premium for an option.

The third area where hedge funds, and macro funds especially, distinguish themselves from real money accounts is in their *choice of assets*. Hedge funds are willing to look for risk premia in many more places than real money managers do, or are allowed to.

In the big-picture sense, I believe the real money funds are right about wanting to earn risk premia as a way of making money. It's really hard making a lot of money being short the risk premia. Every once in a while, you make money because markets collapse, but in the long run you'll make more money being long markets.

Owning assets, or being long, is easier and also more correct in the long term in that you get paid a premium for taking risk. You should only give your money to somebody if you expect to get more back. Net/net it is easier to go long because over portfolios and long periods of time, you're assured of getting more money back. Owning risk premia pays you a return if you wait long enough, so it's a lot easier to be right when you're going with the flow, which means being long. To fight risk premia, you have to be doubly right.

Back to the smart real money funds, Yale has seven asset categories where they look to extract risk premia and Harvard has eleven. The question is, why doesn't Harvard throw in a twelfth category? They should be looking at other uncorrelated markets such as foreign exchange for more sources of risk premia. Once they identify new sources, they can allocate X percent and, in a Markowitz sense, run an efficient frontier to come up with what the correct allocation should be. But they don't do it. Asset categories like foreign exchange or options are not thought of as an asset category where risk premia can be earned.

As a hedge fund, we'll look anywhere for opportunities. The currency markets are a place where global macro hedge funds especially earn risk premia. I can name three risk premia in currencies that I don't think any real money manager has ever attempted to earn on a systematic basis.

1. *High yielding versus lower yielding currencies.* We talked about this earlier when discussing my days running the fund at Bankers Trust. This is a real easy one and there is now a multitude of research about the general propensity for this trade to work. At times it doesn't work, but over many, many years, it does. The market overcompensates investors for higher yield on average to what the future actually brings, so there is a risk premia to be extracted.

2. *Short-dated volatility is too high because of an insurance premium component in short-dated options.* People buy short-dated options because they hope that there's going to be a big move and they'll make a lot of money. They spend a little bit to make a lot and, on average, it's been a little bit too much. When they do make money they make a lot of money, but if they do it consistently they lose money. Meanwhile, someone who consistently sells short-dated volatility, on average, would make a little bit of money. It's a good business to be in and not too dissimilar to running a casino. So there is a risk premia there that can be extracted.

3. *Longer-dated options are priced expensively versus future daily volatility, but cheaply versus the drift in the future spot price.* We need to make a distinction between volatility and the future drift of the currency. Since the option's seller (the investment bank) hedges its position daily, it makes money selling options. Since some buyers do not delta hedge but instead allow the spot to drift away from the strike, they make money on the underlying trend move in the currency. So both the seller of the option and the buyer make money. The profit for the seller comes from extracting the risk premia in the daily volatility, and for the buyer it comes from the fact that currency markets tend to exhibit trending behavior.

The other thing that is pretty obvious in foreign exchange is that daily volatilities are much higher than the information received. Think of it like this: The euro bottomed out in July 2001 at around 0.83 to the dollar and by January 2004 it was trading at 1.28. (*See Figure 4.2.*) That's a 45 big figure move divided by 900 days, giving an average daily move of 5 pips, assuming straight line depreciation. Say one month option volatility averaged around 10 percent over that period, implying a daily expected range of 75 pips. That's a signal-to-noise ratio of 1 to 15. In other words, there was 15 times as much noise as there was information in prices!

Noise is just noise, and it's clearly mean reverting. Knowing that, we should be trading mean reverting strategies. In the short term, it's a no-brainer to be running daily and weekly mean reverting strategies. When things move up by whatever definition you use, you should sell and when they move back down, you should buy. On average, over time you're going to make money or earn risk premia.

In sum, you overpay for options but don't mind overpaying?

Correct, especially when you move out past one-month options. There is a tendency to believe that people overpay for options because the research shows that implied volatility is higher than realized volatility. That has to be the case for the seller to be willing to write you an option—he's got to make some money. The difference is, he's going to delta hedge and you're not, so

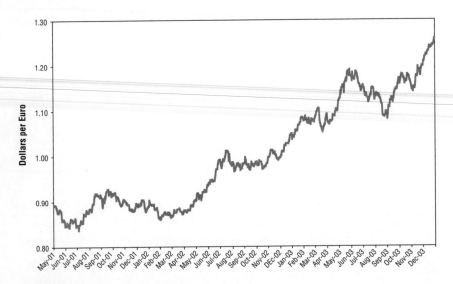

FIGURE 4.2   Euro, 2001–2003
Source: Bloomberg.

you are going to have to pay a little bit extra so that work gets compensated. You have to realize *ex ante* that yes, you are overpaying. The interesting thing is that you are not delta hedging nor are you paying the seller to do all the work. The market is. The seller is making his money off the delta hedge, and you are paying him a little bit by paying him more than what realized volatility is, but *ex ante* no one really knows what realized is.

We had a study done on the foreign exchange options market going back to 1992, where one-year straddle options were bought every day across a wide variety of currency pairs. We found that even though implied volatility was always higher than realized volatility over annual periods, buying the straddles made money. It's possible because the buyer of the one-year straddles is not delta hedging but betting on trend to take the price far enough away from the strike that it will cover the premium for the call and the put. Over time, there's been enough trend in the market to carry price far enough away from the strike of the one-year outright straddle to more than cover the premium paid.

Let's do a simple example. Say the euro moves up 10 ticks every day at noon. The market may consider that zero volatility but a year later, it will be up 22 big figures because there are 220 trading days a year. If the straddles were struck at a rate of 1.20, a year later spot would be at 1.42, which is a huge move. Meanwhile, the guy who sold you the option would say, "Boy, did you overpay for that option. The realized volatility was zero and I charged you 9 percent volatility." In the meantime, you paid 4.5 percent premium for an option that paid 15.5 percent.

It's not a bad trading strategy for being ignorant. Today, it's something that we do consistently. Every Friday, we go out and buy one-year straddles. We admit that we're ignorant but we expect that sometime, over a year, there will be enough trend that we will make money. So, to answer your question, yes, we do overpay for options but that doesn't mean we don't make money. If the option maturity is long enough, trend can take us far enough away from the strike that it's okay to overpay.

How do you size this trading strategy within your overall portfolio?

We're pretty ignorant about that, too. We look at it in terms of how much money we would be willing to lose if, in a year from now, every currency spot price is exactly the same as the previous year. There would have to have been two years of exactly the same price action across multiple currency pairs in order for all the options to be worth zero, so it's nearly impossible.

In light of that, we have decided to allocate 6.5 percent of our net asset value (NAV) toward this strategy. Every week we invest about 12.5 basis points in option premium across five currency pairs. We don't buy the same ones every week but instead buy what we think are the cheapest options that week.

If you allocate 6.5 percent to one strategy, does that mean you generally run about 15 independent strategies in your portfolio at all times?

That's where we'd like to get to eventually. We're not smart enough yet but we're trying to get there by learning from what the real money funds do so well. Again, just look at the endowments at Harvard and Yale as the prime examples of having done something really intelligent. They have averaged 16 percent or so annual returns for the past 10 years, which are just phenomenal returns, especially considering they're without leverage!

We always want to be a step ahead of them and the market, so we've done a lot of research on how we can take what they're good at and improve on it. The best concept we've taken from them is that you have to be invested, because if you're not, you're not in a position to make money. Likewise, if you're running short positions, you're paying away risk premia, which means you've got to be doubly right.

There have been some interesting studies on the reason to be invested across various asset classes. One looked at the S&P 500 index from 1992 to 2000 and found if you were long the whole time, you made 16 percent average annual returns. But, if you were flat on the 10 best trading days, you gave away 5 percent annually and only earned 11 percent average annual returns. That's a huge difference, and it would be so easy to miss 10 days over nine years.

You're moving away from the old global macro style of gut feel, market timing, and trend following.

Exactly. We're trying to move away from that. We think the future is a combination of the best from the real money world and the best from the hedge fund world to create a new paradigm.

The big thing that distinguishes the real money world from the hedge fund world is redemptions. Universities don't have redemptions, nor do family offices for that matter. Both are going to be around for years so they invest for the long term. Meanwhile, the hedge fund industry invests for the one- to three-month time horizon, which subjects managers to taking inefficiency risk and missing out on opportunities that are longer term in nature.

Take value versus growth, for example. Over the long term, value stocks appear to have outperformed growth stocks, but over some three-month periods, boy have they gotten crushed. Over the long term, value stocks will outperform because growth stocks by definition are priced too expensively. The public, in general, invests in stocks that have done well in the expectation that they will continue to do well. That works in the odd case like Microsoft, but most growth stocks will outperform for two or three years before reverting to the mean. Mean reversion works in the medium term.

If you have a real long-term view, number one, you want to be invested in some equities around the world because you want to earn risk premia, and number two, you want to choose those equities that on average will go up more than others, so you should be looking around the world for value stocks in valuable markets.

As a family office, we can take the requisite long-term view. I'm doing this with a 30- or 40-year time frame in mind, so I am free to go out and do things like buy Ghanaian value stocks because I think Ghana is an interesting country. I bought them three years ago and guess what—since then the Ghanaian stock market has outperformed almost every other market I know of and is up several hundred percent. (*See Figure 4.3.*)

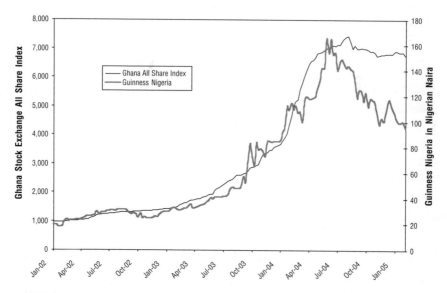

FIGURE 4.3   Ghana Stock Exchange All Share Index and Guinness Nigeria PLC, 2002–2005
Source: Bloomberg.

How do you find a market like Ghana?

I travel, I listen, I read.

Ghana is a good example of the value of reading *The Economist*. There were a few stories about their president—Kufuor—detailing his economic views and policies. He was very impressive and the upshot was that I started looking at it favorably. Another example is Nigeria. A few years ago *The Economist* had something on Nigeria, stating that average beer consumption had dropped from 34 liters to 3 and then rebounded to 4. That signaled to me that there must be a trade there. There's something going on when beer consumption drops 90 percent in a hot country and then starts to rebound. We started buying Guinness of Nigeria, and it's gone straight up over the last three years. (*See Figure 4.3.*) It was as close to a no-brainer as you can get. I'm sure many funds wouldn't want to touch it because of expropriation risk, illiquidity, and various other risks that they might have a hard time explaining to their customers, but to me, all that matters is performance. Nothing else.

How exactly do you structure your portfolio to achieve performance?

We start out knowing we want to be invested and earning risk premia. We separate our portfolio across five big-picture asset classes and admit we are ignorant by starting with 20 percent in each, rather than try to micromanage the way Harvard and Yale do.

One of the five asset classes is of course *equities*. Equities on average have made money around the world and will continue to make money because people don't give money to someone to build a business unless they expect to get more back.

In equities, we start by looking at various valuation measurements like price to book, price to earnings, and price to cash flow. As I have said earlier, it's very important to not be too story-driven. A way to avoid that is by using quantitive screens to determine what is cheap. Once you find things that are cheap, then look for stories that argue why it shouldn't be cheap. Maybe a stock is cheap but it'll stay cheap forever because there's no good story attached to the cheapness.

From a global perspective, we look for countries that we believe are cheap. Then we ask, "Do we like the politics? Do we like the economics? What do we like about it and why? What is changing?"

The next step is to look for big-picture stories. One big-picture country story that we like right now is India. We love India for the long-term story and think its role in the global service sector can really lead to serious outperformance. Where China has done something incredible to manufacturing, we think the same could be happening to services in India over the next 10 to 20 years.

Behind the Indian outsourcing story is the fact that technology and transportation costs have dropped, increasingly allowing for the transfer of services. For example, the National Health Service in the United Kingdom will pay for medical tourism in nonemergency situations. They will pay an English person covered by their health system to go to India to have an operation because there's a long waiting list in the United Kingdom and it's so much cheaper in India. Who would have thought that medical services could be outsourced? It just gets you thinking about what else could be outsourced that we've never considered. Here's another one: Last year, 200,000 Americans filed their taxes electronically through accounting firms where the accounting work was done in India. This year it's expected to be five times that number. These are epochal changes which have all kinds of implications for markets, inflation, and other things.

So we want an Indian allocation in our equity bucket because we think there might be something special happening there. Next we'd look for what's valuable in India and ask why it's going to become more valuable. We also look for what else India has going for it besides services, such as raw materials, and who else in India might benefit from this expected growth, such as the infrastructure companies.

Another big-picture equity theme we've been onto is rising energy costs. Out of the 20 percent Falcon has allocated to equities, we have 10 to 15 percent of that in energy-related equities. And so on and so on.

Our job in our equity category is to find investments around the world that will make money on an absolute basis as well as outperform any global equity index. We use classic hedge fund risk management and cut the position if things start going against us. We'll recognize that if we're wrong, we're wrong, and get out. Bid/offer spreads are not that big, so transactions costs are minimal.

The next big asset category where we can be systematic, earn risk premia, and control our downside is *fixed income*. In *Triumph of the Optimist* (by Elroy Dimson, Paul Marsh, and Mike Staunton), a book about risk premia around the world, there is a whole section on bonds. Because bonds, on average, have paid a positive risk premium over time, you are supposed to be long fixed income. They don't pay the same as equities, but they shouldn't because they aren't as risky as equities. But that's the beauty of being able to take on leverage. When we allocate 20 percent of our risk to fixed income, it doesn't mean we only put 20 percent of our assets into fixed income. There are all kinds of interesting things you can do in fixed income with leverage and still only utilize 20 percent of your capital.

For example, you could put 40 percent of your capital into shorter-duration bonds. When using leverage, you want the highest Sharpe ratio because you're borrowing money against your investment, and the best Sharpe ratios are found in the two years and under the sector of fixed income.

On an absolute return basis, two years and under bonds are not going to pay as much as a 10-year bond because the yields are usually lower. But the risk-to-return ratio is also very different. You could be five times levered in the two-year and get a higher payout with the same risk as a 10-year bond because of duration.

Just from that, a hedge fund can outperform a real money fund with the same risk because the real money guys will not leverage. We spend a lot of time thinking about how we can leverage each individual asset category because each one can be leveraged, although it's very different per category.

Our next big asset category is *foreign exchange*, which we discussed earlier. It's a whole area of risk premia that none of the real money funds are earning.

The fourth asset category is *commodities*. We have a commodity basket where we roll commodity futures contracts, which pays us a risk premium effectively for insuring the commodity producer. Over time, there is a risk premium inherent in commodity futures that is extracted by systematically buying the second contract out, riding it up the curve, and selling it. On average, that pays 6 percent real returns per annum. We've implemented this strategy just recently after reading a study by a Yale professor published by the National Bureau of Economic Research (NBER).

The last major category where we extract risk premia is *real estate*. As a small hedge fund, we cannot go out and buy office buildings but we can buy real estate-linked equities. Real estate-linked equity performance, on average, is not too dissimilar from buying real estate. The equity component is more volatile than the real asset but historically returns have been slightly higher.

The way real money funds generally play real estate is they find a manager to go out and buy real estate and office buildings, rent them out, and manage them. In this way, returns are highly dependent on finding managerial talent. We look for cheap real estate equities around the world. If we find a cheap real estate company, we're happy to buy the stock. We currently have exposure to real estate stocks in Poland, Finland, Sweden, Spain, Hong Kong, Indonesia, Singapore, and Taiwan, yet we don't own a single building or piece of land. We also own stocks of real estate bankers, builders, developers, land banks, real estate investment trusts (REITs), and so on.

How correlated is the real estate allocation to the 20 percent that you have in equities?

We haven't been involved long enough to get a reliable number. All I know is that it has done well, but even that doesn't mean anything. Globally, real estate could be peaking right now, but if it starts coming down, we'll hit our stop-loss and get out.

We're not fully invested in the five asset categories either, so this isn't an exact science. If we got to the point where each of our five strategies had 20 percent of total risk, we'd be really excited. But we're not there yet. We're still fine-tuning our style.

After these five main asset categories, we have a last category which we call *absolute return*. This is where we stick those great, out-of-the-box ideas we come across about twice a year. Sometimes we're lucky and find major mispricings once or twice a year, and sometimes we're unlucky and it takes 18 months before the next one comes along. When we find these fantastic ideas, we're willing to bet up to 10 percent of our fund on one idea. One that we think will double or triple, earning an extra 10 or 20 percent return for the entire portfolio. Over the last eight years, we've found about six or seven ideas like that.

Can you tell me about some of the successful absolute return trades?

In 1997, the gold forward curve was upward sloping, which we thought was kind of weird. Spot gold cost $310 and five-year-forward gold was trading at $380. Given the forward curve and the price of gold volatility, five-year $300-strike gold puts were trading at $3, making the risk/reward of the trade overly compelling. We were risking $3 if gold stayed over $300 and would make $300 if gold went to zero. Gold going to zero is not impossible, if for example, gold as a store of value is debunked for some reason. We bought a bunch of these gold puts and sold them two

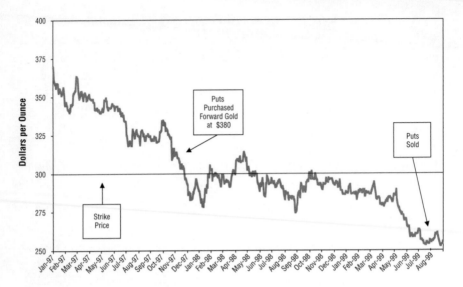

FIGURE 4.4   Gold, 1997–1999
Source: Bloomberg.

years later at $18—when gold was trading at $258—making six times our money. (*See Figure 4.4.*)

Another great trade over the years was betting on deflation by continuously buying interest rate options, which paid out when rates got low. We bought floors in the United States and Europe that paid off handsomely in 1998, and again after the stock market bubble burst post-2000, paying us multiples on our investment.

Another decent-sized investment for us was buying Russian equities in 1999 after the 1998 wipeout. When Russian equity prices got back to 1992 levels, from a risk/reward perspective, we figured it was time to reinvest. (*See Figure 4.5.*)

The absolute return category is there in order to leave us open to making this unsystematic money. The whole idea of being the hedge fund of the future is the ability to combine systematic and unsystematic money making strategies. We start off by acknowledging that we are ignorant, so we need to be systematic, clip some coupons, and earn some

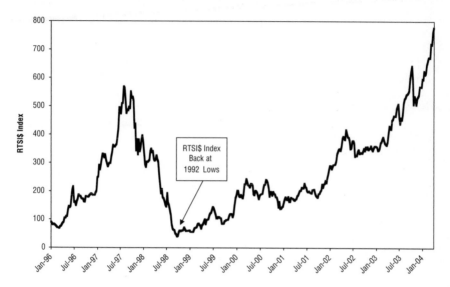

FIGURE 4.5 Russian Equity Index, 1996–2004
Source: Bloomberg.

risk premia. It doesn't matter if it is in currencies, bonds, commodities, real estate, or equities. Of course we have to be smart about it by reading a lot, talking to smart people, and being on top of it all, while acknowledging that we're not that much smarter than the rest of the world. Then, every once in a while, we're going to stumble upon an exciting idea that's going to give us some extra alpha and the ability to outperform.

There's really no excuse to not be systematic and ignore that 6 to 8 percent annual return you can get from just being involved. A lot of people would be happy with an 8 percent expected return but our target is much, much higher than that. Truly significant outperformance is going to come from combining the systematic with the nonsystematic ideas. This occurs when something just clicks due to experience and always being involved. You're reading, you're thinking, you're talking to a lot of people, and then you stumble upon something like Icelandic inflation-linked housing bonds and notice that it's a great bet, so you put a lot of money into it.

Every once in a while something like the Indonesian recap market or

DROBNY GLOBAL CONFERENCE, MARCH 2003

Jim Leitner's Favorite Trade: Inflation Index-Linked Housing Bonds from Iceland

Where can you get high real yields in an economy with a budget and trade surplus, an independent central bank, and with inflation and interest rates coming down? Leitner pointed to Iceland, which has been largely neglected by the financial community.

After five years of strong growth, the Icelandic economy is cooling fast. The central bank, made independent in 2001, has started cutting rates. The krona, which depreciated sharply a few years ago, is still pretty competitive despite having recovered by some 15 percent from the lows, and a very high trade deficit of a few years ago has been transformed into a surplus. On top of all this is the "Alcoa Project," where a good deal of capital investment and capital inflow is scheduled to begin in the next year or so.

The index-linked housing bonds yield roughly 5 percent real, well above the next highest index-linked yield offered in the world (New Zealand at below 4 percent). With inflation at just over 2 percent and falling, the total yield on these puppies is over 7 percent, against a short rate of 5.8 percent.

These bonds are the main liquid bonds circulated in that country, and are guaranteed by the government. Moreover, there is reasonably good volume to get a trade on, with a total outstanding circulation of $4 billion. The main owners and buyers of these bonds are domestics who, Leitner argued, are in pretty healthy financial positions. The risk of forced selling of these bonds seems very small, and upcoming supply should be easily absorbed by domestic funds. So, according to Leitner, these bonds offer an excellent yield, a good currency, and you buy something that isn't widely owned by hedge funds and other international financial institutions.

But the real kicker here is that these bonds are not yet euro-clearable. There are, however, changes coming in the next few months, which could well change this status. Such a change would likely push down the yield on these bonds very quickly as European funds add them to their portfolios. In the meantime, you earn very nice carry waiting for these events in an economy with excellent fundamentals. In terms of funding the trade, Leitner is running it 50 percent domestically funded (positive carry of 1.5 percent) and 50 percent USD funded, with positive carry of 6 percent and with long Europe versus USD currency risk.

Andres Drobny

Turkish currency forwards is going to pique your curiosity. The only thing systematic about finding these unsystematic trades is how we approach the world. We systematically look across the world's markets every day in order to find the unsystematic opportunities. The world is so big that there are tens of thousands of things we can trade and we end up missing 99.9 percent of all opportunities. Unsystematic opportunities by definition are hard to discover because they are unsystematic. It takes a systematic approach of looking at lots and lots of things to develop an implicit database in your head to let you know when something is not priced correctly versus other things in the world.

We've also hired quants to look at the world systematically and use price signals to make us think. They have models that scan 10,000 prices around the world. Every day when I come in, they give me a list of 20 to 30 things to look at that might be mispriced. For example, the other day they had me look at the Czech stock market because there was something going on with the index. I took a look and dug in deeper. The last time I had randomly looked at Czech stocks was two months prior, so this system forces me to think about various markets I normally would not. If I have a list of things that their computer says to look at, like India bank stocks or swaps in Sweden or the Canadian dollar, then I have no excuse not to look. What we're trying to do is develop computer-driven systems to identify price changes that appear nonrandom, not for trading so much but as a research tool. Over time, maybe it will develop into a trading system, which would be great because one thing we all know is that, on average, Commodity Trading Advisors' (CTA) trading models work.

What are some trades that you have in your absolute return book right now? Is India in there?

I would count India in that category of having outperformance potential but not in terms of having a separate 10 percent allocation. We actually want to get India to a 10 percent allocation such that it becomes 50 percent of our equity allocation. We haven't thought of India as a 10 percent nonsystematic bet, although maybe it should be. There are lots of unclear dividing lines between these things. We normally think of these 10 percent absolute return bets more as directly purchased options with a reasonably long maturity. This gives the idea time to come to fruition but with a well-defined downside.

One trade that we have on right now is options on Swedish interest rates, but it's only about 2.5 percent of the portfolio at this point. We see no justification as to why Sweden should be paying a half percent more in yield than Europe. It doesn't make any sense because its inflation rate is lower and its current account surplus is higher. At this point, both central banks have base rates at 2 percent but, five years forward, Sweden is trading at 50 to 60 basis points over Europe.

One thing you have to do with these 10 percent bets is go to the country and try to unearth what they're thinking, what could go wrong, and identify the macroeconomic impulses that maybe you don't understand or can't observe from looking at your screens. Often there is a reason why something like this is out of line. You discover this when you get on the ground and talk to the locals and the experts there. In many cases, there's no other reason except that historically it has been the case and no one has ever come along to say, "This isn't right."

By way of example, for a long time Dutch interest rates were 100 basis points above German interest rates, while the two currencies traded in tandem. I remember going to see the central bank in the Netherlands and telling the central bank governor that I was long billions and billions of Dutch guilders against deutsche marks. I asked him why he had the Dutch taxpayers send me a check every month as there was no reason to compensate the market to own Dutch guilders at that time. They had perfect credibility in the market so there was no excess risk. Two months later they narrowed the interest rate differential and I made my capital gain. The funny thing is, I don't think anyone was ever so candid with him. The same thing could happen in Sweden, so we have a little toehold position there that we're planning to build up to 10 percent. I'll go to Sweden to visit their central bank governor soon thereafter.

Other than Sweden, our unsystematic portfolio is relatively light at the moment. We have a shortage of big ideas at the moment—sometimes you get a few in a year and sometimes you don't find any.

Do you think the influx of money into hedge funds is causing the great ideas to be arbitraged out of the market?

The relative value opportunities are being arbitraged out because there are too many people looking for the same kind of stuff. There is a very limited amount of money that can be directed toward these types of opportunities. Real arbitrage, in the old sense of the word, meant that there was no risk at all. Arbitrage today means a huge amount of risk is required to take advantage of small perceived mispricings.

I want to go with the tide and take advantage of some of the larger, long-standing market biases like value versus growth stocks, or high yield versus low yield. The competitiveness of the world economy is such that mean reversion reigns, so you should buy the guys who are underperforming. Some of them will go bankrupt but many of them will come back up to the mean. Many of the growth stocks will also pull back to the mean as those who are great will become mediocre and those who are mediocre will become better.

This is not an arbitrage in the sense that you can lock in the gain. It's just a truism that, over time, mean reversion works. To take advantage of it, a one-year-plus time horizon is required at minimum, but a five-year-plus time horizon is ideal.

Therefore, all this money being directed toward macro funds and hedge funds is, in a sense, driving out all the easy inefficiencies that are so well documented. The large inefficiencies do not get arbitraged out because there's very little capital that actually gets allocated toward extracting value over multiple years. Everybody who's allocating money to hedge funds has monthly or quarterly redemption clauses, which force hedge funds to manage to those liquidity parameters, and that's not at all the way to wealth.

If all investors allocate money to a one-month time frame, by definition there are going to be fewer opportunities there. Randomly selected, some hedge funds will blow up and some will have great runs but there's just too much competition over short-term trading, which is a timing-driven business. With timing, sometimes you're going to be right and sometimes you're going to be wrong, but it's not going to be consistent over time, nor are the returns going to be good quality on a risk-adjusted basis.

Meanwhile, the longer-term opportunities still exist because there hasn't been that much money allocated with multiyear lockups. If a trillion dollars got allocated to managers with five-year-plus lockups, then we'd see long-standing biases like value versus growth slowly disappear. That's not happening yet and probably won't because investors are way too nervous and shortsighted.

To continuously make money in the big picture, you've got to overlay the earning of risk premia over a wide variety of time frames, instruments, continents, and countries with the sourcing of the occasional home-run type of investment opportunity.

The shortage of ideas this past year has been frustrating. But it's been a great year in terms of allowing me the time to think about this idea of combining real money investing with hedge fund discipline and to look toward the future. These are really exciting times and I think the next 10 years are going to be fabulous, bringing new opportunities into the macro world and allowing us to grow a fantastic business.

CHAPTER 5

THE PROP TRADER

Christian Siva-Jothy
Former Head of Proprietary Trading, Goldman Sachs
SemperMacro
London

What began as a means to get free drinks turned into quite a career for Christian Siva-Jothy. Formerly one of the biggest proprietary traders on the Street, Siva-Jothy admittedly got into the business because going to bank presentations while at university was an inexpensive way to finance a social life. More interestingly, his first job on a foreign exchange desk at Citibank was the day of the stock market crash in 1987. Rather than taking it as an inauspicious sign, Siva-Jothy immediately knew proprietary trading was what he was meant to do. He moved to Goldman Sachs (GS) a few years later, where he eventually became the partner in charge of fixed income and currency proprietary trading.

Goldman Sachs in the early 1990s hardly lived up to its century-old image as a staid investment bank making money through old-line relationships. Rather, it turned into one of the biggest proprietary risk takers among the investment banks, with its traders making huge bets with firm capital in global fixed income, foreign exchange (FX), commodities, and derivatives.

I first met Siva-Jothy when he was still head of proprietary trading at

Goldman Sachs. A friend suggested I contact him, after dubbing him "the man." Soon thereafter, I found myself on the sprawling Goldman trading floor awaiting the often rumored about, almost mythic trader who occupied the glass corner office. Yet Siva-Jothy, I was told by his secretary, was running late. Could I reschedule?

On the way off the floor I ran into an old colleague. As we caught up for 15 minutes or so, I caught a glimpse of a man walking briskly across the trading floor toward me. Compact and bespectacled with close-cropped hair, the gentleman was clad in tan pants and a casual shirt, a far cry from the Goldman uniform of a dark suit and power tie. "Hi, I am Christian, I am very sorry for being late," he began, the first of a series of deeply sincere apologies for having kept me waiting.

Tardiness aside, Siva-Jothy turned out to be quite courteous, going to the coffee bar himself to bring back fresh brew and talking with me for well over an hour. A few months after this initial meeting, Siva-Jothy retired from his partnership at Goldman Sachs, where he had run proprietary trading for the previous 10 years. Over that time, his trades, the size of his bets, the consistency of his annual profits for the bank, and his grace under pressure had become the stuff of legend amongst traders.

Siva-Jothy spent a total of 17 years as a bank proprietary trader, which gives him a different view of global macro markets than a hedge fund manager out on his own, given that a prop trader is betting with bank credit lines and managing risk off of a stop-loss. This interview was conducted after he had left Goldman but before he launched his own fund, SemperMacro. Siva-Jothy offered a rare look at the high-risk, high-pressure culture of Goldman Sachs trading and the differences he sees between running a prop trading business inside a bank structure and running an independent hedge fund.

As I approached his new office off a side street in Mayfair, London, a black cab pulled up to the front door to reveal a congenial Siva-Jothy. He greeted me amiably and fished in his pocket for the £3 fare. The taxi driver did not have change for his £20 note so, while apologizing profusely, he asked if I happened to have any change.

Once inside, we settled in the conference room for the interview session, with Siva-Jothy again providing coffee and a mild manner, chatting and laughing about the people and wild times from his days at Goldman Sachs. About 15 minutes into the interview, his personal assistant interrupted us to hand me the £3 I had paid the cab driver, which he adamantly insisted I accept after thoroughly reiterating his gratefulness.

"After all," he said, "I would not want it to turn up in your book that I stiffed you for a few pounds."

How did you become a proprietary trader?

By accident. I was going to do a postgrad at the London School of Economics in econometrics back in the late 1980s and a good way to get a free drink then was to go to these bank presentations. At the Citibank one, a guy thought I was funny so he asked me to come in and spend a day on the trading floor, which I did. I thought it was just great—it was a big open floor with open outcry and it just looked fantastic. I decided that there was no downside doing it for a year; if I didn't like it, I'd go back to school. Then I just got totally hooked. It was October of 1987. I spent two years market-making forward cable and then moved to the interest rate product group, trading UK interest rates in a proprietary fashion.

Was the October 1987 U.S. stock market crash your introduction to markets?

I had just started after a three-month training course at the London Business School when the crash happened. I was sitting next to a chap to learn from him who gave me a five-bond limit and said, "Get out of my way and trade these." It was moving in one- to five-point ranges, and I thought it was absolutely great. I thought it was going to be like this every single day. The noise levels were immense and it was a very intense atmosphere. It was quite a formative experience, starting during that period.

What was it like at work the day after the U.S. stock market lost a quarter of its market capitalization? People thought the world financial system was imploding.

I was in foreign exchange and we weren't that worried, somewhat naively, probably. I remember the day and the day before, but not much else. The next thing I remember was when the United Kingdom had a minicrash a few years later in 1991. In between those two events there's nothing that really stands out. There are specific things I remember, but it's funny how certain events stick in your mind. They are usually periods when I've had major profit and loss (P&L) swings.

When did you move from Citibank to Goldman prop?

It was in September 1991. I'd been at Citi for three and a half years when I was approached by Goldman Sachs. It's a longish story, but a woman at Citibank knew one of the senior guys at Goldman pretty well. He told her that they were looking for somebody and she threw my name into the hat.

I went over to interview and they actually ended up offering me a job to trade the specials book. I said, "No, I want to work on the prop desk." Apparently I was the first guy who had ever turned them down. Mike O'Brien, who was the partner in charge of London trading, later told me for that reason he was determined to get me to join. About six months later, they offered me a prop trading job and I went over.

Which prop desk at Goldman did you join?

I joined the fixed income prop desk, but because of my forward foreign exchange background, I spent the next few years working in Goldman's J. Aron division (foreign exchange and commodities) prop group as well. Goldman Sachs was very, very different from Citibank. Citibank had a risk appetite, but nothing like Goldman. At Citibank, if you made 15 bucks (US$15 million), you were a hero. At GS, to be noticed your P&L had to be a lot higher.

I remember my first week on the job, I put on a 50 million deutsche mark/Swiss franc position, which was a fairly sedate cross. I'd been a trader for four years at that point and it was the biggest position I'd ever had on in my career. I thought, "I'm going to do it."

I remember the head of trading walking over and asking, "How's it going, Christian—you got anything on?"

I said proudly, "Yes, I'm short 50 Mark Swiss."

He paused, looked at me, and said, "I like a guy who averages into his positions," and walked off.

Goldman had a risk appetite that took me a little bit of time to get used to. It was a bit of a free-for-all at GS in the early 1990s, but the opportunities were there. There were no limit structures per se, no value at risk (VAR) system. It was just kind of get on and do it and hope for the best. There were a lot of characters around in those days who were very interesting.

Can you tell me about some of the characters and mentors?

There was no single mentor—just the openness of the environment was probably the biggest mentor for me. The attitude at GS was "Suck it and see," "If you want to try a big position, try it," and "Make mistakes, but learn from them." That was the culture and the philosophy on the trading side of the firm, which I thought was incredibly powerful. It was a wonderful environment in which to work, but it was to have its downside as we discovered in 1994.

There was one character who stands out, an experienced trader who joined the prop desk in the early 1990s after trading his own account on a brokerage floor. I remember the day he joined, as he sat at the desk next to me. I was trading notional bond futures contracts in 100 lot tickets. When he saw me buy 100, he asked, "Did I hear you say 100?"

I said, "Yes."

He goes, "I've been in this business for 20 years and the largest block I've ever traded is 10. You're a whippersnapper. How can you have a position of 100?"

I said, "I don't, I've actually got a position of a couple thousand" (one thousand lots equals a notional position of $100 million).

At that point, a light bulb went off in this guy's head and he suddenly realized that this was a place where he was going to push the envelope. What he did was leverage the risk appetite that existed at GS at that time.

One of the funniest things I saw in that period was at the height of the big bond rally in 1993. This guy clicked into one of those open box-type lines to the floor and said, "Buy Bunds." Next thing you hear is the broker calling back, "How many do you want me to buy?" He clicks straight back in and goes, "I said buy Bunds, I'll tell you when to stop."

He also had a very comfortable attitude with senior people at Goldman. There was an amusing story with Gavyn Davies, who was the chief economist at GS at the time. Gavyn came into an office where we were gathered to give the prop group his overview of the world and his thoughts on Europe. This trader, with his boots up on the desk, turns to Gavyn and says, "With all due respect, Gavyn, I do my own research. I was in quite a few bars in Spain last weekend and let me tell you something—they were empty." Gavyn was a bit surprised by this in-depth economic analysis. Then the guy added, "I've got another rule that I live by: If you can't drink the water, sell the currency."

There were a lot of amusing stories from this time, it would take a lot of space to recount them all. There are specific things I learned about trading and sentiment from this guy that came from his floor trading experience which I absorbed into my trading style. There were also a lot of other things I had to unlearn.

Can you tell me about some of the good lessons you learned from him?

His appreciation that size isn't important. That it doesn't matter if you're small or big, it's kind of irrelevant, as long as you're comfortable with it. At GS, he basically leveraged up exactly what he had been doing. He was very comfortable in big positions. I mean, this is a guy who went from trading 10 lots to trading lots of 10,000.

How would his trading style fly at Goldman Sachs today?

It wouldn't be tolerated. That period, 1990 to 1994, was a different time. Everyone became a prop trader—all the franchise guys turned into mini prop traders. There were 500-plus prop traders at Goldman Sachs then and they all had on the same position. Then came 1994, which was the turning point in my career. I had a huge loss in sterling/yen that is mentioned in the Goldman Sachs book.

I'd been on a bit of a roll and got carried away with it. I'd had a phenomenal year in 1993—I made well over $100 million and I was a bit full

GOLDMAN SACHS

In December 1993, one of the firm's most profitable traders had been bullish on the British pound, predicting its rise against the yen. The firm's appetite for risk had grown, and he established a large sterling-yen position that would benefit from the strengthening of the British currency against that of Japan. The pound rose gradually against the yen over the course of December and early January, but in February the British currency declined against the Japanese currency by 10 percent over fifteen trading days. By the time the position was fully liquidated, the loss totaled more than $80 million. The chorus of those concerned grew louder, and Winkelman and Corzine began to make more regular trips to London, spending long hours sitting on the trading desks. As risk taking had spread across the firm's trading desks, some of London's traders had now managed to lose most of their previous year's profits—and 1994 was still young.

Source: Lisa Endlich, *Goldman Sachs: The Culture of Success* (New York: Touchstone Books, 2000).

of myself—and 1992 had also been a great year. Going into 1994, I'd built a very large sterling/yen position. It was over £1 billion, which was the biggest position I'd ever run. I had put it on the November of the previous year and was up about $30 million on the position. People were starting to say, "Christian is going to do it again," and it had only moved a few percent. At this point, I had become so confident that besides being long sterling/yen via a mixture of cash and options, I was also selling sterling/yen puts whenever the cross corrected.

Then during the first weekend in February, President Clinton came out and attacked the Japanese on trade policy. He threatened them with tariffs and quotas on cars and car parts. The United States gave the Japanese a real hard time and said, "Look, your currency is going to have to appreciate, or else."

I remember coming in on the Monday morning and dollar/yen had gapped lower 5 percent with nothing trading. If that wasn't bad enough, five days later, on Friday, UK inflation numbers were released, and they were simply awful. Sterling went into a free fall. It was classic—the market found me.

The long and short of it is the position dropped about 10 percent in the space of a few weeks. I was selling out of the position as fast as I could but I was selling just to stand still because I was short these puts. It was a disaster. Markets have a great way of taking it out of you.

So you lost somewhere between $100 million and $200 million of Goldman's money?

Yep. On day eight of this episode, when the biggest move happened and I lost about $40 million in one day, I remember feeling this overwhelming desire to get up and walk out, to pretend it wasn't happening. It was such a powerful emotion. Instead of walking out though, I took a deep breath and liquidated everything. (*See Figure 5.1.*)

The firm was just amazing about it. One of the co-heads of the division happened to be in the London office at the time. I went into his office and he said, "Christian, sit down, what's this all about?"

I said, "I've lost X, I've liquidated everything. What do you want me to do?"

He looked at me and said, "If you hadn't liquidated and come in here, you wouldn't be working at Goldman Sachs anymore. What I want you to do now is go out and make it back, with lower risk limits."

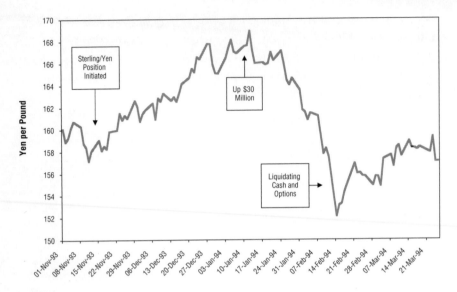

FIGURE 5.1   Sterling/Yen, 1993–1994
Source: Bloomberg.

Simultaneously, the Fed started tightening and the bond markets started tanking. I actually ended up making about 35 percent of my loss back being short fixed income.

After 1994, they dramatically changed the proprietary trading structure of the firm. A lot of people left, and a lot of people were let go. The prop group went from 20-plus pure prop traders down to 3 by mid 1995. They asked me to run the European proprietary trading group and rebuild it but with a very different risk mandate. That was the birth of what I call the "new proprietary trading group."

What lessons did you learn from the sterling/yen loss?

Confidence is a very, very dangerous thing. Simply because you've had a good run doesn't mean it will continue. In fact, once you've had a good run, you're at your most dangerous. Overconfidence is an absolute killer. Markets can take it away as easily as they give it. It doesn't matter how well things are going, you should always kind of pinch yourself, take a step back, and ask, "What can go wrong?" In fact, the better things are going, the more you should look at where your risks are and what the downside is.

Also, you should never be short gamma. I've become very anti any kind of short gamma trade. That includes carry trades, which in my mind are essentially synthetic short gamma trades. I'm a great believer that portfolios in the macro space should always be long gamma, not short. Never, ever be short gamma.

GAMMA

Gamma is the second derivative of an option's value. It is the rate of change for *delta* (the first derivative), which is the relationship between an option's value and the price movement of the underlying asset. When an option is at-the-money (the underlying asset is near the strike price), gamma is high. When an option is deep in-the-money or deep out-of-the-money, there is little gamma. Owning an option is equivalent to being long gamma, whereas writing an option creates a short gamma position.

The most important lesson I learned about trading in 1994, was that liquidity comes at a cost, and a lack of liquidity comes at an even greater cost! I was short some short-dated options to help mitigate my time decay. When the dislocation came, I lost many, many multiples of what I had taken in by selling those options. I learned not only not to sell options, but to actively look for options to purchase in times of stress or dislocation. Leaving a stop would not have helped me in 1994, because the market gapped. However, if I had been long a put, the problem would have been entirely on the shoulders of the counterparty who had sold it to me.

The beauty of trading is you still make the same mistakes; hopefully you just make them on a much smaller scale. For example, now when I get a little bit overconfident, I usually recognize it straightaway and when positions start going against me, I cut them a lot quicker. I'd like to think I'm much more levelheaded now.

As an epilogue, sterling/yen dipped the following year, but over the next five years it went from 130 to 240 with very high annual carry. I take no comfort from this at all, as it just tells me that my timing was out by a year! (*See Figure 5.2.*)

Was it scary to see your particular trade moving the sterling/yen exchange rate?

Markets are going to go where they're going to go. Yes, sure, on one or two days when I was liquidating, it pushed it down, but the moment I stopped selling, it went where it was going to go.

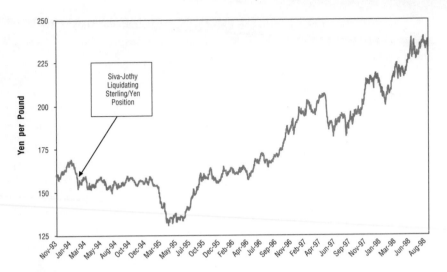

FIGURE 5.2   Sterling/Yen, 1993–1998
Source: Bloomberg.

Markets are immense but if people know there's a big position out there that is being liquidated, they'll go for it. Nick Leeson at Barings Singapore and Long Term Capital Management are the classic cases. The market sniffed their unwinding and traded against them.

Did the sterling/yen experience prove useful later on?

Yes, definitely. The 1998 LTCM/Russia episode for me was the reverse. The firm didn't have a great 1998, but the prop group did and I attribute it to the lessons learned in 1994.

In 1998, GS had a risk arbitrage group that was set up a few years earlier. They were all very young guys, mostly PhDs, who had relatively little trading experience. They had all these risk arbitrage positions on but they were also running all these other positions which were just immense. Meanwhile, we were considered the old guys since we were in our 30s. We used to look at each other and say, "This is going to end in tears." When it did start unraveling, we just loaded up on Eurodollar contracts. (*See Figure 5.3.*)

It was fascinating for me, though, as it was like looking from the outside in. I was watching all these kids make the same mistakes I did in 1994 solely because they had made a lot of money in the previous years. Since 1994, 1998 was our best year, but it was totally swamped because the risk arb guys lost a lot of money.

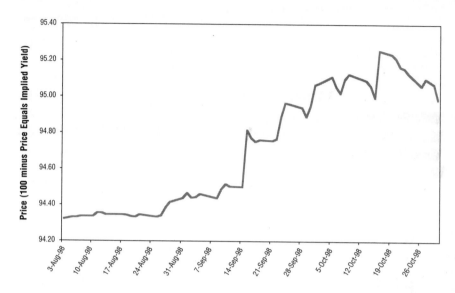

FIGURE 5.3   Eurodollar Futures, Fall 1998
Source: Bloomberg.

In seeing yourself in your colleagues and knowing what they were thinking, you knew to take the other side of the trade?

Yes. As the thing was unraveling, the risk arb group went from up a lot to down a lot. I knew one of the risk arb guys pretty well, and occasionally I'd drop him off on my way home. He was 23 and made approximately $20 million for the firm the previous year. As far as I was concerned that was pretty good. I remember heading home with this guy and asking him how it was going. He says, "I'm up $50 million. What do you think I should do?"

I say, "Look, I don't want to sound like granddad, but the other guys are having a tough year and you're up $50 million. Cut the position out. Trust me, it's a damn good number, you should be happy with it."

He looks at me and says, "But if I cut it, I'll be down 50 bucks."

Those were his exact words. His P&L at the moment was up 50, and if he cut the position, he'd be down 50 because there was no liquidity. When I got home, I bought a lot more Treasuries and Eurodollars, thinking, "This is going to get a lot worse."

Long Eurodollars seems to be your go-to trade.

It's a simple trade and it's liquid. When I see dislocation in the direction of pain to the U.S. economy, I buy Eurodollars—it's not brain surgery.

I remember having a disagreement with a guy in Goldman's risk unit during the big rate-cutting cycle post-2000 in the United States. He said, "Why are you guys always long Eurodollars? Why don't you have some South American fixed income, something in Asia, some diversification?"

My reply was, "When the Fed is in an aggressive rate-cutting mode I want to be long Eurodollars because it's the most obvious trade in the most liquid market in the world. I don't want to be long South American fixed income or anything else when there is a clear trend in a liquid market." (*See Figure 5.4.*)

Over your trading career, have you made more money in fixed income from the long or short side?

Long, and again that makes perfect sense when you look at how markets trade. Bear markets in fixed income are very short with powerful rallies. You can make money during a bear market but you have to time your trades perfectly. You have to have that skill, and it's quite different. As a medium-term player, I would expect generally to make money in a rallying market. Also, being long fixed income is a synthetic long gamma trade. More than 90 percent of the time, if there is a major dislocation to the economy, fixed income will rally. I sleep better at night knowing that.

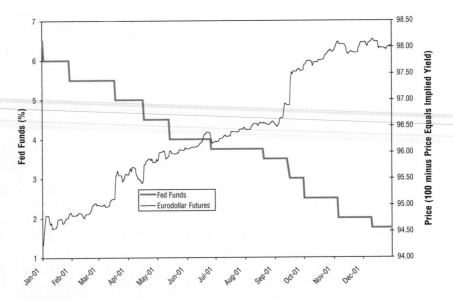

FIGURE 5.4 Fed Funds and Eurodollar Futures, 2001
Source: Bloomberg.

There are other trades where you can make money in a fixed income bear market, such as currencies. There are often great opportunities in the foreign exchange markets when you start getting bear fixed income markets.

What is your time horizon for trades?

It varies. I talk about myself as a medium-term player, but the reality is you can put on a position, an event happens five minutes later, and everything's changed. You have to keep reassessing why you're in a trade and if you should still be in it. If the reasons change or the data changes, you should be out. On balance, my trades vary from zero to three or four months.

How do you generate ideas? Do you read Wall Street research?

Generally not. The problem is, if you get it all coming in, it's overkill. I prefer to be proactive by having stuff sent on specific topics when an idea is crystallizing in my head, as opposed to sifting through all of it. I need stuff that makes me think, which is why a general discussion is much more useful than having a trade idea or worldview shoved down my throat. At the simplest level, I like to see price action. It's very important. It tells you when people have bullish or bearish sentiment. I love watching price. If I could only have one tool, it would be a ticker, or the equivalent.

Do you think it's important to have your feet on the ground when developing a trade idea? For example, if you're looking at a new trade in Switzerland, do you go there?

Generally, no. What am I going to learn about Switzerland in a day or a week? Are you going to walk in to the central banker's office and expect him to tell you he's going to cut rates next week? It's so much posturing.

You've got to know a place really well for there to be value in going back. If you've lived in some place like Switzerland or China for, say, 10 years, then you've got an anchor and can see change or at least know what to look for.

My wife lived in China for a couple of years and we've got good friends out there. I don't go there very often anymore, but I speak to people there a lot who give me very good color as far as what's changed. But that still doesn't give any great insight into whether the central bank will revalue the currency next week, next month, or next year.

There is another problem with traveling for ideas. Being in the financial industry in New York or London, we are already biased by our own financial filter and often have no idea what's happening in the real world even if we see it with our own eyes.

What are your thoughts on Greenspan and central bankers in general? Do you think they've gotten better at their game and have smoothed market movement, or do you think they have smoothed some markets at the expense of others?

They've definitely gotten better at nuancing markets and the Fed is particularly good at it. However, the market seems to believe, "Well, these guys have got all these levers that they can pull to solve everything." That's pie in the sky. They can't solve the underlying issues. They can buy time but little else. I suspect the real problems will hit after Greenspan's departure, as he doesn't want it to happen on his watch.

What is your long-term view of the world right now?

My gut feeling is that there will be a lot of pain because we still have to pay for the 1990s and that worries me. It worries me on a personal level and a family level, but on a business level, it's fantastic. It's the dichotomy of this business that we thrive on dislocation and economic upsets. Macro traders always do better when the world economy is tanking. It's a great hedge, in a way.

Generally, I can't see more than a year ahead because things change so rapidly it's very difficult to have a 5- to 10-year view. I have a rolling one-year view of the world and I impose discipline on myself by keeping a trading diary. Every morning, I go through the same process: If I have any positions on, I ask why do I have the positions? What has changed?

Your P&L tells you a lot, but I don't think it always tells you everything when you're trading medium term because, by definition, you'll lose money at certain points in time. In fact, there will be days and sometimes weeks where you'll lose money, but that doesn't necessarily mean the position is wrong. If I have a trade on and it's making money, it doesn't necessarily mean it's the right trade, either. You can make money for the wrong reasons, but you should be as disciplined taking it off as if you're losing money.

Taking off a trade that is winning for the wrong reasons requires a lot of discipline. When that happens, you should get out of the position straightaway. It's the equivalent of putting on positions because someone really smart that you respect has it on. That's a recipe for disaster because you don't know why you got in or where to get out. These are all common mistakes.

To maintain discipline is very difficult, but that is why I keep a trading diary, to keep me honest. I wish I could say I follow my own rules 100 percent. It seems one is constantly relearning the same trading lessons. The market is always there to keep you in check and is a totally objective judge of your performance. The P&L at the end of the day is yours with no one else to blame. I find it amazing how people always find something or someone else to blame for their mistakes. "It wasn't me, the market was irrational; it's not fair, if the firm hadn't cut me out of this position I'd be up X," and so on. Well, they cut you out of the position because you were down X.

Given your medium-term view, do you express your views via options or the cash market?

I always structure my portfolio to be 50 to 60 percent options. I'll trade cash but opportunistically. My medium-term options are three to six months maturity and then I'll do a lot of overnight options. For example, if I am long the euro currency, I'll sell overnight calls and buy puts when the trade is near my target.

Would you say the average proprietary trader's portfolio management style is to chip away at small trades and then lever up when something big comes along?

Yes. I'm a great believer that there are three or four major macro opportunities each year. If you catch one, your return will be in the high single digits; if you catch two, you should be up somewhere between 10 and 20 percent; if you catch three or four, you're doing incredibly well.

One of the most difficult things about trading is not to trade. That's probably one of the most common mistakes that people starting out in this business make. Overtrading is as bad as running losing positions for too long.

What was your favorite trade at Goldman?

I'm not sure I'd use the word favorite, but the most informative of my career was the sterling/yen trade because every time I go back and look at it, I learn more. It was such a formative experience for me. It had all the elements. It's fascinating to go back to my trading diaries and read through my thoughts.

A very lucky trade that I loved was a trade based on the Bund BTP spread [the interest rate spread between German government bonds (Bunds) and Italian government bonds (BTPs or Buoni del Tesoro Poliennali)]. It was on the winning side, and was a smart trade that I did with another guy. I was and am a great believer in Europe, and one of the things that the market massively underestimated in the 1990s was the political will in Europe for monetary union.

In 1995 we started looking at a convergence trade, and the BTP spread to Bunds at that point was about 600 basis points over. By the time we put the trade on, it was around 500 over. We believed Italy was going to adopt the euro and we thought the spread was going to go to 200 in the medium-term and eventually to parity, so we structured a currency barrier range bet option in mark/lira with a compressing knockout feature.

Our currency options guys gave us this structure for almost nothing and we put it on in decent size as the risk/reward ratio was exceptional. Normally, I don't like these path-dependent, perfection-type derivative structures, but we figured if this convergence thing was going to happen, the profile was a good one.

So this thing paid off well, but because we did all our trades internally, our own options desk got absolutely crushed. They were massively short volatility on this trade and getting doubly whacked as they tried to cover the position because every time it looked more likely Italy was going to adopt the euro, the spread got tighter.

Meanwhile, we were sitting there waving our flags, because we were printing money. Eventually, senior management had to step in and ask us to take off the trade because it was killing the franchise. We took the trade off well before the end of 1999 only because we had to, but if it was on with someone else, we probably would have kept on running it to the launch of the euro. We pretty much ran the Bund/BTP convergence trade to about 50 over. It was a satisfying trade. (*See Figure 5.5.*)

That's probably the longest-term trade I've done. Normally, satisfaction is not intellectual, it's just that quick event trade where you react instinctively, do the trade, and that's it. This one had a lot of thought behind it and it worked.

Can you tell me about a quick event trade you caught?

One that I enjoyed was during sterling's exit from the Exchange Rate Mechanism in 1992. I made very little money betting against the pound, like Soros and everybody else, but I had a massive interest rate bet on that worked great.

I bought calls on short sterling interest rate futures during the event as they jacked up rates to protect the pound. Raising rates when the UK economy was on its knees was an obviously stupid move by the government. As it played out, I bought calls on short sterling at 10 percent and 13 percent. The options were expensive as the Street priced volatility through the roof, but implied volatilities are always massively undervalued during big events. My biggest mistake on the trade was to take the position off too

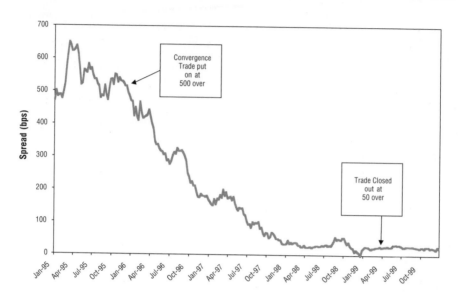

FIGURE 5.5   10-Year Bund BTP Spread, 1995–1999
Source: Bloomberg.

early. I made a lot of money, but if I'd run them for another month or two, I would have made at least twice as much.

Speaking of quick event trades, there's the September 11 trade that was in the **Wall Street Journal** *article. I know for some outside the industry it sounds perverse to profit from disaster, but when you are trading, your job is to react and protect your investors' capital.*

And the markets are going to do what they're going to do. They're not going there because I'm doing it—they were going to go there anyway. No one can move the short end of the U.S. fixed income markets for more than a few basis points; only the Fed has the power to do that.

On the morning of September 11, I was already long U.S. fixed income as I had a structural view that the U.S. economy was weak. It was a decent-sized position as I had been having a reasonable year. I was on the Goldman trading floor in London and I remember hearing someone say, "A plane's crashed into the side of the World Trade Center." The first thing I noticed on the TV was that it was a perfectly clear blue sky day. I'm a helicopter pilot and I've been flying for 14 years. I know that when you've got a plane that's going down, you don't aim for the tallest

TO WEATHER ROCKY PERIOD, GOLDMAN MAKES RISKIER BETS

On September 11, 2001, after terrorists flew the first of two passenger jets into the World Trade Center, Mr. Siva-Jothy, who was on the London trading floor, immediately turned to a colleague and said the disaster hadn't been an accident, according to people familiar with the comment. The weather in New York was clear, and the crash was purposeful, he reasoned. Mr. Siva-Jothy instantly began closing out trading positions that would fall in the wake of major terrorism. He quickly bought options that gave him the right to acquire government bonds at a set price in the future. As news of the attacks spread, other investors fled to the relatively safe haven of bonds, driving up prices and allowing Mr. Siva-Jothy to profit handsomely.

Source: Gregory Zuckerman and Susanne Craig, "To Weather Rocky Period, Goldman Makes Riskier Bets," *Wall Street Journal*, December 17, 2002.

building to fly into; exactly the opposite, you go into the river or you go for a flat piece of land.

I immediately thought, "Terrorist act." I figured this was going to whack consumer sentiment, which was the only thing keeping the United States afloat at that point. I bought Eurodollars and calls on Eurodollars after the first plane hit but before the second. Strangely, I think they rallied no more than 13 basis points on the day. Markets can be unbelievably slow to figure out the consequences of big events. (*See Figure 5.6.*)

It's striking, being a pilot and even being in the office at the time allowed you to do that trade. Had you been out on a coffee break or a meeting, the trade never would have happened.

Maybe, but as I said, markets were very slow to react. It's one of my fascinations with markets—that they are unbelievably slow to react to big events that there is no script for. This was a classic example, but one that I don't really like using, for obvious reasons.

But let's take that event. If the attacks had been in Jakarta or London, the impact on markets would have been much smaller. The United Kingdom had already been through a major terrorist bombing campaign and had grown partially immune to it. The situation in the United States was

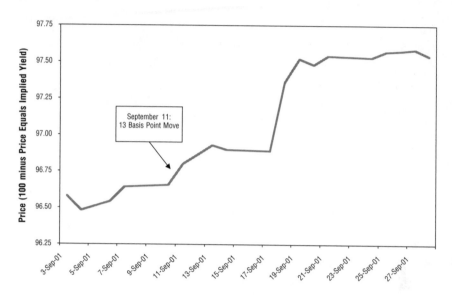

FIGURE 5.6 Eurodollar Futures, September 2001
Source: Bloomberg.

very different; there had never been a major foreign terrorist attack on U.S. soil so the nuance to the trade was not just economic, it was cultural as well. All these things create the fabric of what we do and add another layer that makes the markets so fascinating and interesting. [Note: This interview was conducted several months prior to the London tube attacks, which had little impact on markets.]

You once told me that you can't remember yesterday. Does that help your trading?

It was a standing joke amongst my colleagues at GS. I have a very good memory for certain things, but at times I have the worst memory for market history anybody's come across. If you ask me what the dollar did two years ago, I'd have to go back and look at a chart. I generally see it as a trading plus, because I'm not influenced by recent past events.

History can be a useful benchmark but only if everything is put into the right context. Where are we in the cycle, does X mean something completely different from last time? Is there inflation? Is there deflation?

People spend far too much time saying things like, "This is what happened to the market in 1987 and this looks very similar so I'll put the same trade on," or "This is what happened in 1994 when the tightening cycle started; therefore the same thing's going to happen this time." I don't like that approach. Markets are dynamic and people's reactions are different. It's much more subtle and nuanced than looking at what happened the last time.

Through to the early 1990s I remember, anytime the stock market just wobbled, people would rush out and buy fixed income, because they had been preprogrammed to do that. Now there's a whole generation of traders who know nothing but low inflation: "What's inflation?"

I was fortunate enough to work at GS with a prop guy who's been trading for well over 30 years, Bennett Grau. His first day in the office was the day Bretton Woods collapsed. We've got data and charts to look at, but he's seen and felt the emotion associated with those events, and you can't get that from the textbooks.

So it's a mix. You can take a snapshot of any one single event but it excludes a lot of things, so it's valuable to study history around that event. You've got to take everything in the right context, and that's the difficult bit.

The last time we met, you were still at Goldman and in the midst of an experiment. You had hired a couple of young people without trading experience and given them trading limits. At the time, one of them was the best performer on the desk. What were the end results of that experiment?

A little background first. Back in the early 1990s, Goldman consistently took young people into the prop group and churned them out. The success rate was minimal, 5 percent at most. I stopped the practice because we were damaging the careers of highly talented people. Once they apparently failed in prop trading, they became damaged goods and no one else in the firm wanted them. It wasn't the right thing to do because these people were really talented individuals. Also, the hit ratio was so low that it wasn't worth the effort training them, so I stopped it in 1995 and put in a policy that we would only hire experienced traders that I knew or someone on the team knew personally.

There's a huge advantage to working with experienced traders, as opposed to 20-year-olds, in that it takes a lot less management time. My passion is trading, managing risk and portfolios. My philosophy is to hire honest, experienced traders and let them manage themselves.

What happened to the experiment? We brought a few nontraders from within the firm on board and gave them a limit structure. One was very aggressive, very self-confident, and appeared to have a very good grasp of markets from day one. Basically, this one worked. It worked to the point where she was one of the biggest P&L producers in her first full proper year. She left GS to work for a large hedge fund shortly thereafter.

In hiring traders for the prop desk in general, what characteristics do you look for?

Passion and humility are the main qualities I look for but first and foremost—it sounds a bit cheesy—I ask myself, is this a good person? Is it someone I want to sit next to that I trust and want to work with? Integrity is the single most important thing to me in hiring.

What advice would you give someone who wants to be the head of Goldman Sachs proprietary trading someday?

A lot of this is luck, but humility is probably the most important thing. If you're not humble, you're not going to last very long. You also have to enjoy it. Too many people come into this business for the money, and that's not going to work out over time.

I can put my hand on my heart and say I don't get stressed out by the markets. I don't have bad days or good days. I did get stressed in 1994 when I was either going to break or not, but since having gone through that, I hope I can pretty much cope with anything.

The best compliment anyone's paid me over the years was when one of my traders said, "I can never tell whether you've had a bad day or a good day." That's probably the nicest thing anyone's ever said to me in the workplace. I've seen people get very stressed, and if you're stressed, you can't do this job effectively.

At what point during your trading career did you know that you had skill?

I'm not sure that I do, actually. A big chunk of success in this business is just being in the right place at the right time. In 1994 I was on a knife edge; I could have been fired but was instead promoted. There are certain events where I think, "Bloody hell, I was so lucky just to have been there and not somewhere else."

Had you walked out or been fired in 1994, what would you have done?

I have a fairly eclectic background. I left school to work as a computer programmer for two years before going to university. At university, I initially studied aeronautics and avionics because my passion has always been aircraft, and then switched to development economics. Truthfully, I don't know what I would have done. I just feel incredibly lucky to be doing a job that is also my hobby.

Your original plan was to work for one year and then go back to school. What made you stay?

It was fun. I never really thought about it in terms of success. I just found the markets absolutely fascinating and challenging. I guess I'm still doing it, so I would appear to have some kind of edge.

Are there any books that you recommend to your traders?

My favorite book in relation to the market is *Reminiscences of a Stock Operator*, by Edwin Lefevre. I've probably read it four or five times, and I love it every time I read it. He talks about everything, about risk, about hubris, about passion, everything.

What worries you with traders who work for you?

I used to be worried about having a rogue trader on the team, but my view on that is if you ever lose sleep, then the guy shouldn't be there. In 10 years, I never had a trader blow up on me. I'm actually very proud of that and I generally sleep very well.

Do you think the amount of capital allocated to traders has an effect on their performance?

Most definitely. I've seen it many times at GS. A trader has had a good run, they put pressure on themselves to take more risk, and they become totally overwhelmed. It's as if they have a glass ceiling. I don't know if it's an internal problem or something else. You probably can't rationalize it but I know you can't push people to do more than they want to do. I've spent a lot of time working with some of these people, saying, "Up your risk"; they've tried and it was generally disastrous. I don't know anyone who's made a quantum leap in a short space of time.

You made a quantum leap.

Yes, but in both directions, pre-1993 up, then post-1994 down. It took a long time post-1994 to get back to the levels of risk I was running in 1993 and 1994.

There's a big difference in managing $100 million and $1 billion. You have to have a very good understanding of liquidity, which is one of the reasons I shifted to the major markets or G7. To me, risk is about liquidity, and that is one of the reasons why I am never short gamma.

But I don't really care if I'm trading one million or one billion. It's not about size. What I care about is coming to work and having fun. Absolutely I want to be trading a meaningful amount of capital, but I'd rather be a smaller fund with a higher return than a very large fund with a low return. The economics may not be that different but I know which one I prefer. I would much rather be in the performance category; you've got much more freedom.

Is trading still fun for you?

Yes, trading is still fun. The highs aren't as high as they used to be, and the lows are a little lower. In a perverse way, I find tough times more interesting now than being right and catching a trend. I find it a much bigger challenge when I feel very strongly about something but it's not working. Also, trying to make money back is much more challenging than leveraging at the proper time and making more. Don't get me wrong though, beating the markets is what it is all about, and that means getting it right!

Have the macro markets changed over the course of your career?

The markets have changed and the dynamic is very different. I remember in 1987 we used to watch the money supply numbers closely. People don't even know when they're coming out anymore. The focus has changed dramatically, and you have to have the ability to change and see how the markets are changing and adapt to it; that's a constant process. That's why I think you see some people do well for four or five years, and then just disappear.

Markets are going through huge changes at the moment with the proliferation of hedge funds, and we've obviously got a global economy now. The world markets have become more correlated as a result. I'm not sure it makes it more difficult, just different. Again, it goes back to dynamics—markets are changing all the time.

How has the proliferation of hedge funds changed the global macro playing field?

I remember in the early 1990s, everybody knew who the players were—Tiger and Soros. They had billions of dollars under management and they could drive markets. Even if they were wrong, they could still move a market 5 percent or more in some instances. Today, hedge funds in aggregate have a lot more money under management, but everyone's trying to chase the same opportunity and get through the same door.

Any edge you've got is a big plus. You have to find an edge and push it as much as you can. That can be something as simple as having a different year-end, it can be trading style, it can be systems even. Another source of edge is getting the right, knowledgeable investors behind you. There seems to be a lot of uniformity in the macro space with people all having the same very tight drawdown rules.

I've told investors, "I'm not going to give you a volatility limit, because when there is a major dislocation, we can have very high volatility in the portfolio. But we'll structure the position via options that are skewed so that if we're right we'll benefit from the skew, but if we're wrong, we'll be taken out of the position very quickly. So by definition, there's going to be high volatility when we're right."

If you can get investors to buy into that, it gives you an edge. Too many people are willing to give investors whatever they ask for just to get the capital. I said to an investor the other day, "If you want 1 percent a month, why on earth would you want to invest in macro? You should buy an indexed bond portfolio instead."

Do you worry about the investor community defining your trading?

Yes! It's important to make sure the tail doesn't wag the dog. Investors in hedge funds tend to encourage overtrading, which I want to avoid. I find it interesting that some investors don't like the idea when I tell them that we may well do nothing for two or three months. Friends who have been doing this for many years have told me to be adamant. At the end of the day, you'll have some guys who won't invest with you, and that's better than turning into something that you're not.

I don't think our levels of volatility are such that people will be turned off. We should only have those high levels of volatility if we're doing well, so it's a high-class problem. I'll only say we've had a very large shift in volatility if we've just caught a move and we've levered it up. We will never lever up a losing position.

Do you tell new investors to expect large drawdowns?

Not from what I call our reset, which we will do every six months. I believe you should trade your P&L. From zero to minus 10 percent is unbelievably meaningful, and that's a drawdown that they shouldn't expect. On the other hand, I've told them that if we're up 30 or 40 percent, I am not going to be worried about a 10 percent drawdown as long as we're being rigorous. My philosophy has always been to trade up when things are going well and you have a high-confidence view. There's a big difference between going from 30 percent to 20 percent, and going from zero to −10 percent.

We have our performance fee paid every six months, so essentially we start at zero every six months, as long as we have made money. Our financial year-end is September, and we have another performance payout in March. That way, we are actively trading over the calendar year-end, which is a very interesting period to capture.

One of the things I spent a lot of time thinking about was how to replicate a bank prop style of trading model in a hedge fund environment. Most of the guys who are coming to work with me are ex-bank prop guys, and I didn't want to alter our core trading style too much.

A prop desk's volatility tends to be much higher when making money because the logic is very different between a bank and a fund. Certainly Goldman Sachs saw the prop group as a call option and hedge for when the franchise was doing poorly (the franchise is generally long inventory, whether it's equities or fixed income products).

They very rationally look at history and ask, when do we lose money? Tightening cycles and credit events. During those periods, a bank wants the prop group to make outsize returns, which will compensate for the lack of franchise income. In the years when the franchise is doing well, they'd love it if you could make money, but that's not their main focus. What they don't want you to do in any given year is lose money. So in the years the franchise is doing well, they expect you to be between zero and up double digits, but in the years where there's a big dislocation, they'll expect you to knock the cover off the ball.

At GS, almost by necessity, we ran huge positions during 1998 or during Fed cutting cycles. We'd have big P&L swings but only when we were up a lot of money. We looked at it in absolute amounts. When we were up triple-digit millions and we had a strong view, we'd take a decent drawdown from our high-water mark because we'd see that, all other things being equal, it was just a correction and probably time to lever up.

I don't think you can do that in a fund, so to reduce volatility I'm going to reset the net asset value (NAV) every six months. The reason volatility is reduced is because you're effectively resetting a trader's P&L to zero, so suddenly he hasn't got the $X million cushion to play with.

Will you require your traders to liquidate positions at your reset levels?

No, not at all. What I would expect is, if they've had a really good run, that they reduce risk. The concept is to trade your P&L. Similar to the way it was at GS, if you'd finished the year weak, you had small positions, so no need to change your book; but if you finished it strongly, you had big positions, so you reduced as you came into the new year and looked to build a bit of P&L before you traded big positions again.

People who don't trade don't understand it. I remember the chief operating officer at GS saying to me, "That's totally irrational, Christian, because the opportunities on day one are almost exactly the same as the opportunities that existed the day before I reset your P&L to zero."

I said, "I know, but psychologically it's totally different. You've just reset my P&L to zero so I am going to trade differently. If you want me to trade the same, give me a rolling P&L and a performance structure to match." The reality is that he was intellectually absolutely right, but if you're trading your P&L, it doesn't work that way.

Can you tell me more about your trading style within the new hedge fund structure?

We'll have a range of traders—guys who are medium-term, short-term—and we'll run a model. I've never been a great believer in models, but it's become such a major part of the environment that you have to have a good sense of what they're doing. It will be a very small part of the portfolio, but we'll use it as an indicator. We'll then overlay the primary fundamental portfolio with what I call "event/risk opportunity-driven trades," which are those wonderful event-driven dislocations that you're trying to catch each year.

Do you use traders working for you as weather vanes or indicators of market conditions?

Some traders do that. Sentiment is a big part of it, and you spend a lot of time talking to people trying to figure out whether the market's long, short, bullish, bearish. Psychology and sentiment are a huge part of the markets. No one gets paid for originality—you get paid for making money. I am happy to take other people's good ideas and run with them, as long as I understand exactly why I am in the trade.

When I rebuilt the prop group in 1995, I wanted it to be very small, primarily because I wanted to know the people in it. I wanted to be very careful about who I worked with. I wanted to sleep at night and not worry about tickets in the bottom drawer, so I tended to gravitate toward older, experienced people who I knew and trusted.

I am trying to create exactly the same thing here. I will not work with anybody I haven't worked with or known for a long time. That's important to me. The obvious reason is you know where people are coming from, you know how they trade, and so on. But it's the more indefinable things that matter, such as people's respect and trust for each other.

In an environment where people don't know each other, you can get a lot of tension. People miss trades because they don't want it to look like they are copying a colleague's trade. If you have people who know each other and each other's styles, you avoid issues like that which can affect performance.

People who have confidence in themselves will do the trades they want to do and they'll get out of those trades they no longer like. They may even flip and do exactly the opposite trade, which I'm a huge fan of. I have no issues with one person being long, one person being short, because they've got different time horizons, different reasons—hopefully they'll both make money!

Will you overlay your traders if risk gets too heavily skewed in a direction that you aren't comfortable with, or will you focus exclusively on your own pool of capital?

We will not have an overlay or hedge book. If the aggregate portfolio doesn't exhibit the right risk characteristics, I will make sure that it does by getting the individual portfolio managers to adjust their risk accordingly. Each trader will have their own portfolio and they'll manage their own money. We'll have a basic fundamental firm level overlay, which we may disagree on but it's rare you get disagreement on major fundamentals. It doesn't take a genius to figure out roughly where you are in a cycle and how things look, but if you do, that means it's a very interesting environment.

In general, we'll agree on a broad macro theme—do we think rates are in an up cycle or a down cycle? At the simplest level, that's what we're trying to get to, because historically, we've made most of our money in fixed income. Foreign exchange tends to be a bit of the icing on the cake, and that's perfectly rational. There's always an anchor for interest rates, but no one can tell me for sure whether the euro's fundamental value is one or two or somewhere in between.

Right now is actually one of those points where it seems people are evenly split between thinking we're in for a decent 3 percent growth rate in the United States for the next few years and people who think we're at a peak and entering a downturn.

How will you handle capital allocation decisions with your traders in the hedge fund? Presumably there is a difference between the hard dollars allocated in a fund and the credit lines allocated on a bank prop desk.

At the end of the day, trading is about risk/reward. All my managers have long track records, so I can work back from a comfortable drawdown level for each individual trader and allocate a capital amount based on that. I will work with each individual to get to a number that they are comfortable with. There is absolutely no point in allocating a number that is too big, as the manager would then be in new territory, and experience has taught me that that is when accidents tend to happen.

The structure and ownership of the fund is absolutely critical, and I'll always have less money under management than I know we can manage. I've given away more than 50 percent of the ownership of the company to the traders and management staff, not only to attract them, but to make the business more inclusive. I don't want to manage more than 50 percent of the fund at any point in time because we'd lose diversification. Plus, I don't want to be bigger than eight or nine senior traders. Over 14 years at GS, I've found that to be the optimum number. Once you get bigger than that, you start losing the "team" ethos. All my senior traders are partners, and I'll expect each of them to put in at least $1 million of personal money into the fund over time for every percent they own.

Another thing that is unusual in this structure is that all the traders get paid equally on the money they make. In a lot of fund structures, the senior partners cream a little off the performance fee, which I don't want. I only want to eat what I kill. My passion is trading and I don't see why I should benefit directly from other people's performance.

There is also a fixed cut of the performance fee that goes into a pool for the nontraders. I want everyone to be incentivized. My COO and CFO

are both partners, and I don't want them obsessed with asset growth because that's how they get paid. They'll participate in this pool, which can
be a significant number. I want them to be focused on the optimal balance
between size and return, where return is more important to them than
size, because that's a potentially larger slice of their compensation.

Can you discuss some of the similarities and differences between a bank prop trading desk and a hedge fund?

One thing that is very similar is the ability to ramp up returns when there are
dislocations, as market opportunities are one and the same. The basic disciplines of trading are exactly the same, whether it's in a bank or a fund, other
than the caveat I said about drawdowns. It's difficult to change that dramatically, other than the way we're doing it, which is by the six-month reset.

Since 1994, we never had a down year at GS, but we had some very
volatile years when we were doing very well. That's re-creatable in this
space, certainly, if you get the right investors who understand it. I don't
think any investor wants to have a down year, but you explain to them that
if they want the real outsized returns, they're going to have to accept a bit
of volatility when things are going well.

I really do believe that unless you are willing to push the envelope
when you are doing well, and unless you have investors who understand
that that means higher volatility when you are doing well, you will not be
able to get the outsized returns. There has to be a different return profile,
depending on how you're doing on the year. People who don't accept that
are not going to get those outsized returns.

In terms of differences, banks, contrary to popular belief, don't have set
payouts because it affects the way traders take risk. When you know exactly what you're going to get paid, it takes away from one's ability to push
the envelope. The tendency is to think in terms of certainties. The thought
process goes like this: "Okay, I'm up $20 million. If I push, I could be up
$40 million or I could be flat, but right now I know that X percent of this
$20 million is worth Y dollars in my pocket."

Psychologically, it's very rational. At GS, they wanted us to push the envelope in dislocated markets so they didn't give us the certainty of a fixed
payout. In fact, their subtle, even subliminal message was, "If you don't
push the envelope in times of stress, we're going to penalize you." It was
very clever on their part, because it was that pressure that resulted in the
outsized returns during periods of large market movements.

Some say that investment banks are set up only for the prop group, in that the research group is there to produce something for the salespeople to give to clients to get information from them to then give to the prop group. Will you be handicapped without the bank resources?

I totally disagree with that. I was in the prop business at Goldman for 14 years and I can tell you that the research element was not set up for prop at all. It was set up to drive the sell side and entirely focused on the franchise businesses. The amount of time and resources we got from research people was generally minimal in comparison to the franchise. That's what people tell me is one of the huge advantages of being outside—access to more sources of information and pricing that is much, much better and fairly transparent.

Did the customer flow at Goldman help your trading?

It did in FX in the early 1990s, but as the regulatory regime got tighter and tighter, we got less and less information, to the point where we really got nothing. Also, it wasn't like we were sitting there trying to catch the next 50 pips or big figure. Structurally, we were looking for 5 or 10 percent moves, so flows weren't that useful for our style of trading.

Do you worry about transaction costs or, because you are looking for such large moves, do you deem them inconsequential?

I didn't worry about it at GS because I took the high road. I was a partner at the firm and to increase camaraderie, we did all our trades internally. I didn't worry about paying a pip or an extra tenth of a vol then because it was really just an accounting transfer. I'll worry about it much more in the fund.

What are you most worried about now, launching the fund?

Performing. It's where the rubber meets the road. At the end of the day, it's about making returns.

Also, managing a hedge fund is potentially more public than prop trading for a bank. That probably is going to be the most difficult thing for me. It's very much like when a young person joins the prop desk from a different group. There'll no doubt be a few people who would like to see me fail, and that's pressure, but it's one that keeps me motivated.

Do you feel your competition is with the markets or with other hedge funds?

Ultimately the markets, no question. I'm not going to worry about other hedge funds during the day. The world's big enough and I wish them all well. I'm going to worry about doing well, and that means beating the markets. I'd be lying, though, if I said I won't be looking over my shoulder at the end of the month to check that we have been competitive.

That's all I've got. Want to add any pearls of wisdom?

I'm short pearls of wisdom.

CHAPTER 6

THE RESEARCHER

Dr. Andres Drobny
Drobny Global Advisors
Manhattan Beach, California

In the rapidly changing world of hedge funds and financial markets, the research side of the business is undergoing a tremendous amount of upheaval. Gone are the days when major investment banks shell out several-hundred-page tomes from top analysts who are paid well to support the franchise business. Likewise, the slim staffs of even many major hedge funds often do not permit an in-house research team to address the needs of macro traders who look at the entire world. But upheaval creates opportunities.

Dr. Andres Drobny is an academic economist, former Wall Street chief economist and proprietary trader, and current strategist behind the independent research firm Drobny Global Advisors. He is my business partner, but there is no relation despite the fact that we share an uncommon last name.

I struggled with whether to include an interview with Drobny in this book, for obvious reasons, but concluded that he should be treated like any other top practitioner. Although he is not actively managing money like many other interviewees, his wealth of knowledge and unique background spanning all three market disciplines (academia, research, and trading) is of particular value to this book, not to mention that most of the top global macro traders are reading his reports and talking markets with him on a regular basis.

Drobny began his varied career as a professor of economics at King's College Cambridge and London University, having completed his PhD at the former institution. At the age of 33, he entered the financial markets after the head of research for Bankers Trust saw a letter he had written to the editor of the *Financial Times* and promptly hired him. Within a short period of time he became chief economist and head of research, titles he views as completely meaningless. Later he went to Credit Suisse First Boston (CSFB) to help build a global currency trading operation.

Never at home inside the conservative world of Wall Street, Drobny retired in the spring of 1998 and moved to the beach in Southern California, to the student life again. Always an eccentric, it is obvious upon meeting Drobny for the first time why he did not entirely fit in on Wall Street. He hates neckties, has a phobia about buttons, and never wears shoes. He is incredibly intense, never afraid to challenge someone by waving his arms, making a heated case for something he believes in, and telling people they are wrong. But while he is confrontational and excitable, he is also open to original ideas and intellectually honest.

Bored being a student in Los Angeles, Drobny began to contact old friends from the financial world who missed his wild, out-of-consensus views on markets. He began writing a newsletter that soon grew into an advisory role, which again grew into today's open discussion forum that is Drobny Global Advisors (DGA). Sitting at the center of a living discourse on global macro markets, Drobny facilitates an open dialogue among top hedge fund managers and other leading intellectuals, but unlike other research platforms, he is continually striving to capture the trade. In other words, all views must be captured in tradable, actionable ideas. Theories, views, and opinions are not enough. As banks have reduced proprietary risk taking and trading floors are becoming almost anachronistic, DGA has created in essence a global, virtual trading floor of smart guys from around the world. The virtual group congregate twice a year at the Drobny Global Conference to argue and debate favorite trades with Drobny moderating the discussion.

I first met Drobny when I was working in the Hedge Fund Group at Deutsche Bank in London. I cold-contacted him on *Bloomberg* because I was continually being asked if I was the "crazy, smart strategist from CSFB." We found out that we both had grandparents from Prague; had gone to high school in Bethesda, Maryland; had studied at the London School of Economics; and worked at investment banks in London. As we got to know each other, I quickly found that in a world where everyone claims that he or she is "out-of-consensus" or contrarian, Drobny truly is. He has the academic rigor and varied experience to frame bold ideas in ways that others cannot capture. We soon joined forces, as our complementary skill sets just seemed right, not to mention that my name was already on the door. And the beaches of California were far more appealing than the rainy gray of London.

Five years later, we sat down at his sunny Southern California home to conduct this interview. As Drobny sprawled on his couch, he commented that it felt just like a shrink session.

How did you get started in global macro markets?

I was an economics academic in London and had heard all this talk about "City whiz kids." I got frustrated when my not-so-smart graduate students went to the City and started on salaries several times mine. I wanted to see what all the fuss was about and I needed to see if I was up to the test.

It was 1986 and the USD was falling hard. I wrote a letter to the editor about it, which the *Financial Times* published, and soon thereafter got a call from the head of research at Bankers Trust London about it. We talked for a bit and he hired me as a senior economist in his group.

What led you to academia and economics in the first place?

I have always been a teacher. I love it. So academia was essentially the path of least resistance. Also, I was good at it and got a lot of kudos—at Cambridge, becoming an academic made you a star. I studied history as an undergrad but felt I needed to understand material conditions better. I was always very numerical anyway so it led me to economics. It was a natural fit.

Do you think a deep understanding of economics and history is crucial for success in global macro markets?

No, but it can help. It's one way, but not the only way. One of the things I've learned in global macro is there are many ways to be successful.

Was it difficult for you to make the leap from academia to financial markets?

It was remarkably easy. One of the frustrations in academia is the gestation lag between having an idea and it coming to fruition. The final publication of an article from the original idea can take several years. In markets you can have an idea and within a month you start finding out whether it was a good one or not. So that bit was easy. The other advantage I had was that I was very fresh when I entered the markets at the age of 33. There is often a lot of stale thinking on the research side of markets, so it was very exciting for me to think honestly and outside the herd.

Do you think people in financial markets normally get stale and lazy over time?

Some do and some don't. The really great ones don't, because they have that undiminished curiosity that's always pushing them. To really succeed in markets—and this isn't just global macro—you have to constantly be reinventing yourself and constantly re-create how you approach things. To think that "Ten years ago I did it this way and therefore I'm always going to do it this way" is a huge mistake. Markets are constantly changing; you've got to change with them.

Tell me about your start at Bankers Trust.

It was truly fantastic. I got there in August 1987 just as Alan Greenspan became Fed chairman. The first thing he did was raise interest rates and then two months later, the stock market crashed. It was pretty exciting, although at the time I didn't really know what it all meant. I remember going out to lunch with my boss the day of the crash and when we came back, New York had opened and the bond was up 10 points. Ten points in one hour! I remember him telling me this was not a typical day. I had kind of figured that.

I didn't see the crash coming because I didn't really understand the markets much at all at that point. As an academic economist, I understood what drives currencies, and thus the process of the dollar fall but not really stocks and why they crashed. Also, as an economist, I extrapolated the dollar fall forever, which was a good lesson in 1988 when it started recovering.

So I didn't see the crash coming, but what I did have was a deep theoretical approach to the problems, and that allowed me to constantly look at the big picture. When the crash happened, it allowed me to be pretty helpful on the trading floor because I was pretty raw in my response to data releases and therefore often different from the consensus. Most analysts thought they knew what was going on, and frankly, they didn't because they tend to be risk-averse and follow the herd.

Two years later the head of research resigned and everybody looked around and pointed at me, saying, "You're next." In May 1989 I was made the head of research, which is when I really fell in love with markets.

Weren't you chief economist as well as the head of research?

Those titles are all crap. I've never been one for titles. I think that I was "Head of Research and Chief Economist," but who cares? It's irrelevant.

My difficulty with the promotion was that I also became a manager. I had to run the research group, which was one of the most painful experiences of my life. Markets present an interesting puzzle to unlock, and if you're good at it at a bank, they make you a manager. The problem is, being good at markets doesn't mean you're good at managing. I wasn't a good manager.

How did you perform as head of research and chief economist?

The key was that I started trading my own book. A new head of trading arrived, a really young looking guy named Jim Leitner, who was receptive to my thought process. I would recommend trades to him and he would often put them on immediately, so I learned to be very proactive. I also learned early on that talk is cheap in markets. Everybody runs around with a view, but what leads to success is not having a view but coming up with a direct trade idea. And so I discovered through trading and research how you want to unlock really good trade ideas by having a fundamental view of the process and then comparing that to the perception in the market. That's how you find a good trade.

That year the Berlin Wall fell and the deutsche mark started rallying. It jumped up against all currencies, including the Swiss franc. It was up a lot and everybody was bullish, including Leitner. Then I saw the Swiss authorities respond with pretty aggressive rate hikes and the market didn't really pay attention. The trend was their friend, so to speak. So I saw rates increasing in Switzerland and the market long the deutsche mark. My research group wrote an aggressive piece called "The Swiss Franc at a Crossroads." Mark/Swiss was at what seemed a pretty big technical level and everyone was looking the other way, so I saw the potential for a big move down.

Before this I'd been trading in small amounts in quick moves in and out, usually after data releases. I prided myself at being the fastest in the market to react to data. I could read it quickly, understand its importance, and know to "buy the dollar" or "sell the dollar" on the news.

Then came this mark/Swiss trade, where I put on a 40 million deutsche mark position. It was a puny amount—by way of reference, a small position on the European crosses was 200 million deutsche marks—while big guys like Leitner would run 1 to 2 billion deutsche mark positions. So there I was with my measly short 40 million deutsche mark position, and I immediately got stopped out. I went short again, but this time it fell like a stone as it broke a technical level with the market positioned the wrong way. Within a month I'd made a million dollars on a tiny little position. (*See Figure 6.1.*) It was the first time I'd let a position run for more than a day or so, and I loved getting a trade right when most were looking the other way. That is when I developed a love affair with the Swiss franc. Traders often become attached to things that they've succeeded with.

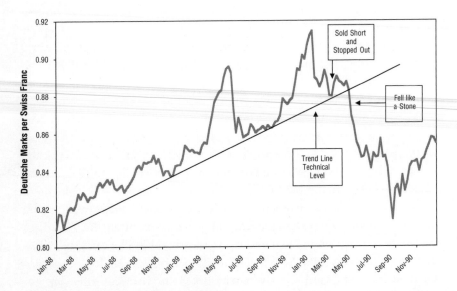

FIGURE 6.1   Mark/Swiss, 1988–1990
Source: Bloomberg.

My style is to use fundamentals to develop a view, but to remember that talk is cheap and views are a dime a dozen. The real trick is to use the view and look for a good trade where few are looking. Even better if the market is leaning the other way.

It sounds like market positioning is a big part of your trade construction process. How do you measure outstanding market positions?

It's a tricky issue. I measure it simply by getting a sense of what people are talking about from listening and reading. If everybody is talking bearish the dollar, even though I'm a bear it gives me pause for thought. This year, for example, I missed the dollar rally precisely because a lot of people were talking about a potential dollar rally, so I didn't get interested. It's not just positioning, it's what the talk is.

When I think of positioning, I try to think about very long-term events and what's happened over the last two, three, or five years to get a flavor of where the positions really are—not this short-term, over-bought/oversold stuff.

I've always liked currencies because there are underlying flows in currencies. A currency with a current account or basic balance deficit that's going up must mean that there's a long building up. A currency with a current account surplus or basic balance surplus that's going down must mean there's a big short building in that currency.

The really great opportunities are often after big trends. I like to find when the trends have occurred and people are leaning one way and some fundamental event starts to occur that means the trend should be changing. That event could be a central bank event like the deutsche mark/Swiss trade, or it can be an economic event like the stock market crash in the United States in 2000, or it can just be pure market exhaustion where something gives. The first two are easier for me to see and understand than the last one. I find it funny, though, how many traders like to look for the last type—exhaustion of a trend. Very tough, I think.

A good example of a big-picture event I caught was the breakup of the Exchange Rate Mechanism (ERM) in 1992. As is often the case with these big-picture trades, I was about a year early on it. The carry trade had developed through 1985 to 1991 because the ERM in Europe created a fixed range for the currencies. When an ERM currency got to one end of the range, the weak currency country had to raise interest rates and the strong currency countries would have to cut interest rates. Relative rates would move because spot couldn't. The forwards would price in a devaluation of a weak currency, but the policy makers wouldn't allow it—the currency forwards would bear the burden of adjustment.

In such a policy environment, the high yielding currencies were a very good buy. The policy makers were committed to holding the parity levels yet market prices assumed they couldn't. When the high yielders were at the bottom of the range and rates went up, it seemed a no-brainer to go and buy them.

It was a great trade, because the low yielding countries had low inflation and low interest rates and the high yielding countries had high inflation and high interest rates. The policy regime was designed to squeeze inflation out of the high yielders. So there was significant carry and the governments had the policy.

But German inflation accelerated after the Berlin Wall fell, and German interest rates started going up a lot. Suddenly, the low interest rate countries like Germany started becoming high yield countries. At the same time, global deflation was building, the U.S. economy was weak, the Japanese bubble was bursting, and the property boom that had occurred in the United Kingdom and in several other countries was giving under the weight of high interest rates. There was pressure for lower rates in the high yielders and higher rates in the low yielders and the carry was being whittled away.

The reward to the carry trade became almost insignificant by 1991 while the risks to the system were building. Risk/reward had gone the wrong way at a time when investors were very, very leveraged in those high yielders, so I started looking for the ERM to fall apart.

The poor risk/reward in the carry trade was also partly responsible for my eventual departure from Bankers. I was on the cover of the *International Herald Tribune* in November 1991 just before they signed the Maastricht Treaty, saying the global economy needs low interest rates and a revaluation of the deutsche mark would do the job. Bankers's management were not very comfortable with me talking against the carry trade. They were sitting there in the carry trade, very involved, while their main research guy out of London was saying the whole thing was going to fall apart! That created a difficult relationship, and ultimately the fit wasn't good because I saw trouble in a place that they wanted to be invested in. I don't know what happened after I left, but I suspect they got badly hurt.

**AS CURRENCY CRISIS LOOMS BEFORE MAASTRICHT SUMMIT:
TRADERS RUSH TO BUY MARKS**

Foreign exchange traders suddenly rushed to buy deutsche marks
Friday, setting the stage for what appears to be a European currency
crisis just two weeks before the EC states are to sign a treaty on
monetary union. The mark rose not only against the dollar, which
has been falling for the past week due to U.S. economic malaise, but
also against the currencies linked to it in the European Community's
fixed-band exchange system. The German currency's across-the-
board gains stemmed from sudden speculation of a coming revaluation of the mark, if not this weekend, then at the EC summit
meeting Dec. 9 in Maastricht, The Netherlands, or right afterward.
Analysts acknowledged that a revaluation of the mark would solve a
lot of problems within Europe, but many doubted it would occur.
"The global economy needs lower interest rates," said Andres
Drobny at Bankers Trust in London, "and a revaluation of the
deutsche mark would do the job."

Source: International Herald Tribune, November 23, 1991, Carl Gewirtz.

*One thing that strikes me about the macro markets in the early 1990s is
that leverage increased while the risk/reward became less attractive until it
all came undone. It sounds similar to the environment today. Do you see a
correlation between that period and now?*

It does sound similar but I don't see a correlation. There is a problem with
assets today because low interest rates and all the liquidity in the system
have led to generalized overvaluation of assets. There's a problem there, but
it's a well-known problem and people are talking about it. In 1991 and
1992, it was really about people sticking to their views rather than thinking about the trade. If you look objectively in early 1992 at the ERM
trade, the risk/reward of being long the high yielder was awful. That's all I
saw. The risk/reward of the carry trade stank, but that's where everyone
was. They wanted to stay there and thought it was great because it had
been great and because they believed that the governments would not
change policy. The governments didn't want to change policy, either, but it

was one of those events where the underlying macroeconomic pressures forced the change. Their policies were leading to deflation and there was no way out but to revalue the deutsche mark.

Today it's different. It's much trickier because people are aware that assets seem overvalued. Everyone is looking for a bubble somewhere. People have much more mean reversion in their minds here so I see the problem as different.

I'm struggling with the current environment because, as in the ERM period, returns to assets are very low and unattractive. However, when I try to anticipate the sell-off—and I keep doing that—I keep finding this amazing stability. Sometimes you have to just sit back and wait for things to happen. This is probably one of those times, but it is hard to sit still and wait.

My main hypothesis has been that it all ends in tears. Ultimately, if there is a sufficient recovery, interest rates go up to a point that assets get knocked and we head back to deflation. Or assets on their own give up and burst. The only other way out of all this debt is to devalue it via genuine goods price inflation, but that seems hard to achieve. If the authorities are lucky, they will be able to muddle through with lowish inflation, stable asset values, and okay growth over a long period, but during that process the world economy will be very vulnerable. It's never been accomplished before, but maybe this time things are different.

Today, the pessimists are actually now the optimists. The pessimist says house prices are going to collapse. Think about it. It's actually not that pessimistic, because if assets give without interest rates going up, then interest rates can stay low, helping cushion the process. So, oddly enough, the optimistic case may turn out to produce the worst outcome. Interest rates will have to rise more than is priced into the markets, which could cause a nasty tumble in assets and, ultimately, the global economy.

Do I sound confused? Perhaps. And that makes macro trading tough right now. It's critical to differentiate between views, opinions, and biases, and actual trades. If your views are a little confused, you really want to back off on your trades. You only want to trade when you've got good risk/reward and you feel you understand the process. Analysts are particularly bad at telling us when they are confident about something and when they aren't. That's a mistake. Sometimes things are clear, sometimes they are not, and it's important to recognize the difference.

Do you think global macro markets were easier back in the 1980s and 1990s than they are today?

No. I think they're difficult at this juncture.

I have typically found success in times of trouble because there is an innate optimism by people in financial markets that everything is going to be okay. It's partly a self-interested optimism. I'm not so inclined. I can take it or leave it, so when there's been trouble, I've found my greatest success. To me the 1990 to 1993 period—where I saw the problems building—was very similar to the 2000 to 2003 period, where I also saw and understood the problems that existed. So no, they're not easier or more difficult. Right now they're more difficult because it feels like we are in the eye of the storm, but it's been a frustratingly long period of stability for me, that's for sure!

Where do you see the world in 5 or 10 years?

I don't have a clue. I really don't know, which is beautiful because it leaves me free to listen to new news and to actually hear the message. I have a bias that is deflationary and that this all ends in tears, but increasingly I've been finding that bias holds me back, partly because a lot of people think that way. So I really don't know where we are headed right now, but I find it very liberating not to know.

What is your time horizon in markets? How far ahead are you looking?

I don't think in terms of time horizon at all. I think in terms of the potential for the move. Sometimes things happen very quickly and sometimes it's grudgingly. I think in terms of pressures rather than time horizon. The only place time comes into my thought process is with carry, because the forwards are per unit of time, so it influences the risk/reward of the concept.

What drives markets—speculators? Government? Central banks? Economics?

Speculators definitely don't. The idea that speculators broke the Bank of England in 1992 is ludicrous. The inevitable collapse of sterling from the ERM was because they were trying to maintain 10 percent interest rates when the economy needed 5 percent interest rates. It was not sustainable.

There's an old debate in economics as to whether speculators are deviation "dampeners" or deviation "amplifiers." Milton Friedman, the eternal optimist, argued that if people see an anomaly, they'll pick on it and limit how far that anomaly goes. I think both are right at different times. Sometimes speculators add to volatility; other times they dampen it. The important point is, they don't influence the trend. Underlying pressures combined with policy decisions drive market events, so you have to keep an eye on underlying pressures all the time.

Which big market event has impacted you the most?

Each one is different, but I guess the one that still reverberates is 1992. I always go back to the ERM and the crash because I saw it ahead of time. I remember what I was thinking at the time, during the frustrating period before the thing broke and as it occurred. I also learned a great lesson there, which was never to underestimate how far a move can go. When sterling broke, who would have thought that cable would go from 2 to 1.5 in that event? Who would have predicted the levels these currencies got to? They just kept going and going and going. (*See Figure 6.2.*)

Why do you love markets? What is it about markets that is so interesting to you?

Finding a good way to exploit a view by finding a good trade is a fantastic challenge in and of itself. There are few moments more exhilarating than

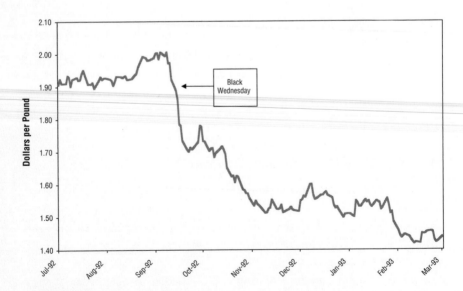

FIGURE 6.2   Cable, 1992–1993
Source: Bloomberg.

really catching something in the market, neatly and nicely. But there are few more depressing times than when the markets are confusing and you don't have a handle on them.

The other thing that really grabs me about markets is I'm a control freak. I like to control the environment around me, and markets are a real challenge because you can't control them. When I understand them, I feel empowered. When I don't, I feel very lost.

But being a control freak, why are you drawn to something that is constantly in flux?

When you understand the process, then the whole out-of-control process is oddly very much in control. Because as a control freak, you're always looking out ahead of you, you're looking out ahead for trouble, and that's exactly what you have to do in markets, is try to look forward. So much of market talk, market analysis, and trading is based on what's happened in the past. "The yield curve is flat, therefore it tells you it's a recession," or "The yield curve is steep, which tells you there's going to be a recovery." Those types of historical examples are of very little value, so a control freak is always trying to look forward and trying to look ahead.

What do you think differentiates a good analyst and a good trader?

The good trader knows how to actively manage the risk and run a position. A good analyst should help find the trade or look for pitfalls in the trade. The key difference is in their stomachs. The great traders I know are able to manage large position sizes. That's what makes them great. They also need to be bright, aggressive, and forward looking. Being able to manage large positions is a very rare talent, which is why there are very few great traders.

My skill is in finding trades, not managing them, so I used to run only small positions. What having trades on did was make me profoundly honest. Markets, if you have a position on, make it very painful to be lazy. They force you to be thinking ahead and watching your back. Having a trading book allowed me to think ahead and always use my fundamental insights to end up with a market view. I learned over time that my skill is finding good trades. What I'm not good at is running trades. I didn't enjoy it. I'm a very risk-averse person so when a trade was in profit, I'd immediately start thinking about when I was going to lose it all. Better for me to move on and look for the next one and let the big guys do the hard work of actually managing the risk.

What did you do after leaving Bankers Trust?

I followed other Bankers people over to Credit Suisse First Boston in the summer of 1992. Alan Wheat, who was running the show, hired Marc Hotimsky to build a foreign exchange business, and he in turn asked me to join him to help do a little bit of everything. I was the strategist, but I was also a partner in the hedge fund. I traded a little bit, but increasingly my trading got in my way. It was 1992 to 1993, things were happening very quickly, and I was on it. There was a lot of money to be made as it was a great time for macro.

But I wasn't on it at first! My first trade at CSFB, the first thing I did in late August 1992 was get us long the Finnish markka. It was a disaster. The Finn mark had already devalued the year before, so I said to myself, "Well, the Finnish markka already devalued last year and the other currencies haven't." My trade was to buy the Finn mark, I think, against the Swedish krona, and in the first week of September, the Finn mark devalued again and we got crushed. (*See Figure 6.3.*) I can still remember Hotimsky standing next to me really pissed off. I thought he was going to kick me off the floor, literally.

So my first trade was a big loser, but we turned it around fast. If the

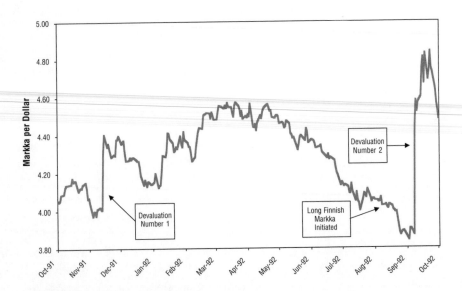

FIGURE 6.3   Finnish Markka, 1991–1992
Source: Bloomberg.

Finn mark was going down a second time, then the others simply had to give. The system couldn't hold much longer. I got the message about the ERM and we got aggressively short the Spanish peseta, the British pound, and the Swedish krona.

I understood that the carry trade that had helped hold the ERM together also involved a lot of Japanese inflows. During the late 1980s, this Japanese wall of money had come to Europe, so as the ERM started to fall apart and the Japanese bubble imploded, I looked for the wall of money to work in reverse and retreat back to Japan. So the other trade I saw was to sell the European currencies against the yen, which also proved to be a really big winner. Everyone thought the yen would weaken due to the implosion of the Nikkei, yet the opposite happened! (*See Figure 6.4.*)

So my start at CSFB went very, very badly, but markets are a great discipline. We made pretty big losses in that first week of September, but we made five to six times the gains over the rest of that year, and then into 1993 we made really big money. We had a killer year, in part because we were on top of the process and knew where to find good trades.

Then came 1994, which was a bad year for me. It was the year of recovery and rate hikes in the United States. My approach was to be long the

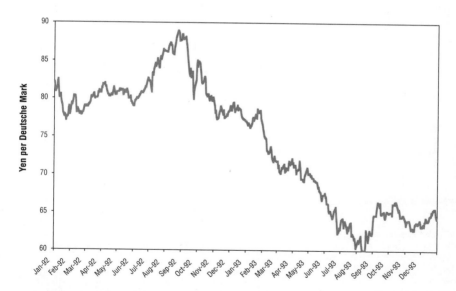

FIGURE 6.4 "Europe" versus Yen, 1992–1993
Source: Bloomberg.

dollar and short bonds because of Fed rate hikes. I remember Marc Hotimsky reminding me all year that my trade wasn't making any money. I
caught the bond market sell-off, but unfortunately gave it all back with the
dollar sell-off that year. (*See Figure 6.5.*)

How did you approach proprietary risk taking at CSFB?

The trick was to have a diversified group of people trading, which is pretty
much what the funds of hedge funds do today. We'd have a gamma trader
sitting on the right looking for the big moves, a carry trader sitting on the
left making regular income, a guy who exploits options strategies in the
middle, and then our big back book, which Hotimsky and the hedge fund
would manage.

We then used our prop traders as weather vanes or as information
sources. There are no genuinely unique ideas out there. There are similar
types of ideas, and so for me the trick was to be able to take an idea from
area X and apply it to area Y.

If you have very smart guys prop trading, you can learn what the market
is doing in part by knowing their styles and seeing who is profitable at any
one time. My role was as an idea generator, a catalyst, an information

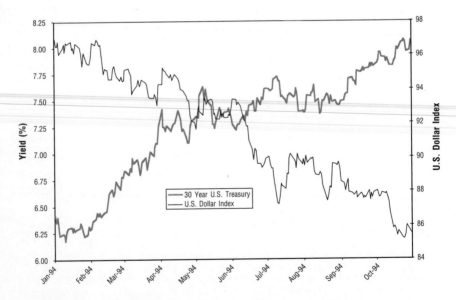

FIGURE 6.5 U.S. 30-Year Treasuries and U.S. Dollar Index, 1994
Source: Bloomberg.

sharer, and making sure we were on it. I'm pretty good at filtering information as I have a good handle on what's important and what isn't, so I would be able to pick up on what our traders were doing and express the good stuff in our back book and internal hedge fund.

How did your run at CSFB end?

I got tired. The foreign exchange business broadened out to incorporate an emerging markets business, but I didn't want to travel as much, especially to emerging markets. I found myself increasingly wanting a change of lifestyle. What the bank said to me was, "Okay, stop doing the strategist thing and just run a prop book yourself," which I did. I hired a trader and the two of us traded markets, but without much success. It was too painful for me to always be running a position.

I came to this racket at the age of 33. I'd been reasonably successful in a short period of time, made more money than I ever thought I'd need. I was tired of banks, I didn't like wearing a tie. I tried just prop trading but frankly, it wasn't working out that well. So we worked out an exit strategy for me to quietly leave the firm. I set off into the sunset, having retired thinking that I'd left markets forever, almost exactly 10 years after I'd entered.

Why did you start a global macro newsletter?

I got bored. I thought it was going to be fun leading a student life again. I moved to the beach in California, goofed off, took a bunch of classes, did some volunteer work, but I eventually got bored. I started looking at markets again, approached some old friends, and asked, "What if I started writing a newsletter?" They loved it, I started writing, and the business began from there. The newsletter has since evolved into a community discussion among smart people, partly as a result of my own need to interact with traders.

Do you think hedge fund managers today are handicapped not being in a trading floor type of environment?

It depends on the trader. Some people work on their own and manage their inputs very closely. Those people could be working on the beach in Hawaii and still be successful. Other people need to be in the mix of it because they need to constantly be fed by what's going on around them. I'm in this category, but nowadays there is an abundance of available information so you don't have to be on a trading floor.

While at Bankers Trust, I was the first guy in the markets to start a daily document about markets. Daily documents didn't exist then, but I had this European morning commentary which was my regular thoughts on whatever came up. Nowadays you get 50 daily documents, so the information flow is there and you don't need to be on a trading floor anymore to get it. What I need now and what I think others need is a dialogue with other traders.

A lot of people are starting their own firms today and there are very good reasons why they're doing that. The problem with starting your own firm is that you might get a little bit isolated. Even though there are 50 sheets that you get every morning, giving a review of what happened or everybody's views and biases, what there isn't as much of is the ability to interact with other smart people who are managing money.

You said earlier that "talk is cheap." How do you respond to the notion that writing a newsletter is like paper trading or just cheap talk?

The truth is that when you retire, you always have a trade on because you have to manage your personal portfolio. Then it becomes a question of being honest. In my sheet, what I do is have biases and trades. The biases are the talk that tells you where I think things are going. The trades are attempts at finding good risk/reward bets that are not inconsistent with my biases.

One is the cheap talk, the other is the way to try to extract value out of the market based on my views. The idea is to give people a big-picture thought process but also keep myself very oriented to the trade, because that's how I have added value in the past and hope to continue to add value. By thinking like a trader does. When I can do that successfully, then I'm going to help people navigate the markets and make money.

That's also why, when I don't feel I understand the market, I get quiet. There's no sense in pretending to understand things when you don't, and there is no need to be in trading or writing at those points. Just like a trader, I go through hot and cold patches. Part of really good trading is understanding when you're hot, and then you've got to lever up. And when you are cold, the key is to reduce size. When I'm cold I reduce, which in my case means reducing my output. It's still pretty much the same process as when I was at CSFB.

How do you do your own research?

I read a variety of things. I read the *Financial Times*, I read *The Economist*, I read heavier literature, I read the occasional academic piece, I read other independent research. I also read the research provided by many of the banks because that gives me a benchmark of what people are thinking, and from there it allows me to look at reality and see what people are saying.

The way I do my research is, I do my reading, then look at market prices and see what the markets are doing and what people are talking about. Then I try to see what is missed or misread out there. The market may either be getting it wrong because it's looking at the wrong variable or it may be missing something. When people are excited by the dollar, they may be missing what's going on with the yen. From all of that is where I can piece together a trade idea.

You often talk about "favorite trades"—where does this come from?

One of the things I did at Credit Suisse was interview a hell of a lot of people. You have to ask people unique things to get to know them and to get to know how they think to see if they fit in. One question I asked everybody was, "If you had to do one trade to get rich today, what would it be?" It was a very provocative question and the answer revealed a lot about the individuals. I can still remember the best answer I ever received. We hired the guy and he ended up being a huge success.

So the "favorite trade" idea came from that. If you've got to glean everything down to one trade, it really helps isolate the basic concepts that someone is thinking about and also helps you learn something about the individual. It helps you see if they think big. If someone's favorite trade has the potential of making 2 percent, you know the guy is never going to be a big player. If someone's trade can make 20 to 30 percent, at least you know that you're getting somewhere. The favorite trade concept grabs the basic contours of their thought process and also tells you something about that person.

Ultimately, what you're looking for in a hedge fund, a prop trader, or even a salesperson talking to the hedge funds, is someone who can see the big move. That's why "favorite trade" is a fantastic concept.

What is your favorite trade right now?

Short-term, I like selling bonds. My bias is neutral, so I can go long or short. Right now I think there's so much liquidity out there holding up the system that rates will have to rise to soak it up. As that process takes place, asset values will be challenged. It's what I have called a bumpy path to deflation.

Bigger picture, it's going to be the same trade I first wrote about in October 2004. The trade is to sell the yen against the other Asian currencies. It's a very unexciting trade because it's a carry trade and it's a slow mover, but it has been working.

The argument goes as follows: Back in October–November 2004, the yen was trading at its strongest point against the other Asian currencies, similar to levels it reached during the yen surge of 1995 and the collapse of the non-Japanese currencies in 1997. The other Asians went down hard in 1997 and never really recovered. Yet today Japanese rates are still at zero while the interest rates of the other guys in the same region have been increasing. So the forwards price in further yen strength against the other Asians, even though these guys have increased interest rate protection, solid current account balances, and very cheap currencies. The yen could go down a long way as Japan recovers until they start raising rates. These other guys are already way ahead of it, so it strikes me as a fundamental anomaly that exists. The price is right to put the trade on and the forwards are to the trade's advantage. I first started talking about it when the world was very bullish the yen, which also helped.

What has been your favorite call since starting your newsletter?

My best trade was presented at our first client conference back in April 2002 when my favorite trade was to buy the euro against the U.S. dollar. The beauty of the trade was not the view, because I'd had that view and I'd been wrong. The beauty was the timing. When equities tanked and the Fed slashed rates in 2001, I thought the dollar would crash but it didn't go down much at all. In fact, I had another letter to the editor published in the *Financial Times* in early 2002 which tried to make sense of why I, and others, had been wrong on the USD.

Much of my presentation involved asking "Why now? Why is the dollar finally ready to go down?" The reasoning was very straightforward. The hypothesis was that the dollar had held up surprisingly well during the recession of 2001 because the sharp fall in profits created a cash squeeze on U.S. companies. As a result, they were forced to repatriate capital from abroad. By early 2002, however, the talk in the market was that companies were flush with cash, which was seen as helping support the recovery. I didn't buy that one! Instead, I translated that into the idea that firms no longer needed to repatriate capital and the USD was now free to go down. That allowed me to catch the beginning of a really tremendous move in the dollar. (*See Figure 6.6.*)

Aren't you always bearish the dollar?

I tend to be bearish the dollar, yes, because it's a trend. The dollar's been going down ever since Bretton Woods broke down in the early 1970s. That's a pretty good trend and for good reason. The United States has had an inflationary economy throughout this period. That shows up either in terms of actual inflation or, as today, in a huge current account (C/A) deficit. The deficit is a sign of excess demand for goods. (*See Figure 6.7.*)

So yes, my bias is typically bearish. I do change my bias when I want to do something against it, which is what I did in 2004 when I went to neutral. At that point, everyone was very bearish and short the dollar, while I wanted to buy it, so I had to go to a neutral bias to free myself to buy it for a trade. So it is a bearish trend and I find it hard to believe I'll ever be bullish the dollar, but if I'm neutral that would allow me to buy it on occasion.

The only reason to be bullish the USD is if real U.S. interest rates get

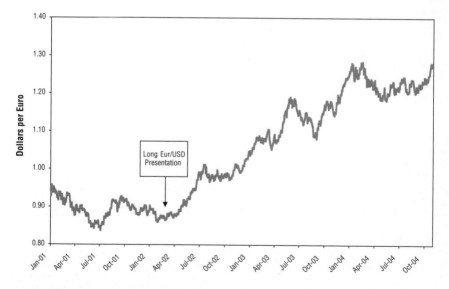

FIGURE 6.6   Euro, 2001–2004
Source: Bloomberg.

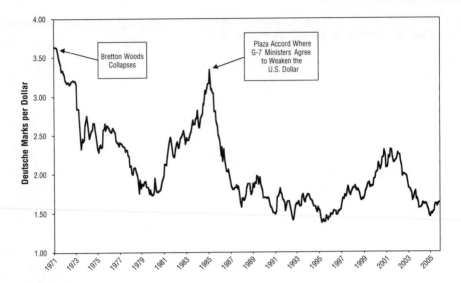

FIGURE 6.7   U.S. Dollar vs. Deutsche Mark, 1971–2005
Source: Bloomberg.

very high. That would both attract capital inflows and hold back spending and thus the excess demand in the economy but, with U.S. real rates very low, the better trade is to sell bonds if you think that's going to happen.

More generally, my approach with biases and trades is that if I move to neutral, then I can buy or sell the asset. But if I have a bias, then I only allow myself to have no position or a position consistent with the bias. It is a discipline that forces me to think deeply about the views underlying a trade. It also is a way of avoiding market whiplash!

Going back to favorite trades, my favorite trade ever was not in the markets but it was a classic macro trade. I bought this amazing penthouse on the Thames in London in 1993 at about 15 cents on the dollar. The bottom had finally fallen out of the property market, exactly as policy turned to be much more supportive of property. Sterling had just devalued and rates were slashed. It was a great anomaly.

But, as is typical for me, I sold out way too soon! I sold it in 1998 at something like 70 cents on the dollar. I made a bundle, but also left a lot of money on the table. It's probably trading at something like 150 to 200 cents on the dollar now. I saw a great trade but struggled to hold on to it. That's my style.

Why do you think you've been successful in picking market inflection points and finding anomalies?

First, because I'm a countertrader by instinct, so if the world is leaning to the left, I'm thinking about what could make it go to the right. Secondly, because most changes in market trends take place for real economic reasons. If you keep a close eye on those underlying conditions, you can catch the changes and find the catalyst for a turn in trends.

Another reason is that most analysts spend their time describing and defining the current equilibrium in the markets. I prefer, instead, to look at things that cause changes in the market equilibrium—something that prompts a shift in the environment. The biggest moves occur when we move from one equilibrium to the next.

In terms of portfolio construction, which global macro trading style do you prescribe to: the one where there are three or four good trades a year and you're looking to hit two or three of them, or the style where you're running a diversified book of many equal-weighted trades at all times?

I am the former. I am a believer that the really fun way to do this is to look for those 20 to 30 percent events, and there aren't that many of those. As a practical matter, you have to live your life and be making a return, so you've got to have some carry trades. Eighty percent of the money shouldn't move around that often. It should be in carry trades or lower-risk stuff that brings in some income. Then there's the remaining 20 percent of the money that's out there looking for the 20 to 30 percent return. That's where one should spend one's energies. To me, global macro is about finding those big trades.

When putting together what you think might be one of those big percentage trades, do you think it's important to travel to the countries you are trading to check them out firsthand?

Just the opposite. I typically find that domestics misunderstand their own economies. I find I get much better perspective by looking at the fundamentals from a distance. That means I will miss things that could be seen on the ground—if a country starts to recover, you might see it on the streets first. But my approach is pretty theoretical and I prefer to keep an analytical distance. Likewise, when I want to get a flavor of a bond market I will often ask an equity guy what he's thinking. People too close to a situation can get emotional and I'd rather look from a distance.

How do you define global macro?

Global macro is trading based on economic/political/sociological factors, so-called "fundamental factors" that move market prices. You can also define it in terms of what it isn't. It isn't looking at individual companies. Although individual companies might affect global macro, or might reflect global macro, it's not really what we're trying to do. It's not really about individual stocks, per se, although it can be about stock market indexes. It's also not technical trading. In global macro you can use technicals as an aid to building good risk/reward bets, but you have a lot of systematic traders out there who I wouldn't consider part of global macro.

How do you differentiate between global macro and relative value?

They are intersecting sets. In global macro terms, a relative value trade that I like is long long-dated UK Gilts against long-dated U.S. Treasuries. The reason that trade is attractive is that cyclically the UK economy has been weakening, while the U.S. economy has been surprisingly robust. More importantly, on a secular basis, the United Kingdom has moved from being a high-inflation country to a very low-inflation country. The UK inflation rate is strikingly low. (*See Figure 6.8.*)

The U.S. dollar, as the reserve currency of the world, is in decline. When the British pound was the reserve currency of the world and in decline, there were periodic currency crises and an uptrend in underlying inflation, and a trend up in the relative interest rate against the rest of the world.

So long UK Gilts against U.S. Treasuries is a relative value trade that fits in the macro sphere. There are other relative value trades that people do, but they may be doing them simply because of price. This bond is priced 3 basis points higher than that bond kind of thing. That's not global macro, in my opinion. So they're intersecting sets.

I'm attracted to relative value in global macro because trading has taught me that I can be very wrong. That's the great discipline that running your own trading book as a research guy gives you. The reason I often go to spread trades or a relative value concept or a hedged bet—which some people think is kind of wishy-washy—is because I ad-

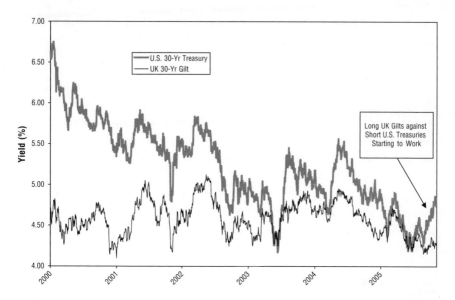

FIGURE 6.8   U.S. 30-Year Treasuries and UK 30-Year Gilts, 2000–2005
Source: Bloomberg.

mit that I can be wrong. What I like to do is look at what might happen, or how do I cover myself if I am wrong? That thought process often leads me to relative value. The great traders of the world make a little money even when they're wrong, and they make a lot of money when they're right.

How has global macro changed since you started?

Macro has changed in some very simple and straightforward ways and the first is, the instruments have changed. For example, we used to trade intra-European currencies and that's been eliminated. Secondly, like everything else, people have become more specialized. So unlike 15 years ago when there were just a few big global macro traders, the very famous ones, what you have now is more specialization. You have people who are currency specialists, relative value specialists, bond specialists, or option specialists. More than anything, macro has changed in that there are a lot more people doing it, which in a sense has forced specialization.

Do you think that the flow of capital into global macro strategies and the number of people trading global macro markets have made it more difficult to make outsized returns?

The amount of capital going into market speculation in general means that the law of diminishing returns works. You get weaker people coming into the system and that leads to a bifurcation of the market between the really good ones and all the others. Distinguishing between the guys who really shouldn't be there and the guys who are just okay becomes difficult. The really great ones stick out and that's why you get a bifurcation in the fees different hedge funds can charge. You now see a few superstar fund managers who are able to charge a 3 or 4 percent management fee and a high percentage of the profits. The rest are becoming commoditized.

Do you think the performance of superstar fund managers is affected by increasing amounts of money under management?

Sure, it has to at some point. Take an extreme case where all the money is in the hands of one guy who is the only person trading markets; it then becomes very difficult to make money. The point is that the amount of money must have an effect. When and where depends on the individual, and that in some ways depends on the style and the stomach. Some guys have a style and a stomach that allows them to be able to trade billions without much trouble.

What advice would you give to a fund of hedge funds manager who is looking to make an allocation to global macro for the first time?

I would say to think of it just like we did at CSFB when building the proprietary trading desk. You want to diversify. The simplest version is you want a carry trader, a fund that earns regular income; and you want a gamma trader, one that looks for the huge move. You want someone who's going to make you the regular money when things are normal and quiet, and the guy who's going to make you a lot of money when things really move. That's how you develop a diversified portfolio. Not by diversifying through markets or by geographic regions but through how they trade. The great trades in global macro are when you combine carry with gamma. When a high yielding currency is cheap, for example, is when you can get tremendous outsized returns.

Why do you think asset allocators find global macro the most difficult of the hedge fund strategies to understand?

Number one, it's not easy to assess quantitatively because it's nonsystematic. Second, because the differences in the managers are very important in terms of how they trade rather than where they trade. Third, because the largest group of managers is in the mixed area between the guys who really shouldn't be doing it and the guys who are doing all right but will never be superstars. It's very hard to distinguish those guys. There are just very few really good ones who have the intellectual capability to find the trades and the stomach to be able to run them, so I think that it's a genuinely difficult process.

Who's the best global macro trader you've worked with?

Jim Leitner, because he has the intellectual ability and curiosity to find the really compelling risk/reward ideas; because he looks for big moves; because he's always shown himself to have a very open mind—he likes to hear contrary ideas; and most importantly, because he's got the stomach to carry all of that in size. There are very few people who combine all of those.

I remember in 1991 when I went to Jim saying, "Look, ERM is going to fall apart," and there were jitters at the time and the French franc was trading at its worst point in the band against the deutsche mark. He went in at the beginning of the year and bought billions and billions of French francs, because he saw a market bearish, it was at the bottom, and he didn't think the system was going to break. So he had the analytical skills, the curiosity, and the stomach to go after it when things looked awful, which he taught me is typically the best time to do a trade. And, by the way, he also was able to get out before the system broke down, and he made money as the breakdown occurred.

Have you had success over your career in finding good traders to hire?

I've had some success and some failures. I don't really have a magic wand on this one. I can tell who's a good trader once they are trading and I'm working with them and talking with them regularly. Typically the guys that I find very good are those who have strong views but differentiate those views from their trade. They pick good risk/reward trades. Another characteristic of a really good trader is the ability to change their mind.

Do you think the current practice of writing a detailed monthly investor letter affects a hedge fund manager's ability to change his mind?

It shouldn't. Most investors shouldn't mind a manager who loses money when he's wrong. What they want is a manager who loses small amounts of money when he's wrong and makes a lot of money when he's right.

By the way, a lot of these guys write these monthly reports the wrong way, in my opinion. They should be writing them to themselves as a sort of personal clarification process. Writing is a cleansing process and a great discipline. When you're writing something and it doesn't make sense, that's where you learn something and you say, "Wait, why doesn't it make sense, what don't I understand here?" You're not writing to convince people or to be elected to anything. It shouldn't be spin. So the more honest the writing is, the better it is for the manager.

I've seen some strikingly honest and helpful reports and I've seen some very questionable reports. When someone writes a report and says, "The markets were irrational," or "There was a lot of noise in the markets," I get very nervous because markets are always somewhat irrational, and of course there's noise in the system. The point is to find the logic behind the moves. If markets have been irrational, that will often present opportunities, not excuses! When someone writes, "I didn't understand this and this happened to me," then that's fine, that's interesting. The key question then becomes "Why didn't you understand it?" The goal is to constantly be learning. Markets are a real challenge and you've got to keep learning just to stay still.

The other thing that I loathe in these monthly reports is overconfidence in the views. You can have a great trade but your view will become right or wrong. It gets proven in the future, so being overconfident in a view is a warning sign. You can be very confident in a trade because it has very good risk/reward characteristics and the idea makes sense. But a good manager is always asking the question, "What if I'm wrong?" The great ones always seem to do this.

What are some other danger signs that an investor in global macro hedge funds should be looking for?

It's the point of a stop-loss. Repeated mistakes are a sign to pull out of a trade. Irrationality is always a time to get out of a trade. You've got to have a stop-loss because you've got to be able to say, "I may be wrong at some point."

The worst sign is when a manager is right but doesn't make money. Again, the best of the bunch is often the guy who is able to make a little money when he's wrong because that means he was able to get out of trouble. Then it's a question of whether he can find that pearl of a trade to make big bucks.

What are your theories on risk management in general and stop-losses specifically? The reason I ask is because you talked about your mark/Swiss trade earlier where you went short, got stopped out, and went short again. In that case, what was the point of a stop-loss?

My theories aren't that evolved. You get stopped out because you want to minimize your losses. Typically what happens is, the market spikes against you, it comes back, and you get back in because you feel that it was the noise that got you out of there. It's the hardest time for a manager when you've been stopped out but you still believe in the view. So what do you do? You have to get back in again but with a very tight stop.

Each trade is an expected return equation. It's just simple theory of uncertainty mathematically expressed as the expected return of a certain set of variables. That expected return is influenced by the boundaries of the trade—that is, where the trade can go and how far away the stop is—and by the probability you attach to it going the way that you think it's going to go. Therefore, strength of view is relevant. If you get stopped out, think it through, and still have very strong views, then the expected return is still pretty good but with one very important proviso: You have to add in the loss to your trade because you've already incurred it. Thus the risk/reward must be less the second time than it was the first. Your risk/return ratio should at least be 4 to 1 in any given trade (the great traders think in terms of 8 to1 or 10 to 1). After you've hit the 1 a couple of times, all of a sudden what was a 4 to 1 trade is now a 4 to 3 trade, at which point you should move on to another trade, even if you don't want to.

Do you think managers should have specific rules regarding when they can get back in a trade after a stop-loss gets hit, such as a cooling-off period or the trade has to move back your way by X percent?

On a specific trade, no. On a portfolio level, if you get stopped out of all positions due to a bad run, then I do believe in the concept of brain damage. When managers takes big losses, they should get away from the markets for about a month because your brain cannot help but be influenced by what just occurred. It's just like after a car accident that was your fault; what you want to do is drive real carefully for a while because you're not driving sensibly at that point.

I'm also a great believer in stepping away for three to four weeks to clear your head anyway, at least once a year. I think everyone should do that. If I were a fund of funds manager, I would force my managers to do that because it's good to clear your head. At Bankers Trust, there was a forced vacation rule for traders.

What advice do you have for someone who wants to be a trader or hedge fund manager?

Talk is cheap; think in terms of risk/reward rather than just direction; and think big move, not little stuff. Be very honest with your thought process. Markets are hard. When we are totally honest with ourselves, we place ourselves in a position to read the news clearly. If you're stuck in a view, you're going to kid yourself, disbelieve new news, and probably panic too late. That's the other dictum, by the way, that I've learned or that I pass on: If you're going to panic in markets, panic early. Panicking late is a recipe for disaster.

CHAPTER 7

THE TREASURER

Dr. John Porter
Barclays Capital
London

John Porter is the biggest risk taker at Barclays, one of the United King-dom's largest and most venerable financial institutions. Whether it is home mortgages, savings accounts, credit cards, or corporate loans, Porter takes in everything that has interest rate risk. His job is to turn that risk into profit. His mandate is unique among global macro style traders in that he is able to trade with a true medium-term view without the constraints of daily mark-to-market. For example, if a two-year government bond he owns sells off against him, he is not forced to cut the position due to investor pressure, stop-loss rules, or other exogenous constraints. Rather, Porter can continue to collect coupons and hold the security until it matures at par because everything he trades is part of Barclays' inventory or balance sheet.

Porter is a deep thinker with a nontraditional background for a top trader. American, he studied at the highly selective École Normale Supérieure (which produced such famous graduates as Samuel Beckett, Jean-Paul Sartre, Jacques Derrida, and others) and received a doctorate in psychology from the Sorbonne, both in Paris. He also holds a master's degree in international af-fairs from Columbia University and an undergraduate degree from Harvard. After his studies, he spent several years as the chief investment officer of the

World Bank, overseeing a $20 billion global fixed income portfolio, and worked for hedge fund pioneer Louis Bacon at Moore Capital Management in Paris, where he was a strategist and portfolio manager.

I interviewed Porter at the Barclays Capital headquarters in Canary Wharf, London. He strikes a professorial image befitting his several advanced degrees and very much looks the part of a bank treasurer or political figure, with a magisterial crop of white hair and a reflective, highly articulate manner. He is commanding and extremely curious, someone who has both taken a circuitous path through the markets and has seemingly enjoyed every minute of it. Indeed, for his recent 50th birthday party, he treated 500 of his closest friends to a blowout party with live entertainment provided by Roxy Music.

He was meticulously well-prepared for our interview, something it was not hard to imagine permeating his professional mien. In order to prepare for our discussion and an open line of questioning, he took one of his junior traders out to lunch and gave him the opportunity to ask anything and everything about his background and experience. My own encounters with Porter have shown me a man who invites challenge and debate.

During our discussions, it came up several times that he considers psychology the most fundamental aspect to understanding financial markets. Indeed, his own specialty in the field provided him with an edge that has translated into compound annual returns of 30 percent gross of fees (on a sizeable allocation of risk capital) since he took the helm as Barclays' principal risk taker in 1998. As a bank treasurer, Porter is a macro trader concerned primarily with front-end interest rates and carry, or interest income he earns on his portfolio while waiting for the big directional macro moves. He can afford patience, since being inside a bank allows him to be a "horizon trader," so dubbed by another market practitioner because of his ability to truly manage for the intermediate term.

But making money in financial markets does not seem to drive a man like Porter, whose wide interests have already led him to excel in a number of different fields. Rather, as he himself readily admits, he is merely "passing through," although, given his broad and diverse background, passing through to where is anyone's guess. I asked him if being the Federal Reserve chairman would be of interest to him one day and he smiled. In the interim, this little-known element hidden away inside one of the world's most prestigious financial institutions helps to shed some light on market psychology and risk in the global macro markets.

What did your junior trader ask that you thought was interesting?

He asked, "What makes you unique? If the market is a zero-sum game, why should anyone be able to beat the market?"

Well, in a zero-sum game, you have winners and losers. With a certain ability, one can be among the winners. What makes me unique is probably my background. I have a PhD in psychology and a master's in economics. I was always more academically oriented and planned on going into teaching and research, which I did for a year. Trading wasn't something that particularly interested me—I actually didn't start trading until I was 35 years old.

I started in the treasury department for the World Bank, which was one of the best training grounds in the world then. Because the bank was one of the largest clients in fixed income at the time, we had great coverage from the sell side. There were 26 different currencies, each independently benchmarked, so there was a lot to learn about the specificities of each particular market. The portfolio was managed very aggressively and we had the ability to trade all these markets with very little experience, so I learned on the job.

When I needed money to send my children to college, I joined the hedge fund Moore Capital in their Paris office to look at European convergence trades. At Moore I learned a lot about money management, especially with regard to using leverage. Because Moore decided to close the Paris office in order to move to London, I chose to leave in 1996 to join another hedge fund for a few years before going to Barclays Capital to manage the bank's portfolio.

Managing Barclays' bank portfolio is the perfect vehicle for my trading style. I feel I have an advantage in the medium-term, which requires staying power, and the bank affords me that. Staying power can be confused with a lack of discipline, but it depends if you survive and are profitable. There's an old trading adage that says, "One man's staying power is another man's foolish lack of discipline," and I recognize that.

What I am doing at Barclays nowadays is engaging in time horizon arbitrage. All investors these days are replicating the same very short-term style. Whether it is hedge funds, funds of funds, prop desks, or real money, the good old days of a strategy session to discuss portfolio changes are over.

Nobody can do that now. Everybody is held to parameters that don't allow for any volatility in earnings. To me, that's a good thing, as long as I don't have to follow that formula. I believe that by executing a strategy that nobody else can, I will outperform. Does that make me any better? Not necessarily, but it gives me an edge.

An analogy I like to give is a jam-packed cocktail party where everyone enters the room through a very large door. There is also a small door in the back that nobody notices. If someone yells "Fire!" the logical thing to do is exit through the large door. The problem is, if everybody heads that way, you might get trampled. The proper strategy then becomes to head toward the small door in the back, even though it's not the most efficient exit strategy in terms of actual physics. The moral of the story is, when things get crowded, you need to adapt your strategy in light of everybody else.

Can you give me a specific trade example highlighting the staying power that Barclays affords?

When I joined Barclays in June 1998, there was a fantastic opportunity to buy 30-year German Bunds and sell 30-year UK Gilts, as the Gilts were trading expensive to Bunds. I did not invent this as it was a very popular trade at the time. Regardless, I felt very comfortable with the trade because (1) I knew why the anomaly was occurring and (2) the positive carry was huge at around 250 basis points. In other words, 30-year Bunds could be financed at 2.5 percent more than Gilts.

This striking anomaly was occurring because UK investors were paying up for Gilts due to regulatory reasons (the Minimum Funding Requirement ruling) that artificially held down yields.

MINIMUM FUNDING REQUIREMENT (MFR)

This regulation, passed in Great Britain after the Maxwell pension scandal in 1991, was meant to guarantee that assets in company pension plans were always enough to cover their liabilities (i.e., obligations to retirees). As a measurement tool, the legislation uses the yield from long-term UK Gilts. To abide by the obligations created by the MFR, pension plans purchased these long-term bonds, causing their price to go up dramatically.

The risk on the trade was the fact that it was crowded. Another risk was UK base rates dropping below European rates. There was no precedent in history, which doesn't mean it can't happen, it's just one of the risks.

The trade would work and we would get paid if there was a slowdown in regulatory-induced buying. Moreover, we were long the wild-card option of the United Kingdom joining the euro, which would immediately cause the spread to collapse. In the meantime, we were happy to wait and collect the carry.

This trade made a lot of sense for Barclays because, as a UK bank, we have the benefit of using accrual accounting, which only accounts for the current income, or carry, on our positions. So I put this trade on in pretty big size. It had a DV01 (dollar value of a basis point) of £800,000 which, duration weighted, put the notional position size at around £650 million. It was about a quarter of the overall risk in the portfolio and one of the riskiest positions the firm had on.

As soon as I put it on, it went against me significantly on a mark-to-market basis. Long Term Capital and everybody else had it on as well, so when market conditions forced them to unwind their portfolio, this trade blew out. At one point, I was down £60 million on the trade.

During the blowouts, though, I was able to lock in 350 basis points of carry for two years, so the breakeven on the trade was getting ridiculous. We were making all this carry, but the mark-to-market was negative. Given the bank's generous accounting treatment and my confidence as to why the trade was going against us, I continued to run it.

We took the majority of the position off six years later in mid-2004 and made approximately £180 million for the firm. I have to admit, there were times when I was nervous because I'd just joined the bank and was getting pressure from risk management. But I told management, if I were you, I'd be issuing 30-year Barclays paper because a sub-4 percent yield in 30 years is only occurring because of regulatory reasons and the LTCM unwind. I couldn't really convince them but I was able to stick with the position, mainly because the net present value (NPV) of the book never went negative. (*See Figure 7.1.*)

So one of your advantages here at Barclays is the accounting treatment that allows you to hold on to a position as long as the current income stays positive?

Yes, but that doesn't mean we are happy to lose money as long as we get current income. Along with our attraction to current income, we do have

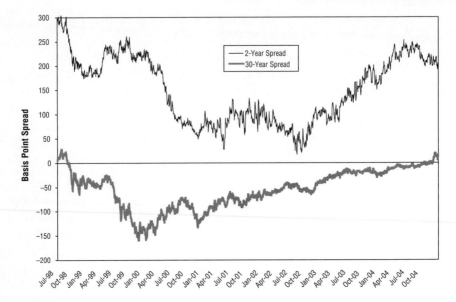

FIGURE 7.1   30-Year and 2-Year UK/Germany Spread, 1998–2004
Source: Bloomberg.

an absolute return focus. I've done this at Barclays for seven years now and absolute returns have been very good and we have never taken any horrific losses.

Essentially, we do the traditional banking function of interest rate mismatch. Barclays has separated areas of comparative advantage, cut up responsibilities, and consolidated all interest rate risk from various areas of the firm. For example, the Barclaycard people are much better at marketing credit cards than managing their interest rate risk, so we do it. As a bank, we want to make sure that whenever we lend money, we get it back with a spread.

3-6-3 RULE

This is an old, informal rule at banks in which 3 percent interest is paid on savings accounts and 6 percent interest is charged for loans, allowing the bankers to be on the golf course by 3 o'clock in the afternoon.

All of the firm's interest rate risk from the retail bank, the mortgage guys, the Barclaycard, and so on, is transferred to Barclays Capital, and I take on the majority of that risk. The remainder is used to grease the wheels of the other areas in capital markets: fixed income, commodities, FX, credit, and so forth.

My group is mandated to run a gap risk whereby effectively we lend long and borrow short. That doesn't mean we blindly offset Barclays' interest rate liabilities. Indeed, we will take the positions in areas where Barclays doesn't have any natural presence or exposure, such as New Zealand, for example. Our risk is not limited to Barclays' outstanding liabilities. We are actively managing risk and seeking a positive absolute return while being limited by the firm's value at risk (VAR) model, regulatory capital limits, and balance sheet limits.

We look to maximize current income for a given unit of risk. As a result, we tend to be in the front end of the yield curve as opposed to the back end because it's better to roll one billion one-year notes for 10 years than to buy 100 million 10-year bonds ceteris paribus. The VAR would be the same if they had the same volatility but with the one-year notes, you get much more current income.

By concentrating risk in the front end of the yield curve, the only thing that can really make me right or wrong is a central bank. A central bank has the ability to enhance or diminish my carry, and we want carry. Everything else is just noise.

Our area of core expertise is the one-year, one-year interest rate forwards. One-year, one-year interest rate forwards are where the market is predicting where one-year interest rates will be in one year's time. It's the one area where the potential for large overshoots still exist, so we focus on it. Inherently, it's the most volatile part of the yield curve because it's the area around the future expectation of the central bank's base rate.

If you had a perfect central bank with perfect cyclical foresight, the 10-year rate would stay at 4 percent yet base rates might vary between 3 and 5 percent. When central banks start to move, the market often prices in an acceleration of that move, and it's always those one-year, one-year forwards that tend to exhibit the greatest change. Most interest rate cycles are between 16 and 24 months, so it's the back months in the Eurodollar futures where the meat of the cycle occurs and where the market often extrapolates more than what will actually occur.

When my colleagues talk about how bad the market feels, I say, "I don't care how it feels. We're not here to take the pulse of the market. We're here to look at how much carry we can get for this position relative to expectations about where we think central banks are going." As such, we try to take the other side of market distress when people are blowing out of positions because we don't have to worry as much about the mark-to-market of the position.

In the absence of everything else, we are here to make income every day. If we're making money from the positive carry but the mark-to-market is against us, we'll hold the bond position to maturity.

There's another old saying that "The road to ruin is paved with positive carry," and I recognize that, too. When I'm worried about a central bank I will reassess our medium-term view, but I want to maintain that medium-term perspective because that's where I feel I have a comparative advantage. If I focus on something more "now," I'm afraid I will lose perspective.

Perception is a very interesting thing in psychology. Small moves appear big to some people, while other people won't even notice them because they have a different perspective. The more micro you're shown, the more small moves appear big. You need a reference point.

Over the last seven years, on a mark-to-market basis, we have run a successful and robust strategy. Will this always be the same? We've been through different market cycles and it has worked, so that is encouraging. But as interest rates and volatility continue to decline, there are questions about the viability of our strategy, or any strategy for that matter.

Other than the fact that you can hold on to positions longer, are there other advantages for you being at a bank, such as primary information?

For me, the value being inside a bank is the comfort factor. There is a lot that is taken care of at a bank in terms of cost and infrastructure. I find it less valuable on the information side. I actually don't talk to that many people because I know their views and find them to be a distraction. I spend most of my time reading research, but I tend to read more independent research simply because it provides an unbiased view.

All I'm trying to do is arbitrage between what a central bank is going to do and what the market thinks it's going to do. I like to know what traders are doing, but that's not really relevant on a daily basis. What is important is to get a sense when everybody is leaning one way. That doesn't necessarily mean that I will countertrade it, but it's good to be aware of market dynamics when timing the entry and exit of positions.

Do you talk to other hedge fund managers for information?

No. I'm friendly with them and see them out socially or at Barclays functions, but I don't have any regular idea exchanges with anyone. I just don't find it advantageous. A lot of my time is actually taken up with bank administration stuff.

Does administration stuff detract from performance?

Some admin responsibilities are good because they give me something to do when there's nothing to do. The problem with sitting at a desk all day staring at the markets is that sometimes you do things you don't really want to do simply out of boredom.

What specific instruments do you trade?

All plain vanilla stuff. Government bonds, swaps, bank paper. Instruments where I know I will get my principal back if I hold them to maturity. We don't do any corporate bonds, except for bank paper. In the United Kingdom, all credits are 100 percent weighted for bank portfolios, which means that we can't leverage credit.

How is what you do different from a fixed income or relative value hedge fund?

Relative value hedge funds and hedge funds in general are all about leveraged selling of volatility. We do the opposite. Too many hedge funds today are selling volatility, and volatility is so low that it makes little sense to be selling it now. The return does not justify the risk.

You can see evidence of overpopulation in hedge funds by looking at how tight high yield spreads are. Hedge fund managers are under immense pressure to perform, so they can't worry about market distress. Their competitors aren't worried about risk, so they all have to be in the same trade, eking out 50 basis points a month or else investors will pull their money, anyway. One way to make 50 basis points a month is with credit spreads, but the risk is tremendous. Low levels of volatility in the past have preceded major market disruptions—1998 being the classic example. (*See Figure 7.2.*)

My strategy is to try to take advantage of market distress to lock in as much carry as I can. Most of the time, I'm not going to be invested and there's not going to be any return, but I will make significant returns at the

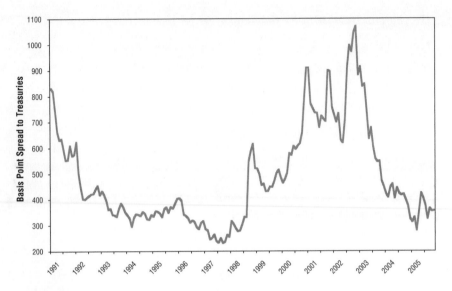

FIGURE 7.2   High Yield Spread, 1991–2005
Source: Bloomberg.

moment of distress by taking the other side. In doing so, I should be able to make very large returns over time which, when averaged out, will allow me to perform as well as, if not better than, the best hedge funds. In other words, as everybody's going through the big door, I want to go out the small one in the back.

Interest rate trends aren't what they used to be, and even though volatility's down on a secular basis, you have pockets of extreme and violent volatility. The goal is to catch these moves. Obviously it is easier said than done, but that's how things must be approached now.

To make money today, you need different investment strategies that go against the conventional strategies. To get the required latitude to execute those strategies, you need very savvy and astute investors and/or a long lockup period. We've just launched a fund to take outside money and our plan is to be very selective choosing our investors so we can do this.

Are we in a hedge fund bubble right now?

From a cyclical point of view, I do think we are in a hedge fund bubble now. I believe we will see a decline in the number of hedge funds and a net decrease in assets managed by hedge funds in the short term. It shouldn't necessarily result in something cataclysmic in the financial markets but I think at some point, investors are going to conclude that the returns don't justify the fees. Over the long run, the asset class of hedge funds is here to stay, just like the mutual fund industry, but I think we're close to a cyclical top right now simply because so many people are doing it. The problem is, with the management fee, it's just too easy. Why not launch a hedge fund if you can raise a billion dollars and get paid a 2 percent annual fee? If things don't go well, so what? You have $20 million in your pocket minus a few expenses.

If you think the number of hedge funds will shrink and you worry about getting your focus shifted from the medium-term to the short-term, why are you planning to launch a fund and take external money?

I have told every interested investor that external money is going to be managed in exactly the same manner as the bank portfolio. We tell them that we can have a 15 percent drawdown although the possibility is low.

I also say, "Please don't invest unless you're 100 percent comfortable with our style." We haven't had to institute a lockup period to date because I'm currently only talking with investors who know me well and understand my style. We may have to implement one as we take on more investors.

But again, you are managing a lot of capital here at Barclays. Why take on more and all the hassles that go with it?

Growth. I keep bumping up against internal capital constraints. I can manage a larger capital base and, from Barclays' point of view, it would be good to diversify my asset base since I currently take the majority of risk for the firm. It's a win-win since I get to stop bumping up against capital constraints and Barclays gets additional fee income with less risk. Also, this is an additional business challenge that I felt I needed outside of the day-to-day of the markets.

Back to the lunch with your junior trader, were there any other interesting questions asked?

Another question was, "What makes a great trader?" which is actually not the right question. The right question is, "How does one embody the qualities to become a great trader?"

The most important quality of a trader is discipline. That is a sine qua non of trading; one must have discipline. It is even more important than idea generation. The key over time is to have the discipline to capitalize on your successes and minimize your mistakes because, ultimately, the game is about preservation of capital.

The market is a completely objective observer of human behavior. People often try to rationalize mistakes in the market by saying things such as "The market is overreacting" or "Who could have seen this coming?" but once you start to rationalize, you're wrong.

The most disciplined trader I know is my former boss, Louis Bacon of Moore Capital. He used to always say, "You're not here to be right, you're here to make money." I kept saying to him, "In life, I'd rather be right." It took me a long time to realize that I could still have that philosophy, just not in the trading arena.

Can trading discipline only be learned via mistakes or can it be instinctive?

It can come naturally, although there is a certain degree of experience that is necessary. I believe if you have shown yourself to have great discipline, then there is a chance that you can become a great trader. I am still a relatively undisciplined trader, but I've been able to attain the level of discipline necessary to enable me to stay in the game.

Have you had success in hiring disciplined traders?

I believe I have. People who have worked here and left have gone on to do very well.

I look to hire very junior individuals and go very much outside the typical investment banking hire. I like individuals who have discipline instilled in them from athletics or the military. People who are constantly evaluating risk and hopefully have the discipline to know when a decision is wrong and can change quickly.

The typical hire in an investment bank is not of interest to me. The MBA or the PhD in finance or particle physics did not save investment banks from Long Term Capital or the NASDAQ bubble. Psychology is the one discipline that explains these events and it is not embodied in these types of education.

Psychology is by far the most important area in the markets. Markets people want to be quantitative and model human behavior, but the problem is, human behavior is not stable. When people interact as groups, human behavior becomes subjugated to that of the overall group.

There's a great story about a famous local trader at the Chicago Board of Trade (CBOT). One day, he was on the floor of the CBOT and a U.S. inflation number came out that was totally unexpected. Pure pandemonium ensued. When all the noise died down, he walked out of the pit having made $10 million and said, "By the way, what was the number?" That, to me, captures it all.

Did you come to this conclusion before you entered financial markets or after trading for a while?

I got there after taking what I observed in the markets and tying it back to what I studied as an undergraduate in experimental psychology. At the World Bank, one of my colleagues was into charting the bond market and when I first saw his charts, they reminded me of the stimulus and response graphs we got from our conditioning experiments on rats and pigeons.

From a trading perspective, it's very simple. There's stimulus, response, reward, and punishment. To every trading action, there will always be some kind of initial response which will have decreasing marginal responses. Thus one has to be increasingly reinforced to elicit the same response. The longer an individual has been rewarded for a given response, the longer it will take to extinguish the response when the reward is no longer forthcoming. Then we introduce the concept of punishment. With punishment, conditioned responses get extinguished more quickly. This provides a framework to analyze markets but it doesn't necessarily predict where things are going.

A good example is the U.S. stock market from the late 1990s to today. In the mid 1990s, investors started to like stocks again for some reason. Earnings growth or the prospect of a technology boom served as a stimulus. The response to that stimulus was to buy stocks. Stocks went up, reinforcing the initial response. The reinforcement caused another response—buy more stocks—and so on. Even market dips acted as stimuli in the late 1990s as people were positively reinforced for buying the dips. There was positive reinforcement over many, many years. The longer this continued and the greater the amount of positive reinforcement, or capital gain, the greater the amount of time required for the buying response to stop.

It's the same with rats and pigeons. If a pigeon is shown a green light which precedes the dispersal of food, the pigeon pecks where the food is. If this is done over a long period of time, continuous positive reinforcement, then the pigeon will still peck upon seeing the green light even if there isn't any food dispersed. The longer this is done, the longer it takes the pigeon to stop pecking once the food is no longer forthcoming, despite the green light. To extinguish response more quickly, punishment is introduced and the pigeon is given an electric shock when it pecks upon seeing a green light when there is no food.

When I first started trading, I actually wanted to trade like an economist, but I quickly learned via punishment that it was not possible. In the U.S. stock market example, the conditioned response was extinguished post-2000 as the market went down, incessantly, punishing investors for owning stocks and especially for buying the dips.

Did you know the NASDAQ was a bubble in 2000 because of your psychology background?

Yes. With regard to financial or asset bubbles, you have to know it's there and hopefully that will be enough to keep you out of trouble. The only thing I did during the tech bubble was sell all of the stocks from my personal account. My thought process in 1999 was that the Fed was entering into a hiking cycle so stocks should stop going up. I sold in February 1999, which was a year too early. But then again, when the great financier Bernard Baruch was asked the secret of his success, he said, "I always sold too early."

How did you incorporate the tech stock bubble and subsequent crash into your fixed income trading?

Once tech stocks started to really sell off, I knew the Fed would be on the move lowering rates. Once they started their easing cycle, the stock market became less relevant to me. At Barclays, I keep my trading limited to fixed income simply because it's the area I know best. Individuals who deviate from their area of expertise in markets are often the ones who get themselves in trouble.

When the bubble popped, I put on a U.S. yield curve steepener—long U.S. two-year notes, short U.S. 30-year bonds. Two-year notes at that point were yielding around 6.75 percent and the curve was inverted by 75 basis points. I wasn't overly bullish bonds at this point but I thought the yield curve inversion had to normalize.

Although about 95 percent of my profits are from directional fixed income positions, I consider myself a relative value–oriented trader because I feel it's important to properly place directional positions along the curve in order to maximize the probability of success. When I put on this curve steepener, people thought I was out of my mind. As it turned out, I put it on at the absolute low in terms of inversion. The spread went from minus 75 to plus 365. (*See Figure 7.3.*)

Did you pull a Bernard Baruch and get out too early?

Yes. I only rode it for about 125 basis points or so.

If you are mostly directional, why didn't you just buy two-year notes?

The only time I'll enter into relative value trades is when I'm confident each leg could be profitable on its own. Essentially I was running two positions. People who trade the curve delude themselves into thinking they're in a hedged position. The yield curve is 90 percent explained by

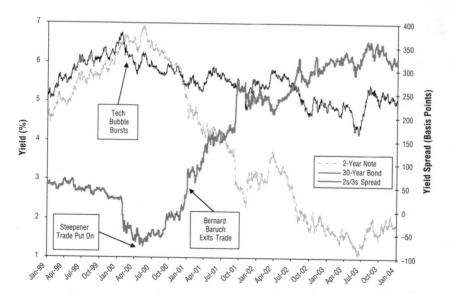

FIGURE 7.3   U.S. 2-Year Note versus U.S. 30-Year Bond, 1999–2004
Source: Bloomberg.

the direction of interest rates. If you have on a curve steepener, you basically think the bonds are going to rally, and if you have on a curve flattener, you think the market is going to sell off.

What do you look for that denotes a good directional macro trade opportunity?

The most important variable to me and my trading is the probability that a central bank will move interest rates in line with the market. That's where I focus my macro calls. It provides a decent anchor because it's something I can truly get ahold of as opposed to trying to understand supply, demand, or some other micro variable to the macro story.

When you find a good macro trade, do you use various instruments to express it or do you just choose the instrument you think will perform best?

Unless I can see compelling reasons why a position should be diversified, I believe you're fooling yourself if you have a lot of positions on. The more positions, the more potential for losses. If there's an instrument that you think will capture 80 to 90 percent of your thesis, why distract yourself with a bunch of positions?

Is your portfolio usually long volatility or short volatility?

Long vol on average. We went short vol last year, because it was the only way we thought we could make money. Now I wouldn't do it, just because vol has become too cheap. I am comfortable going short volatility when we are long the front end of the yield curve, because if there is a blowup and we get hit on our short vol, front-end interest rates should rally. But I like to be long that risk, not short, so I can sleep well at night.

A famous trader once said, "If you can't sleep at night, that means your positions are too big." That's why I can sleep. I make sure that I don't run positions that make me feel uncomfortable.

How exactly do you structure your portfolio?

What we do is maximize current income per unit of VAR while maintaining a certain level of diversification. Liquidity is important, although we need less liquidity than others because our portfolio is not marked-to-market, but there is a point where we'll recognize that we're wrong so liquidity is still important. We do a qualitative assessment of all our positions and think through what will make each of them right or wrong. Then we look for other positions that might serve to offset our positions if they all go wrong. We then look at the impact of those new positions on our overall VAR while keeping in mind the problems associated with VAR—that is, that it is a backward-looking indicator and assumes correlations are stable.

The problem with VAR is captured in a discussion I recently had with my risk manager prior to a U.S. employment report. We were short U.S. Treasuries going into the number.

RISK MANAGER: You should put on a curve steepener because you have to reduce your VAR number.

PORTER: You've got to be kidding. We're a day in front of the employment number. If that number prints big, trust me, this market is not going to steepen, it's going to flatten because it will force the Fed to hike.

RISK MANAGER: If you put on a flattener, you'll be over your risk limits.

PORTER: So you want me to put on a trade I think will lose money just so we get under our VAR limit?

Obviously, he smiled sheepishly and walked away. That sums up the problem with these VAR models. It's very important to employ a quantitative framework to evaluate risk, but it's also very important to be able to overlay that with common sense, which can only be gained through experience.

The whole trading game is geared for very young individuals, but experience should trade at a greater premium. That's probably part of the reason the market has a short memory.

Can you use the market's short memory to your advantage?

Definitely. It's one example why markets aren't efficient. Another is because people don't even remember things that they've lived through. It's not so much that markets have short memories but it's somewhat related.

I remember after September 11, the world was coming to an end in many people's minds and bond markets rallied massively. Gloom was everywhere, but I never shared that gloom because I understand the great adaptability of the human species and that this, too, shall pass.

When zero percent interest on cars came out post–September 11, causing record car sales, it showed that no matter how depressed people are, they will buy something if there is a bargain. We got very short bonds after that car sales number. Retail sales came out next and it was a repeat of the car sales number. At this point, the market caught on and the bond market sold off like nobody's business.

Extreme moves like September 11 have happened and will happen. That's where older guys like me have an advantage due to experience. It's important to realize that things don't always have to be a certain way.

I did my thesis on the development of memory and communication of children and have always tried to develop a good memory for myself. One of my advantages in markets is that I have a good episodic memory for remembering exactly what happened in the bond market and why. That's why I don't use charts that much—I just remember these things.

How have markets changed since you started?

We just had a 20-year period of paper asset appreciation and physical asset depreciation. That's over. In 1980, financial stocks were 5 percent of the S&P 500. Today they make up 20 percent of the index.

In 2000, I said to my children, "I hope you've enjoyed your life up until now because you've lived through a period of peace, prosperity, and wealth creation that's a historical anomaly. Even if you don't have the prosperity and wealth, as long as you can live without war, you're doing really well." Then September 11 came. Compared to the 1990s, it doesn't get any better than that and it won't.

From a financial markets point of view, we're in a range type stock market with downward bias. People will become quite disillusioned with the financial markets. At some point, people are going to look to do other things, like public service, the Peace Corps, or that type of thing, as opposed to getting an MBA or going into investment banking. These things tend to go in waves.

As for geopolitics, I don't subscribe to the fall of the United States versus China. I still believe the United States has enough dynamism and openness that it will continue to attract the best and the brightest. China could be a very strong factor and maybe we'll have a tripolar world. It'll probably go back to the way it was before there was one predominant superpower, and that's probably a good thing. From a humanistic point of view the Soviet Union was terrible, but from a balance of power and geopolitical standpoint, it was a very good thing. It's always good to have an offset that keeps everybody in check and honest.

What trading strategy has the greatest probability of success going forward?

A very experienced stock picker. A guy who, on a micro basis, can analyze which stocks are overvalued and which stocks are undervalued and trade accordingly. We are going into a trading market versus a trending market. All those ridiculous people who are indexed are going to get killed, as are trend followers.

There may come a day where my asset class won't deliver, in which case I have to recognize that. Failure's lurking around every corner, and there'll be a time when the bank's management will expect something out of me that I might not be able to deliver. Hopefully it will be because I couldn't get it out of the market. The only thing I really have to lose now is my reputation, so I won't try to do more than I should just because somebody expects a certain return.

Does the increased correlation in global bond markets hurt your ability to produce returns?

It goes in fits and starts. There are periods of synchronized growth and there are periods of unsynchronized growth. Some of our markets are more correlated now but others are less so.

The two ends of the U.S. yield curve are negatively correlated, which is unprecedented. The central banks of New Zealand and Australia are going in different directions, as are their economies, which is unusual. And Europe is not as correlated with the United Kingdom as people think.

We monitor correlations as they might have an effect on the short term, but they often don't play into the big picture because they are backward looking. I often put on trades that don't make sense in the current correlation environment as a hedge into a potentially stressed environment. For example, I believe that if all my other positions are wrong, then, say, New Zealand will perform if there is a significant move. We can't forget about putting that New Zealand trade in the portfolio because even though it's not an interesting market right now, if all of a sudden something happened, that New Zealand position would kick in and help us defuse some potential losses in other positions.

Again, what we do is different from most hedge funds. We manage money in a true portfolio context with a medium-term focus. Hedge funds operate on a day-to-day basis. They will claim to have on a series of medium-term trades in a portfolio context but they are really trading with a bank prop trader type mentality.

Are you surprised by the lack of academic rigor in financial markets?

Yes, particularly in behavioral finance. There are a lot of very interesting biases in human behavior that tend to be quite consistent and should be applied to the markets. Nobody is really doing this, however. I don't necessarily use behavioral finance directly in my trading as it's more a qualitative thing than a quantitative thing.

For example, I like watching my young traders because they all make the same mistakes. I don't mean this unkindly—everybody has to go through it. But at the beginning of one's trading career, there is a general tendency to want to be with the crowd. I'm only interested in what they have to say for that reason.

I also use behavioral finance to look for the concept of why people think the way they do. The *concept* is very important. Markets can be overbought or oversold but they can't start trending until there's a new concept. Concepts eventually become exhausted, which is usually when they make the paper or magazine covers. In other words, when a certain concept becomes fully popularized, it no longer has any value to the market. It goes back to stimulus and response. At some point, the same stimulus will elicit a monotonically decaying response until nobody cares. I want to know what the relevant concepts are and why people are positioned the way they're positioned in order to help me judge when things might change. Behavioral finance explains why markets do what they do.

Economics is still an area of human psychology. Why is something worth what it is? Supply and demand; but so what? Why do diamonds attract significant sums? Somebody must like them, but why? Well, they just do. So it's all psychology.

Do people buy gold because of psychology? Do you believe there is inherent value in gold?

I don't think there's any inherent worth to gold so it's all psychology. That being said, I recently bought gold for my personal account because I felt the risk was incredibly low. I liked the fact that all the central banks, including the Bank of England, were selling. When central banks engage in market-based activities, they are great counterindicators. I also liked the economic growth of India and China, both of which are large gold users. Indian women wear a lot of gold and the Chinese have gold all over their buildings and shrines. I figured, if these people ever get the purchasing power to buy gold, it will go up. Again, a psychology thing. Why do they value gold? Who knows, they just do.

Do you find it valuable meeting with central bankers in spite of their counterindicator status?

Yes. I have very good relations with central bankers because I'm a bank portfolio manager, not a hedge fund. Central banks have a duty to Barclays because we're part of the clearing system. I've also got a similar background to a lot of them so I always start our chats by mentioning my 10 years of service at the World Bank to make them comfortable.

All I want to know from them is what they are looking at. As long as I'm focused on the same things they're focused on, I feel more comfortable that I'm making the right trading decisions. They don't have to slip up for me to make money.

The difficulty is, everybody's too caught up in the game now. All of a sudden, every single word is important. Central bankers have all just fallen into the trap where they feel they have to be so communicative and so transparent to the market that in the end it probably does them more harm than good, particularly the European Central Bank. If I were they, I wouldn't say anything.

Besides central bankers, what other tools or indicators do you use when trading fixed income?

People will laugh at this but I might as well throw it out there because some people associate me with it. I look at lunar cycles and like to know when the moon is full.

There is nothing mystic about me—I'm not into astrology and I don't ask people for their signs—but I once read this empirical study on the very statistically significant correlation between full moons and trend reversals. I trust the guy who did this study and I find it quite interesting. And it makes sense that the gravitational force of the moon can have an effect on human behavior. Obviously the gravitational pull of the moon is huge. It changes the tides, it affects the menstrual cycle, and people who work with Alzheimer's patients say their patients act differently during full moons.

There have been a couple of times when noting the full moon has been a good thing for my trading. Trading is all about confidence. The more confident you are, the bigger your position can be and the greater your staying power. But you have to know why you're confident; it can't be foolish confidence like arrogance or invincibility.

Look at it like the mosaic theory, where you put together different pieces of a puzzle to help you formulate a decision. The full moon just happens to be one of my pieces. I don't trade off it, but I'll always ask where the moon is, particularly if we're at an extreme level on a trend.

What was your worst trading mistake and what did you learn from it?

There were a lot of them, but I'll give you one that occurred at Moore Capital in 1994. I had on a Eurolira calendar spread where I was short the front contract and long the second deferred. I thought the back months or forward rates were too high vis-à-vis Europe and that this anomaly would dissipate as time went on with Italian rates converging to euro rates.

It was one of those trades where things weren't going the way they were supposed to go. Italy had a weakening currency with a weakening economy. The front end should have sold off relative to the back end because the central bank in Italy was either going to hike rates to defend the currency or at least keep rates steady so as not to kill the economy.

Instead, the opposite happened. The front end rallied and the back end sold off, so my trade went significantly against me. I decided to leg out of it, but the leg I was long was going down and the leg I was short was going up, so it was hard to decide which leg to get out of. I had a certain amount of company in this trade so the pain was intensified.

I didn't know what to do, so I called up a trader friend, who used to be a broker, for advice. He said, "It's very simple. Call up a broker that you've never spoken to before and ask him to unload it quickly. The broker is only going to care about the commission so he's going to get it done as quickly as possible. The last thing you want to do is give the trade to one of your friends on the sell side who is going to try to work it for you, thus take longer, and probably cost you more money in the end."

When things go badly for reasons you don't understand or for reasons that you understand but that aren't the reasons that you initially got into the trade, you really should cut the trade as soon as possible. I crushed the market getting out of my Eurolira trade and lost a bit more money on the way out, but at least I was out.

From this experience, I learned that the stop-loss is by far the most important aspect to a trade. Going back to discipline, the stop-loss is a very difficult thing to implement, but if you have a proper stop-loss, you'll never blow up. You'll be out long before you get anywhere near the end.

Besides the Italy trade, what else happened to you during the 1994 bond market rout?

Nineteen ninety-four was the worst year of my life. I was almost physically ill it was so difficult. I never got sick but I was running to the bathroom every three minutes. Some background first: I was one of the first traders at Moore, other than Louis Bacon, to have my own capital to trade. This was in 1993 and the conversation went like this:

BACON: Why do you want to trade?

PORTER: You're a much better trader than I am, but I feel you have to allocate me some capital. If you don't, I'm just going to remember the trades that you didn't do that worked and completely forget about the ones I recommended that didn't work. I feel strongly that I should be able to trade an account that you can track.

BACON: Fair enough, makes sense.

I remember being bearish bonds in 1993, thinking the market was totally overdone, but I tried to go short and it didn't work. The problem was, I felt intense pressure to succeed because I had just talked Louis into allocating capital to me. So I got in with the crowd, jumped on the trend, and went long bonds. I was long the UK ultra longs and Italy, as discussed earlier. As a result, I finished very strongly my first year and was up 50 percent on my capital allocation.

BACON: This is fantastic. I have decided to triple your position.

PORTER: The market seems quite pricey at these levels.

BACON: You're not at the World Bank anymore. You're not trading to a benchmark. If your capital is tripled, your positions should be as well.

So it was effectively tripled. As it turned out, global bond markets melted down in 1994 and the markets that I was in were the ones that got trashed the most. I was down 15 percent on my new capital which, when tripled, was 45 percent of my original allocation. Louis was very upset and I felt like a deer in the headlights.

BACON: This is totally unacceptable.

PORTER: I realize that, so I cut all my positions, but I'd like to start up again.

BACON: Okay, but you can't be that undisciplined anymore.

At this point, I looked around at all the people getting blown out, started seeing all these anomalies turning up and started doing relative value trades partly because I didn't have any confidence in my directional trading. By September, I was actually up on the year. Then I tried to resign.

PORTER: I don't want to stay, but I'm happy to say that I didn't lose any of your money.

BACON: What do you mean you're resigning? This was a phenomenal performance. In 1994 there were two types of people, those who lost a lot of money and stopped trading, and those who lost a lot of money, tried to get it back, and lost even more. I don't know of anyone who's done something like what you've done.

PORTER: I'm very honored, thank you, but . . .

BACON: Stay.

So I stayed, but it was the worst year of my life. I'd just moved jobs and countries after 10 years at the World Bank so, on top of my poor trading, I went through all the so-called stress positions in life other than death and marriage. I'm glad I went through it, though, because it is the most important trading experience I've been through. It's amazing—in the end, the worst experience of my life turned out to be the best experience of my trading life. Remembering that experience always keeps me from getting sloppy.

The main lesson I took from that experience is that things can always get worse than you can possibly imagine. You can never say that something is not possible, because anything is possible in the future. In light of this, you always need a disciplined stop-loss in place.

It's amazing how many successful macro traders today had their seminal trading experience in the 1994 bond market rout.

Which is bizarre, because you had one of the greatest trends of all time. You were never threatened but still almost nobody caught that trend.

What was the best trade of your career?

My favorite trade was in February 1999, a few months after the Long Term Capital unwind, when people thought the financial system was imploding. I was in a Barclays Capital management committee meeting and they asked for my views.

PORTER: I'm very bearish on fixed income.

COMMITTEE: How can you be bearish when the world's coming to an end?

PORTER: You were right four months ago, but it's still here, and that view is now fully discounted and irrelevant. I think the Fed actually made a mistake with that insurance ease back in November because everything was over by then.

COMMITTEE: So what's in your portfolio?

PORTER: We have a very large short position in 10-year UK Gilts.

COMMITTEE: Don't you think that's dangerous?

PORTER: Here's how strongly I feel about being short fixed income. I will bet you that the U.S. 30-year bond contract will hit 110 before it hits 130. It's currently at 124.75.

COMMITTEE: Are you crazy?

PORTER: Nope. I'm willing to bet anything you want as long as you don't highball me, and I'll even give you 2-to-1 odds. That's how strongly I feel.

COMMITTEE: You are crazy. Why don't we bet a box of cigars?

PORTER: Fine, happy to bet anything. Cigars are fine.

In October 1999, the bond contract printed 110.08.

COMMITTEE: Where are we on that bet?

PORTER: Here's the chart. From the day of the bet, we've gone from 124.75 to 110.08 today.

COMMITTEE: Give me a copy of that chart. When you lose your bet, I'm going to use this graph to light the first cigar.

PORTER: That's a very bold and audacious statement. I'm very happy you said it, because when people start to say those types of things, they inevitably lose.

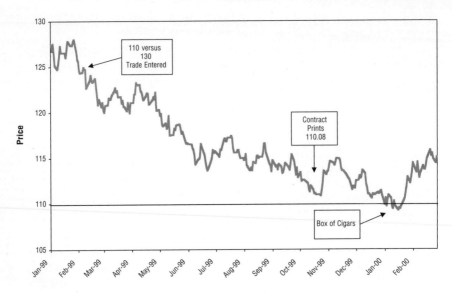

FIGURE 7.4 U.S. 30-Year Bond Contract, 1999–2000
Source: Bloomberg.

Sure enough, in early 2000 we hit 109.24. (*See Figure 7.4.*)

After they got knocked out, I said to the committee, "I've got good news and bad news. The bad news is, you got knocked out of the bet and owe me a box of cigars. The good news is I put Barclays' money behind my view as opposed to yours."

That was my greatest trade ever. It was a very outrageous call with unbelievable odds against me that turned out to be right. Also, we made a tremendous amount of money that year and I won the bet just before bonuses were paid, which helped.

It sounds like you were somewhat influenced by John Meriwether on that bet except that you learned from John Gutfreund's mistake and put a cap on it!

Exactly, it was my *Liar's Poker* moment.

What market books do you recommend to your junior traders?

I'm a semiproponent of the Chartered Financial Analyst (CFA) program, simply because I believe it's a good program that covers all areas of finance.

LIAR'S POKER

JOHN GUTFREUND: "One hand, one million dollars, no tears."

JOHN MERIWETHER: "No John, if we're going to play for those kind of numbers, I'd rather play for real money. Ten million dollars. No tears."

Source: Michael Lewis, *Liar's Poker: Rising Through the Wreckage on Wall Street* (New York: Penguin Putnam, 1989).

In terms of fixed income, one has to know the mechanics, and Fabozzi is the classic.

My favorite is *When Genius Failed,* by Roger Lowenstein (New York: Random House, 2001), which is about Long Term Capital. I make all my traders read it and I say to them, "No matter how smart you think you are, you're never going to be smarter than these guys. They were the Dream Team, but look at what they didn't understand." The clear problem with the LTCM guys was that they tried to overly formalize economics into mathematical models. They held the view that a scientific, quantitative approach was the only approach.

It's funny how people are very reassured by numbers just because they're numbers. They rarely look at where the numbers come from or how stable they might be. Numbers can give people a false sense of security that something scientific has been done, when it hasn't. This approach clearly worked for LTCM for some time but they totally lost sight of the one area that could ruin them: psychology—and more importantly, social psychology. In the end, it turned out that their own internal psychology and the psychology of the market destroyed them.

I believe markets are nothing but psychology, and *When Genius Failed* captures this. It shows the extremes of the market and why one can never say "never." In retrospect, there's no better background for trading than psychology and economics, because that's what it all boils down to. After I finish here, I'll go back to academia and formally study behavioral finance and economics. I feel that I have a fantastic background to do so, having been an academic in psychology and economics as well as a practitioner.

What would you like to be known for?

I'd like to be known for having made a contribution to the advancement of human thought. I'm just passing through the investment world. I didn't purposely get into trading and I don't know when I'll get out of it. I'm doing it now because I enjoy it but I don't feel that being a great trader is that important. I don't look up to great traders. I don't think traders do a necessary job, nor are they contributing anything significant to society. They fulfill a function but they are no more useful than banks.

Would you like to be a central banker someday?

Yes, that would be a very interesting job.

Federal Reserve Chairman Porter.

I don't know if I'm worthy of that. Greenspan has one of the most agile minds in the productivity era and his ability cannot be cloned. It would be a very tough act to follow. The post-Greenspan era cannot be forecast and it's going to be very interesting, given all of the imbalances out there. Thankfully, history only judges you for your time in office.

CHAPTER 8

THE CENTRAL BANKER

Dr. Sushil Wadhwani
Former Monetary Policy Committee Member
Bank of England
Wadhwani Asset Management
London

D r. Sushil Wadhwani's appearance is closer to a tenured university professor than a swashbuckling master of the universe, which is perhaps not surprising given his stature in financial academic circles. Wadhwani is of interest to this book for his academic perspective, but even more so for his insider's view of central banking and interest rate policy making. Wadhwani performed his public service for several years as a member of the Monetary Policy Committee at the Bank of England (BOE) soon after it was made a politically independent institution. It seemed that the BOE was interested in having a financial markets practitioner in its ranks as it pulled away from government policy.

Reading central bank tea leaves is one of the most important components of global macro trading as interest rate policy ripples through world economies and affects most financial markets. Thus, a hedge fund manager who spent time inside the policy-making arm of a major central bank that macro traders follow in earnest was a man that I needed to spend time with.

In 1999, Wadhwani was selected by UK Chancellor Gordon Brown to replace Alan Budd as one of the four "outside" members of the nine-member policy-making group at the Bank of England. Prior to the BOE, Wadhwani worked for hedge fund legend Paul Tudor Jones as a proprietary trader, a role he came to after working at Goldman Sachs in London as director of equity strategy.

Wadhwani invited me to his new offices in the City of London, overlooking St. Paul's Cathedral and a stone's throw from the Bank of England. His old-world gentlemanly politeness and thoughtfulness made it far easier for me to place him in a classroom at the London School of Economics or a boardroom at the Bank of England than the trading floors of Goldman or Tudor. Indeed, his soft-spoken manner permeated our discussion, revealing the antithesis of a hard-charging trader. In a world seemingly dominated by testosterone-charged personalities ever tempted by fast lives, Wadhwani prefers to spend weekends watching cricket and being with family. An admitted pragmatist, he views economics as a means for understanding how the world works and the framework of the field as a tool for positively impacting the behavior of society. He is frank about not overestimating his own impact or worth, admitting that, although discipline and rigor of method are crucial determinants of success, luck also plays a major role.

Nevertheless, he is a giant in the macro world. A premier academic who became a trader, then a central banker, then a trader again, he has operated as a practitioner both inside investment banks and hedge fund complexes and now on his own. A gentle giant, maybe, but certainly a giant.

You once said, "Life is 99 percent luck and 1 percent everything else."
Do you still believe that?

Yes. As I look around the world, at my own experience, and seeing where a lot of people I know ended up, it is an inescapable conclusion that luck played a principal role.

When I was studying at the London School of Economics, for example, I was very fortunate that there was a professor who helped me become a researcher. The economics department used to go away to Windsor every year and I just happened to be sitting next to him on the coach. At the end of the coach trip he asked me to come and see him to chat about offering me a research assistantship. He took great personal interest in me and encouraged me at every stage.

That's been true persistently throughout my career. I went to Goldman Sachs because I met their chief economist, Gavyn Davies, through an introduction by the aforementioned professor. He invited me to be an academic consultant and then got me a job at Goldman's. It was through Goldman's that I met Paul Tudor Jones.

So it seems my life has been a whole series of happy accidents.

Has your academic background helped or hindered you in markets?

I'll start with hinder. Long before I came into the markets I knew that a lot of conventional finance theory didn't work, but it took me a while to realize that markets didn't necessarily react in the most rational way to a piece of macro news. What is much more important is positioning and sentiment.

An example that really brought it home to me was a tax change related to dividends in the United Kingdom, which I was predicting should have meant equities would go down meaningfully. I was positioned accordingly but when it was announced, the stock market went up big-time, much to my intense surprise. Three months later, people finally absorbed the consequences of the tax change and prices did ultimately fall. Today, studies blame the underperformance of the FTSE index to that particular tax change, which is now many years ago, but on the day, believe me, I lost money trading that.

It is experiences like that which taught me that whatever the ultimate effect of a piece of macro news on a market price, I had better not lose sight of all the other things that could be affecting it.

So in that sense, an academic background, at least in the early days, was a hindrance because I had this tendency to think exclusively in terms of what *should* happen, which sometimes is very different from what will happen.

Having the academic background certainly helps in identifying some of the forces that affect market prices. It's also helped by giving me the skills to build quantitative models. Ultimately, most of the trading decisions I make are discretionary, but it gives me a lot more confidence if some of the models are on my side. Meanwhile, about 30 percent of the money in my fund is managed purely by the models.

I first started on these models purely out of academic curiosity back in 1986 when I was an academic consultant to Goldman's. Today, obviously, the models have been refined and are wholly different from the models back then. So yes, certainly the academic background has been helpful.

What other academics have influenced your thinking the most and in what ways?

Keynes—unquestionably. I've read and reread bits of Keynes so many times I've lost count. Every time I've reread it, I felt I learned something I'd missed before.

Even reading simple things like the transcripts of an annual talk he did in London on financial markets are fascinating. He effectively ran what we would call a "global macro hedge fund" but he called it a syndicate, which traded currencies, bonds, equities, and commodities.

There was a period in his life when he was running the King's College endowment, the syndicate, and was the chairman of an insurance company whose portfolio he also managed. All three investment pools had very different objectives and time horizons, so he framed different investment policies to suit the particular investment pool, all the while writing his academic articles and talking to policy makers.

His insights were so deep yet simple to understand. Take his notion of the "beauty contest" to explain price action. When I was a student, I found that much more useful in terms of trying to understand market prices than anything conventional finance textbooks were teaching.

Talking about Keynes makes me think that no matter how much markets change, the basic underlying fundamentals of money management remain the same.

Correct. The stories change, technology has changed, and I guess the degree to which things are crowded has probably changed. The enduring features are how long markets can remain irrational, how long you can have bubbles, and the degree to which the same investor biases are influencing prices.

Are you surprised by the lack of academic rigor employed by financial market practitioners?

When I first left academia and came into the markets, there were a number of common market practices that I treated with some skepticism. If someone came to me with a head-and-shoulders pattern and

BEAUTY CONTEST

The concept of a "beauty contest" in financial speak comes from a passage that John Maynard Keynes wrote in *The General Theory of Employment, Interest, and Money* (1935) to describe the behavior of stock market participants. Keynes compared the art of selecting stocks to correctly predicting the winner of a beauty contest held by a number of the English newspapers of the day. The newspapers would publish photographs of one hundred or so women and ask readers to choose which five would match the consensus selections of the other readers. Keynes wrote, "It is not a case of choosing those [faces] which, to the best of one's judgment, are really the prettiest, nor even those which average opinion genuinely thinks the prettiest. We have reached the third degree where we devote our intelligences to anticipating what average opinion expects the average opinion to be. And there are some, I believe, who practise the fourth, fifth and higher degrees." In other words, selecting a winning investment becomes a psychological game of predicting what investments others will select. Keynes believed that, ultimately, investment and market prices are determined by the herd-like "animal spirit" of investors.

price target, I would sort of smile indulgently and think, "They'll learn." I quickly learned that my attitude was dead wrong. Markets are very humbling.

I must confess that I've been impressed at how well purely technical traders can do and how well purely technical trading systems do over time. I've been impressed by the persistence of these profits.

To some extent, academia has moved in the market's direction. When I was a student, virtually all of my professors told me technical analysis was bunk. Now, you can read a lot of academic articles testing simple technical trading rules, showing that they do, on average, make money.

To the extent there is a significant body of people who look at technicals, it's incumbent on me to be aware of the patterns because there will be models and individuals selling or buying at certain levels. Therefore, the truthful answer is, I do look at these things, as any market practitioner should.

Are there any other differences you observe between academia and markets?

In academic life, if you're doing your job properly, you are potentially making a much bigger social contribution. First, you're training the next generation, which is a valuable thing. Second, you are coming up with ideas that may have a big impact on subsequent events. I've certainly seen some of my former colleagues have a *huge* impact on social welfare on the basis of things written 25 years ago.

Do you feel that your role in the Bank of England similarly created social benefits?

That would be arrogant, but it was certainly nice to have had the opportunity to be part of a process where the United Kingdom was engaging in what was a relatively new experiment whereby credibility building was very important.

Many credit that experiment and the independence of the Bank of England for the current prosperity in the United Kingdom. That is a social benefit.

It was certainly an important reform. I wouldn't have joined otherwise, but it would have been much more difficult if we hadn't already had the labor market reform of the 1980s. It was a very benign environment because unemployment was coming down and so was inflation, which made it much easier to set interest rates. You got much less criticism.

I don't want to underplay it because it has played an important role. It has brought inflation expectations right down to the target and that has had a lot of beneficial effects. In the old days, when oil prices went up, there was always a risk that you needed to tighten policy to ensure that inflation didn't get out of hand. Now we've had two significant oil shocks since the Bank of England has been independent, and in neither case did they have to tighten policy, because wages and prices were well anchored by subdued inflation expectations. That's a good outcome.

There are other benefits from the reduction of inflation volatility, such as businesses being more willing to invest, and you don't get unfair redistribution because of unexpected inflation. Likewise, the Treasury is no longer worrying that much about macromanagement and macrostability, so it can concentrate on other policies designed to help the long-term growth rate of the UK economy.

Have central bankers gotten better at their game and, as a result, reduced market volatility?

In some countries, that's true.

I'll speak to the United Kingdom first. In the old days it was very difficult for the government to raise interest rates at certain points in the electoral cycle due to short-term political considerations. That meant imbalances were allowed to build up, which then led to macroinstability, which then bred opportunity for people in this industry.

I'm not saying that we don't have imbalances now; we've got them in spades. But imbalances were allowed to build up because policy was reactive, not sufficiently preemptive, which meant that you'd get this boom followed by a bust. It made output, inflation, and interest rates excessively volatile, but it also gave you nice trending moves that people in the market could exploit.

What's happened now is we don't have the political business cycle affecting the interest rate cycle, which means that policy is more preemptive and therefore interest rates need to move up and down less than they used to. You get fewer of these long-lived trends that can be exploited by macro funds. That's true in the United Kingdom and it's clearly true in many other countries including Canada, Australia, and New Zealand.

It's less true of the United States, where central banking was already a bit ahead of the pack in setting interest rates independently of the political cycle. It's also less true of Germany and Switzerland because they were already doing it as well. Within Europe, Spain, Italy, and so on have all come into the fold via the European Monetary Union. Many other countries have caught up including some in the less developed world as well.

Historically, central banks have been viewed by the market as a source of alpha. Do they offer less alpha now?

Other things being equal, that's got to be true.

So having been a central banker contributing to this process, why then start a global macro fund when there are fewer opportunities?

Because other things aren't equal. The current type of central banking has certainly reduced certain kinds of instability. However, because so-called "modern" central banking is focused on consumer price inflation and not so much on asset price inflation, the result in a number of these places has been that huge imbalances have built up. Now, these are different kinds of imbalances from what used to occur in the past, so it's not the old-fashioned variety where you had an artificial boom followed by a bust. What you've got now is huge asset market distortions, and one of these days, the chickens will come home to roost, and when they do, there'll be huge opportunity.

An obvious imbalance is the U.S. current account deficit leaving the U.S. dollar overvalued, and that is where most people in our game made money in 2004. There are other imbalances everywhere: the housing market in Australia, New Zealand, the United Kingdom. These are all things that one day will correct and may already be correcting, but it is always difficult to know when a bubble is bursting. Meanwhile, these bubbles cause macro dislocation and therefore opportunity.

I was talking with a hedge fund manager in Stockholm recently about this phenomenon and together we came up with the term "paradox of perfection," meaning that as central bankers have perfected their game, paradoxically, that perfection has encouraged excessive risk taking and created other issues and imbalances elsewhere.

Absolutely right. That's a very good way of putting it, and some central banking circles have been worrying about precisely these issues recently. When you create an environment with low inflation and low volatility in output growth with stable or rising employment, if you take your eyes off the ball vis-à-vis asset price misalignments, you are then storing up trouble.

It's possible they will get out of jail. Alan Greenspan clearly thinks he achieved a soft landing by reacting preemptively to the burst bubble. The jury is still out on whether the United States is out of the woods, and with all these imbalances, you've got to wonder. Although, it is wholly possible that I'm being too alarmist about these asset price misalignments.

The fact is, in either case, there's plenty of opportunity for macro funds, and in some ways, the imbalances we've got now, globally, should offer more opportunities for us to make money going forward.

What should Greenspan or the Bank of England have done with regard to asset prices?

It's a mistake to target asset prices or to necessarily give it too much weight in the inflation numbers. What I argued at the time was that they should have been willing to take these asset price imbalances into account more concretely in terms of monetary policy.

The sort of thing one might have done when UK house prices were heading into bubble territory would have been to announce to the British public that you're not just going to set interest rates on the basis of your two-year forecast for inflation. Rather, you're going to take a longer-term view. After all, the government has given you a brief to hit the inflation target at all times, not just a two-year horizon. You know that if you allow a bubble to be created, you're storing up instability for later.

To prevent that instability, in principle, interest rates could have been held higher than they were and higher than was necessary for inflation to hit the target two years out. The defense to the public could have been, "Fine, we're undershooting the target on a two-year horizon, but that's because we are much more focused on stability over time."

If we had done that, it would have had a very important effect on housing market expectations. As in any bubble, shaping expectations formation is critical. Chairman Greenspan should have done more of that vis-à-vis the stock market after his "irrational exuberance" speech in December 1996.

Greenspan has always argued that it's better to deal with the bubble after it has burst than to worry about preempting the bubble. I just take a different view because you can see bubbles emerging. Now, we've got the advantage of the Fed transcripts and we know that, even in late 1995, they were worrying about an emerging bubble in the stock market. So the difficulty in 1996 and 1997 was not that they didn't spot the bubble; they spotted it and just deliberately chose not to take action.

What did your experience as a central banker give you that you hadn't gotten previously at Tudor or Goldman?

Mostly just the personal pleasure that I derive from having done it. As a student and as an economist, you talk about policy makers doing X, Y, and Z, so it was great to actually have a chance to have some impact on policy.

In terms of other things, I would hope that I have a better understanding of how central bankers think and respond to information. Sometimes the markets are very excitable and move around with individual pieces of information. Within a central bank you realize that the effect of individual pieces of information is often much smaller than the markets think, especially when you get a big outlier which causes a market reaction. There is a tendency within a central bank to smooth data because what is very weak one month is often very strong the next month. The tendency is to look at the information received over the month as a whole.

How much were market prices and market movements used in the decision-making process?

We all watched the markets and price action but, ultimately, we set policy on the basis of what we thought was right for the economy, rather than what happened to be discounted in the market. Sometimes a colleague would say, "We shouldn't put rates up this month because it's not discounted by the market. Why don't we put out a hawkish set of minutes and raise them next month?"

The majority view usually prevailed against that. We always thought we should do what's right for the UK economy now—why wait a month? If they get surprised, fine. There'd be a lesson to learn and the lesson is they should watch the data closer.

Since I've left, I do discern a greater tendency to guide the market. That's something the United States has always done but the United Kingdom seems to be doing increasingly these days. Guiding the market and managing what's discounted in the market has become more important with the risk of deflation. If we ever got into a situation where deflation were a serious threat, communication and credibility would be paramount.

Is deflation still a big risk or do you think we're out of the deflation woods?

It would be complacent to say we're out of the woods. One mustn't lose sight of the fact that inflation is still pretty low in most countries and we could only be one big shock away from deflation risk again. And we all know big shocks happen. Meanwhile, the swings between the reflation/deflation poles can be wide once you get to that zero line in inflation, which is another new opportunity created for global macro traders.

What central banker has impressed you the most?

Oh, by a long way, Chairman Greenspan, even though I fundamentally disagree with him about what he did vis-à-vis asset prices. His feel for the economy is almost unparalleled in terms of knowing where things are going. He has a very commonsense, eclectic attitude toward policy setting and doesn't get hung up with a particular dogma. He is very pragmatic and willing to change his mind quickly, which is key.

Which global macro trader has impressed you the most over your career?

Am I allowed two people? If so, I have learned a great deal from Paul Tudor Jones, whose encyclopedic knowledge of market history and ability to spot the appropriate parallels early is second to none. There was also a man at Tudor called Mark Heffernan and he's certainly one of the most insightful and forward-looking traders I've ever met, someone who was often able to spot trends well before they materialized. It was almost like a sixth sense with him. I always thought of him as a leading indicator for most price builds. He is incredibly well read and very disciplined with great risk control. Paul and Mark are really the best I've seen in the business.

What trading lessons did you take away from your time working with Paul Tudor Jones?

One of the key things I learned from him was that good defense is paramount. That's something he drilled into you. Another one of the key lessons from Paul was intellectual flexibility. However strongly you believe in something and however coherent the case is, you need to be (1) willing to accept that you might be wrong, and (2) able to take the position off even though you may not be wrong in a medium-term sense.

This applies in spades to a profitable trade. You've made some money, it hasn't quite got to your target, but something happens that makes you think it isn't going there now. Rather than giving up all your profit by letting it go back to your stop, be flexible enough to take it off.

There are famous stories about Paul's flexibility out there and I've witnessed it firsthand many times. You'd talk to Paul in the morning his time and he'd be long something. The next day, that market would have gone down and you would fear he had lost money, but when you spoke to him again you would find that he had changed his mind and had gone from long to short. That's tremendous flexibility. It's very important in this game that one doesn't get hung up and anchored to a view.

Meanwhile, academics have a tendency to get anchored. Now I still trade with my medium-term views or else I wouldn't have confidence in my trading, but I've learned to be flexible enough to temporarily suspend the medium-term view, take the position off, and wait for a better reentry level when necessary. It's how I've merged my academic experience with my market experience, with a little help from Paul.

Does Greenspan have the same sort of flexibility as Paul Tudor Jones,
which would enable him to become a good hedge fund manager?

Greenspan is very skeptical about the ability of anyone to outguess the
market. He has all the intellectual firepower and flexibility to be an excellent fund manager, but one also needs self-belief. His well-advertised skepticism about outguessing the markets could come in the way of taking a
big bet. If you don't believe in what you're doing, it's very difficult to sit on
a big position.

When hiring, are there certain skills or qualities that you look for that
denote success in macro?

I look at whether I think the person will have good risk control. That's
number one for me. The second thing I look for is some sort of edge
in their skill set. The third thing that we look for here is that they'll be
easy to get on with. Someone with sharp elbows won't work out here
for long.

What keeps you up at night running your own fund, and how is that different
from what kept you up at night as a policy maker or as a trader at Tudor?

As a policy maker, you worry about the next decision and about whether
you're making a mistake. It could potentially affect millions of lives, although you remind yourself that ultimately 25 basis points is not going to
have such a big impact.

With the fund, the stress is very different. You've got clients who have
put a lot of faith in you and you feel very responsible for their money and
your own money in the fund. You worry about things that could go wrong
because exogenous events do occur and they can derail any carefully
crafted strategy.

Running a fund is a privilege, though, because it gives me independence and gives me a chance to build things in a way that, rightly or
wrongly, I regard as appropriate. So it's a huge privilege to have been given
this opportunity by clients, and I've got to make sure it works out over
time as well.

Do you take vacations?

Not enough. Even when you are on vacation, you're watching markets all
the time. It's much easier to take vacation over Easter and Christmas, be-

cause on average there's less happening. Otherwise, it's difficult—you're constantly worrying about being out of contact in some shape or form. Global macro markets are always moving.

How do you define global macro?

Global macro has evolved to mean the license to do anything.

I started my fund at what I call the narrow end of global macro, meaning traditional macro directional bets in equity indexes, interest rates, and exchange rates. The intention is to move in the multistrategy direction, because *virtually everything has a macro dimension to it.* I see no reason why one shouldn't have all strategies under one umbrella, especially because you learn so much from each other.

When I was at Tudor, I learned enormously from our long/short equity people because they were often picking up trends in individual economies long before it penetrated the macro data. Likewise, the fixed income relative value chaps were also incredibly helpful in finding the optimal place in the curve to express a macro interest rate view, which was very powerful in terms of having the best macro trade. So I'm all in favor of multistrategy.

Can you further explain your "traditional macro" trading style?

I segment my portfolio into two bits. One is the tactical, short-term portfolio and the other is the long-term core portfolio, where I'll often sit for a long time in options.

There will be long periods of time where I'll have a number of smaller, hopefully distinct bets where the intention is to make some pennies along the way. Then, when something big happens, I overlay that same set of trades with a big bet and hopefully make bigger returns that particular month. I often have 20 to 30 different smallish bets running through the portfolio. Obviously they have some sort of correlation to each other but I try to make them distinct.

Do you use sophisticated risk management and allocation systems when structuring your trades?

I utilize a whole host of sophisticated systems as well as simple calculations, like if every single position in my book hit its stop and all the options expired worthless tomorrow, how much would I lose, and am I comfortable with that number? If I'm not comfortable with that number, then I must look at my risk again.

In risk management, I've often found that simple insights from experienced traders are much more valuable than the most sophisticated analytics that you get from academia, which may let you down at precisely the time that you need them.

Are there certain variables that you look for that signal when it's time to make that "big bet"?

To begin with, there has to be a big valuation misalignment. Then I wait for some catalyst to provide confirmation that the misalignment might be about to correct. The catalyst could be technical, it could be news, it could be flows. Something that makes me think that a trade that has been on my radar screen might be about to come into play.

Where do you get your information to locate the misalignments?

It's a mixture of things. We have a reasonable size research department within the firm and I rely a lot on them. I certainly read Street research. There are some good ideas that come out of there and you get a sense of what the consensus is thinking. I talk to other managers; I talk to other non–Wall Street consultants; I talk to bottom-up analysts, who may be seeing things in their countries or industry. Sometimes I talk to policy makers, or ex–policy makers. A whole host of people.

When you get your catalyst, will you make the big bet with several instruments or will you pick the one instrument you deem optimal?

It's always nicer to try to pick the instrument which you think is going to be the best, so I try to concentrate my firepower on the one where the reward/risk ratio is the most compelling.

Do you remember what your best risk/reward trade was?

I do—it was luck, actually.

In November 1997, 33 out of 33 economists were looking for no change in interest rates in the United Kingdom and, as expected, the short sterling strip priced in no change in rates. The Bank of England had been hiking but in September they came out with a statement saying they were going to pause. So as far as the world was concerned, these guys had paused and that's how this strip was priced, flat as a pancake. Then, virtually every economic number after that was strong. Still, the short sterling strip didn't move, because they had told us they had paused.

I remember two days before the announcement, thinking there was nothing priced in for the Monetary Policy Committee (MPC) meeting and that I could actually sell the front contract (December) such that if I was wrong and they did nothing, I would lose a tick and a half, and if I was right I would make $23^{1}/_{2}$ ticks.

So I decided to take a little bet on it, and they hiked 25 basis points. I think I made 5 percent that day, which for me is a good day—a very good day. It never happened to me again, that sort of reward/risk ratio.

Did you tell your Bank of England colleagues that story when you subsequently joined?

No, dear God no! That would have gone over incredibly badly.

What was your worst trade?

My worst trade was dollar/yen in 1998. This is something I always feel really ashamed to admit, but I got seduced by stories and Street research that said dollar/yen was going to 180.

China started complaining because they hadn't moved their peg so they were becoming uncompetitive versus the rest of the region. Ironically to us today, they'd kept the peg partly under U.S. pressure. The United States was worried about another round of Asian devaluations which, given what had happened in the region, would have been terrible.

I remember one or two people saying to me that they thought the United States would intervene because of China's complaints, but I'm afraid I didn't pay enough attention. Then, in the middle of June 1998, the Fed intervened, along with the Bank of Japan. It was in the afternoon and dollar/yen dropped like a stone, ending the day eight big figures lower. (*See Figure 8.1.*)

That was painful, but it got worse because a lot of other people were long dollar/yen, so you got one of these correlated sell-offs where things that shouldn't be correlated became correlated due to position unwinding.

It was a pretty ugly day in terms of my P&L, but my biggest regret is that I broke all my rules of appropriate risk management. Number one, I knew dollar/yen was in elevated territory in terms of my valuation models, yet I got seduced by a story and junked my valuation models. The

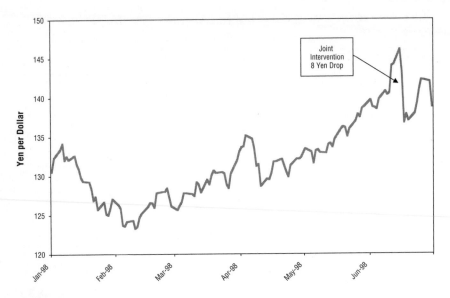

FIGURE 8.1   Dollar/Yen, 1998
Source: Bloomberg.

second mistake I made was not paying attention to the political rhetoric. When something's going up or down in a straight line and you start getting political resistance, you'd better pay attention.

Do you read Wall Street research with a grain of salt after that episode?

Yes, I do, but it's very important to read it because you've got to know what the consensus is and what people are saying. In terms of trading, though, one has to do one's own research and make up one's own mind.

Why did you break your risk management rules—greed?

Yes, exactly. The honest answer is that when a trade is going reasonably well, you become a bit complacent, which you shouldn't. Yesterday's P&L is yesterday's P&L, and that's history.

When the intervention happened and it gapped lower, did you get out?

Yes. No questions asked. I had my stops and it blew through them, but I got out at the first opportunity I could. When the stop is breached, you don't ask any questions, you just get out.

Have you ever ignored a stop or reinitiated a position after getting stopped out?

I've never ignored a stop in the sense that, if it goes through a stop, you just take it, because otherwise there's no point having the stop. Now you ask the most subtle question about whether you reinitiate, which then begs the question about why bother having a stop. I usually give myself a 24-hour break before I'm allowed to do that.

The rationale behind the break is I want to distance myself from things and have no position. I want to have a clean slate to think through all the arguments and see whether this would now be justified as a new trade. Getting back into a trade to make back losses is a bad argument.

Well, the good argument is that a good trade now has a better price.

Yes, but it may be there for a reason, so you've got to be confident that you know something the market doesn't. To balance that, I usually structure a trade with a mixture of spot and options. The spot positions have stops which are unquestionably honored if I'm wrong. If the options become nearly worthless, I still own them so they can come back if I turn out to be right in the medium term.

You wrote a paper in 1991 criticizing the inefficiency and "short-termism" of the financial markets. Do you still believe that?

The inefficiencies in many markets are still there. Obviously, some of the particular anomalies may have been arbitraged away, so it may well be that simple things like January effects and small cap effects work less well. It's possible that you make less money now in some crowded strategies, like fixed income relative value or convertible bonds, but it seems there are still anomalies around and perhaps some new ones.

Ultimately, a lot of these inefficiencies are a product of things that haven't changed, such as the lack of long-term investing in markets. All of us monitor rather shorter horizons and don't have the ability to hold things to maturity; otherwise a lot of the anomalies you see in the world wouldn't exist. So the "short-termism" is still very much there, which leads to the persistence of some anomalies and the appearances of new ones.

The efficient market guys say if there's a $100 bill lying on the pavement, it always gets picked up. My view is that it sometimes gets picked up and sometimes new $100 bills appear.

Are global macro markets a zero-sum game?

In large part, that's true, because there's got to be somebody else who's on the other side. In the equity markets, there is genuine wealth creation. Almost by default in most markets it's close to a zero-sum game, but that's exactly who you are trying to exploit, the person on the other side of the trade.

Do hedge funds have an advantage against the person on the other side of the trade?

Yes. Take a mundane example: A hedge fund manager can move much more quickly to a piece of news than a larger institution. Larger institutions have committee meetings, run position reports, and all sorts of stuff until, finally, a few weeks later, they'll move. It's certainly true that nimble hedge funds have an advantage over the central banks, who also move much more slowly and are not profit-seeking entities.

What kind of inefficiencies and anomalies do you look for—structural, regulatory, legal?

All of the above and especially behavioral anomalies, such as the shortage of investors with a long-term trading horizon.

Let's discuss that one. To profit from this anomaly, would your ideal scenario be having investors locked up for five years or just managing your own capital?

Either of those could help. The former is very difficult to get. The latter, well, a lot of people that I respect do that. They feel it's the only true way of making money over time because you can genuinely position for the long term. It is a true path to making spectacular returns, if you're right.

That's a big if though.

Oh, it's a big if, absolutely. I've seen people blow up.

That's the classic joke—what's the difference between a long-term trade and a short-term trade? The long-term trade is under water.

Yes, absolutely. On the other hand, I do know of some people who have gone down that route and done astonishingly well. Their numbers are not in the public domain, but if they were, you would see incredible success.

Where do you see the world in a long-term sense?

The key questions for a macro chap are: What will happen about the U.S. imbalances? How will the world adjust to China and, to a limited extent, India? Will Japan ever reemerge to self-sustained growth and avoid deflation?

I'd like to believe that the United States will muddle through, but the imbalances are getting so big, it seems more gloomy scenarios are looking more likely.

In regard to how the world adjusts to China, I think the economic adjustment will be easier than perhaps some of the political issues. As they become more powerful, there are various potential flashpoints and a lot of potential for friction, especially as they become more and more self-assertive, which I think they will.

In Japan, things have clearly looked up, but they have stored up such huge problems. Perhaps what you're going to have is a lot of inflation in Japan, which may be the only way they'll come out of this mess.

CHAPTER 9

THE DOT-COMMER

Peter Thiel
Former CEO and Cofounder of PayPal
Clarium Capital
San Francisco

Peter Thiel is bit of an enigma in global macro. Whereas some managers earn distinction because they are successful and secretive, Thiel is unusually open about all things related to his business, Clarium Capital Management, a San Francisco–based global macro hedge fund. Since its launch in October 2002, initial investors have more than tripled their money and fund assets are now well over $1 billion. Clarium was the standout performer in global macro in 2003 and again in 2005, with net returns over 50 percent both years.

Thiel is very different from most other global macro managers in others ways as well. Rather than having spent his entire career within an investment bank or hedge fund before moving on to launch his own fund, Thiel founded PayPal, a dot-com company, in 1998, in the middle of the biggest financial bubble of recent memory; listed on the NASDAQ well after the bubble burst in February 2002 with a $1 billion market capitalization; and then sold the company to eBay six months later for $1.5 billion. When asked, Thiel credits his global macro vision with his success as a former technology entrepreneur. As a result, many of his major trading themes since starting Clarium have centered on the lingering impacts of the bursting of the bubble. He has been right on most of these themes, such as long bonds, short the U.S. dollar, and long energy, leaving only his short equities view as a prediction that has yet to come to fruition.

Thiel is a deep thinker with varied interests. He has degrees in philosophy and law from Stanford, has practiced law, traded derivatives at Credit Suisse Financial Products (CSFP), and ran his own venture capital fund prior to starting PayPal. He is also classified as a master in chess and is a former California math champion. In addition to running Clarium, Thiel is active in the Libertarian party and often hosts salon gatherings at his home with prominent intellectuals such as Milton Friedman. And he is only in his 30s.

Success breeds naysayers, and some have questioned Thiel's ability to consistently turn in outsized returns, asking if he is lucky or good. But debating luck or skill may be superfluous—he just may be particularly well placed to perceive, articulate, and express one overarching view since he launched his fund: the deflationary impacts of a post-bubble world rippling through the economy and the financial system. Indeed, he has profited from the bubble on the way up and on the way down.

I went to see Thiel in Clarium's offices on California Street in downtown San Francisco, which was filled with what I call *Thiel's army*: young, highly intelligent, loyal, hardworking colleagues. Many scored 1600 on their SATs and were valedictorians of their high school classes—brainiacs who funneled through Stanford, then into Silicon Valley, and now into what is rapidly becoming a prominent hedge fund. Why not be loyal, when many of his employees have come from PayPal, where Thiel has already made them one fortune?

Thiel's confidence comes across when he speaks, but more bold evidence of his assurance in his abilities is observable by his waiver of a fixed management fee for all investors in his fund. After all, he explains, he would still have to manage his own money even if he did not accept any outside investors. He wants to be paid for success, however, and takes 25 percent of all profits versus the industry norm of 20 percent.

As the bumpy path in the post-bubble world continues to unfold, imbalances build, real estate froths, and equities look increasingly vulnerable when juxtaposed against a shaky economy and rising interest rates, Thiel may very well keep steamrolling along.

Let's start with your widely varied background. How did you get into global macro?

My path wasn't direct. I started in philosophy, moved to law, and then traded derivatives before getting into macro in 1996. I knew when I launched my first fund that macro was right for me. Macro was, and remains, the most promising way to invest; it's also a good fit for my skill set.

When I came to macro in 1996, the luster of the swashbuckling Soros era was already fading, but I was convinced that macro was still the place to be. Macro comes with a broad mandate: A macro manager can extract value wherever it exists; he isn't pigeonholed by some narrow brief as in convertible arbitrage or the like, where managers wear style-imposed blinders.

Macro demands that a manager think broadly about the world, and that's where my varied background has been helpful. My route hasn't been direct, but it gave me the necessary breadth of experience.

When did you know you were good at macro?

In the spring of 2000 when we were raising money for PayPal. The company had an excellent product but needed time and money to grow the business. At the same time, we were concerned about the equity bubble we saw inflating on our Palo Alto doorstep. We believed it would pop and that it would thereafter be difficult to raise funds, regardless of product quality. With that in mind, we raised $100 million in March 2000, at the very peak of the bubble, which was more money than anyone thought we needed in the short haul. The deal closed on March 31, the last day before the market began its slide in earnest. (*See Figure 9.1.*) The extra cash gave us the runway we needed to finish building PayPal into a robust business. Had we done what everybody else was doing, which was to ignore the forest and just work on our particular tree, we wouldn't have seen this enormous forest fire coming and we would have been burned along with everybody else. That really drove home the importance of the macro view.

Essentially you raised more money than necessary in order to shore up PayPal's balance sheet to prepare for the coming storm?

We raised more than many thought we would need at the time of the offering, although we were careful not to give up too much equity. I had

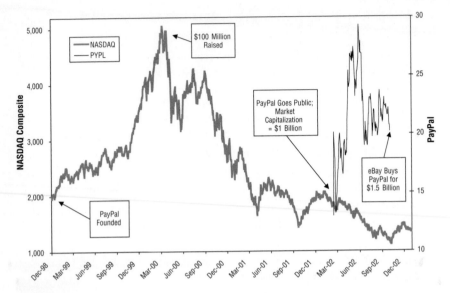

FIGURE 9.1   NASDAQ, 1998–2002; PayPal, 2002
Source: Bloomberg.

watched the bubble inflate from the very start and knew from Japan's bubble experience that the unwind would be very hard. Any second bite at the apple might not be on favorable terms. Had we not raised the money when we did, PayPal's future would have been much less assured.

What were some of the clues that the end was nigh?

Aside from the well-known indicators—eye-popping valuations and so on—the anecdotal evidence was incredibly powerful. Investors were behaving in very irrational ways. People came into PayPal trying to invest, without knowing anything about the business. An investor in South Korea wired money with no signed documents. And all around us in Palo Alto, the center of the financial cyclone, the same sorts of things were happening on a massive scale.

Interestingly, one factor contributing to (or rather, failing to restrain) the bubble was a lack of global macro investing. By the late 1990s, many of the big macro funds, like Quantum and Tiger, had closed, often after losing money betting against the bubble. At the same time, stock indexing reached its peak, with flows reaching their highest level ever in March 2000. Passive indexers bought in blindly without thought as to whether the indexes themselves were overvalued. The balance was totally lopsided—without global macro, there wasn't a lot of money pushing back against the bubble.

You have said PayPal was a combination of luck and brilliance. Do you think the same combo is required in money management?

As they say, chance favors the prepared mind. Being in Silicon Valley as the tech boom began was a very fortunate turn of events. But capitalizing on those opportunities required recognizing them in the first place and then building a team to see our insights to execution.

The same is true with global macro investing right now. There are some very large imbalances in the economy and correspondingly good opportunities, but it's up to us to work hard and capitalize on them.

How did you make the decision to start a global macro hedge fund after years of running a tech start-up?

After PayPal was acquired, I decided to manage my own money and to focus on macro analysis more systematically. We considered launching Clarium as an aggressive family office for me and some investors who had been with my first fund, but it made sense to take on outside investment, because our ideas were scalable and with size comes opportunity. So we launched Clarium and opened it to outside investors just a few weeks after the acquisition closed.

Why is global macro the best business to be in now?

There are two essential reasons: Global macro offers the best investment opportunities and it is probably the most stimulating style out there. Enthusiasm for global macro waned a bit in the late 1990s even as the hedge fund industry mushroomed. That left global macro undercapitalized, which creates enormous opportunities in a world where other players ignore the systematic distortions from the bubble that still tug at the fabric of the economy.

Because of that big-picture view, macro is intrinsically very interesting. There isn't much that's more engaging than thinking about how the world works. And part of the joy of global macro is that it is driven by a search for the right questions as well as for the right answers. Being able to pose your own questions, questions that are answerable and where the answer tells you something new and important about the world, is very exciting.

Will you start getting worried about the viability of global macro when people start wiring you money without their subscription docs signed?

If that were to happen, we would worry, but we are a world away from that. Having been through the last bubble, I can say with confidence that global macro is nowhere near that point.

How does building a hedge fund compare with building a tech start-up?

In many important respects, the experiences are similar. Both involve themes that take time to play out, and both reward managers and investors willing to take the long view. A start-up is about building a business, which is a multiyear proposition. Similarly, we develop themes that may take months or even years to mature. Both require a coherent vision and patience.

How is your research process similar to or different from what it was at PayPal?

Both start with the same, open-ended search for a great idea, but the processes diverge quickly thereafter. In an early stage tech company, the options are limitless: You can work with business, government, or consumers; you can pick your product; you can locate wherever you want. But as time goes on, history starts to dictate the future. The chess metaphor I use is that at the start of a game, you can play any set of moves, but as the game progresses, you become locked into a strategy. At a macro fund, optionality remains broad. Every day is a new day—you can trade any product, in any country, largely unconstrained by what happened last week, last month, or even last year. That can be daunting, but it's also what makes the job so interesting.

Hedge funds are more challenging. At a fund, everything is completely transparent—your positions may be visible to investors, which means you can be evaluated in real time. Because of that real-time monitoring, life at a fund can be much more emotionally volatile than at a start-up. Fairly large daily swings in the P&L are normal, but they can cause both euphoria and depression in our staff, and managing those emotions is an important part of running the fund. As for our investors, we try to be clear and direct about the time horizons and risk, so that they are comfortable with our style. Our best relationships are with investors who appreciate macro's longer horizons.

*If you think some investors are too shortsighted, why take
institutional capital?*

There is no such thing as a universal investor or a universal fund. If you
can find an investor who is comfortable with your style, that investor is a
resource. We're fortunate to have investors who understand our approach,
and we're glad for the resources they bring. Investors are also a fine source
of information; they are incented to give you good information, even if
you end up arriving at different conclusions.

*What qualities should investors be looking for when selecting a
macro manager?*

It can be difficult to quantify what share of returns is attributable to manager skill and what share is due to chance, even if a manager has a long
and enviable record. That makes the usual quantitative due diligence difficult. Instead, investors should listen very carefully to a manager's arguments and consider: Does the analysis make sense? Is it cohesive, is it
novel, and are the conclusions well supported? The investor should try to
understand the manager's thought process; if it seems sound, then the relationship will probably work. That's how investors have gotten comfortable with our strategy.

   Investors have to balance adequate due diligence against participation in
fund returns. Achieving that balance is harder for macro investors, because
macro funds only trade a handful of themes over long periods, so it may
take several years of data to achieve the level of comfort one might have
after looking at another type of fund over just a few months. But in waiting those several years, the investor incurs a significant opportunity cost in
the form of profits forgone and because managers who have been successful over the course of many years often tend to close their funds to new
investors. Once an investor reaches a reasonable, if not entirely perfect,
level of comfort, it makes sense to invest.

*Do you forgo an annual management fee to encourage investors to pull
the trigger?*

I wanted to minimize agency problems as much as possible. To accomplish
that, we charge no annual management fee and I have almost all my liquid
personal net worth in the fund.

   Something that has troubled me is the long history of agency problems in finance. Financial firms often have incentives that are opposed to those of their clients. The classic example is the stockbroker who is incentivized by trading commissions to churn a client's portfolio. One of the more striking recent examples is the annual management fee imposed by many hedge funds. In the early 1990s a management fee made a certain amount of sense, because assets under management were usually modest and the funds needed the fee to defray operational costs; moreover, the robust returns of that era more than offset the fees. Today, the situation is reversed: Funds can scale up assets very quickly but returns are lower. In the current environment, managers may derive a substantial amount of revenue from management fees despite structurally low returns. And as returns drop, the 2 percent management fee becomes much more painful for the investor on a relative basis.

That said, there are situations where a modest management fee makes sense for all parties; for example, where scale or investor servicing demands a relatively large amount of firm resources. But in most situations, the incentive problem lingers. I think fees will be an important issue in the future. We've tried to put the fund on the leading edge of aligning our interests with those of investors.

How large an asset base do you think you can handle?

The goal is to build a world-class hedge fund that generates the best absolute returns possible—that's the limiting factor. But given the size of the macro distortions we study, we think we can effectively allocate many billions. That's one of the advantages of macro—while it's impossible to deploy more than, say, $100 million to some styles, macro can deploy a huge amount of capital.

You currently run a few concentrated themes. Will that still be the case if you are managing several billion dollars?

Yes. The number of themes is not likely to grow in direct proportion to assets. Markets have become highly correlated—emerging market spreads are linked to junk bond and credit spreads, which are in turn correlated with the USD and high tech equities—and the tightness of those correlations is historically high. As a result, very broad diversification is neither practicable nor desirable. However, the interlinked distortions are extremely large, so the themes are highly scalable. Often, a substantial portion of our performance for a given period is driven by a limited number of trades, but that is often the case in life or investing generally.

Where do you get your fundamental information from? What drives your research process?

We have nine people on the research team and they spend an enormous amount of time reading, watching the markets, and testing their theories. I also read extensively, but I spend quite a bit of time talking with people internally and externally. Once our internal research generates an interesting idea, we talk to experts, dig further, and try to get a broad perspective.

Has your Silicon Valley network helped the investment process?

Silicon Valley serves as a very powerful sentiment indicator, but that's probably about it. When things in the Valley are going crazy, the market is usually overbought. When everyone in the Valley is pessimistic, it's often a good time to buy.

Tell me about your best trade other than the PayPal venture round.

Our best all-around trade to date has been the long-dated crude oil call, which I described at your Santa Monica Conference last year. (*See Figure 9.2.*)

FIGURE 9.2   Crude Oil Futures (WTI), 2004-2005
Source: Bloomberg.

DROBNY GLOBAL CONFERENCE REVIEW, APRIL 2004

Peter Thiel's Favorite Trade: Long Long-Dated Oil

Peter Thiel, of Clarium Capital Management, suggested buying shares in oil sand companies in Canada. The idea is to create a synthetic call option on long-term oil. The Canadian oil sand companies are high marginal cost oil producers whose valuation can be explosive if oil were to rise substantially over the next decade.

Both the demand and supply curves for oil are very price inelastic. Global growth is increasingly dependent on the Asians (e.g., China), and they are inefficient users of oil. So demand should be moving up steadily through the next decade. And there is really no simple or cheap alternative to oil. Rather, he argued, the best alternative product to cheap oil is more expensive oil! So when prices go up, demand really doesn't fall much.

But perhaps it's on the supply side where the biggest dangers lie. The peak in global oil production is near, and reserves may well have been depleted more rapidly than originally thought. U.S. production already peaked and there is increasing evidence that oil reserves have been exaggerated. The OPEC quota system, for example, works by setting production for each country as a percentage of estimated reserves. That creates an incentive to overstate reserves.

These factors are combining after a 15-year period of low oil prices in real terms. The result is a market mind-set that the price of oil will remain in a rough $20 to $30 per barrel range, with occasional spikes. The oil curve is thus still quite inverted, despite a likely trend toward higher prices. The biggest anomaly, therefore, lurks in the back months of the oil curve. But the problem is that the market is pretty thin in precisely the part of the curve where you want to get long oil.

Peter's answer is to buy these Canadian oil sands companies that convert tar into oil. They are high cost producers, and that's where the beauty of this trade lies. They are not that valuable with the price of oil around current levels, but their valuation should shoot up if oil prices move higher and stay higher than generally expected. At a certain price point, the cash flow of these companies will suddenly surge. So you get what is essentially a synthetic call on oil prices by owning these companies.

Andres Drobny

The best pure quantitative macro trade we've done so far was our short of Japanese government bonds in June 2003. At the time their 10-year government bond was yielding 45 basis points, so going short was pretty much a free one-way option. We figured our worst case was that the bonds didn't move down, and the price in that scenario was a little carry. But the more likely scenario was for yields to go up a lot (and prices down). Japan is a world apart and it's hard to tell what's going on, but this trade seemed straightforward. We started shorting Japanese government bonds (JGBs) at 60 basis points in yield and then increased the position at the lows at 45 bps. The timing was good, as we got on the majority of our position within 1 basis point of the all-time low. (*See Figure 9.3.*)

The aspect of the trade that we were happiest about was our entry point. The trade looked good from 1.5 percent yield on down; that we got in at nearly the low in yields was very helpful. This is one of the really tricky balances in trading: when to put a trade on. Often, if you wait for a great entry level, you miss it altogether, but sometimes patience pays off.

Do you manage that balance by using options?

I am not sure there is an answer to the problems of timing and exposure management, but we don't think the answer is derivatives. I used to trade

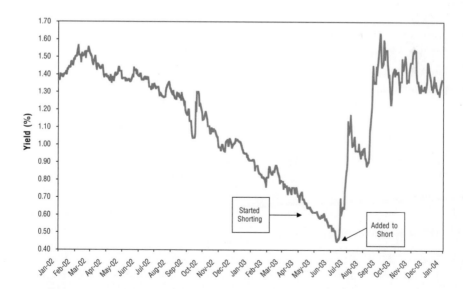

FIGURE 9.3   10-Year Japanese Government Bonds, 2002–2004
Source: Bloomberg.

and structure derivatives for Credit Suisse Financial Products (CSFP), so I understand their shortcomings. Trading options directly is usually an inefficient or lazy way to express a theme or hedge a trade. We tend to use them more as nonprice indicators in our research. We'll look at what's happening in derivative markets, swaps markets, swaption markets, and so on, for information as to how people are positioned in the underlying markets. But options as investments are usually not very compelling.

Can you tell me about your risk management philosophy?

We've drawn from the lessons learned at LTCM and stress-test all positions in our portfolio. We assume that all positions correlate perfectly and make sure we limit our losses in a disaster scenario to about 15 to 20 percent. To accomplish that, we adjust the overall size of our portfolio and place stop-losses on each individual trade. Strict stop-loss implementation is probably the toughest discipline in a fundamental global macro fund because, when the market moves against you, the trade just looks better and better in the context of your long-term views.

If we were to get stopped out, we would step back and try to determine whether the analysis needs refining or if it was simply misconceived. But we do not get obsessed about a single trade.

Even though we have a stop-loss on each trade, it is not a trailing stop-loss. If the trade has accrued a lot of profit, we are comfortable with it moving more against us. We don't want to lose a lot from the entry point of a trade but, if it is in the black, we're willing to ride out short-term drawdowns so we can hold on for the longer term. If an investor is truly in for the long term, the downside risk is mitigated.

For every trade, we also try to identify what I call nonprice indicators that we feel should be going a certain way as the trade progresses. For example, when we short equity markets, we track volatility indicators and various sentiment indicators that tell us if people are getting more optimistic or pessimistic. When price is used as the only indicator, things devolve into an ineffective charting exercise.

What was your worst trade?

In early 2004 our long-term view was that the unwinding of the financial bubble would create deflationary pressure, so long bond positions seemed attractive.

CLARIUM INVESTMENT THEMES, Q1 2004

- Deflation: Buying 10-year U.S. Treasuries.
- Dollar collapse: Long a basket of foreign currencies such as the Japanese yen, Brazilian real, New Zealand dollar, and Australian dollar.
- Oil to rally sharply: Buying shares in major oil companies, Russian oil companies, and Canadian oil sands companies.
- Equities and especially financial stocks are at the top of a wide range: Short equity indexes heavy with financials such as the S&P 500 and the German stock market index (DAX).

However, research on Fannie Mae's fixed income portfolio led us to believe that the U.S. bond market was vulnerable to a massive short-term sell-off. So, even though our long-term view was bullish Treasuries, in the short term we were concerned about weakness in the market. Given that, we shorted U.S. debt in February 2004. Soon thereafter, a very weak employment number came out and fixed income experienced one of its strongest rallies in many years. We exited according to our stops, although bonds sold off promptly thereafter. After a month, our indicators suggested that it was time to return to our core long bond thesis, and we put the trade on, capturing the subsequent rally in Treasuries. (*See Figure 9.4.*)

The trades reminded us once again of the old saying that timing is everything. One of the dilemmas with our post-bubble hypothesis is that while the enormous distortions affecting the market must eventually unwind, they can get bigger before reversing course. Balancing long-term and short-term views on the pivot of timing indicators is very tricky. For example, we think there's a housing bubble in the United States today, but we thought that two years ago. Since then, home-builder stocks have gone up by a factor of four, so it would have been a disastrous trade if we had put it on then. Lacking a good timing indicator until recently, we refrained from trading the housing bubble. Sometimes good trades are the ones you don't put on.

What is your current view of the world?

There are two ways to think about the world: Either we are living in a normal world or else something extraordinary is happening. If you think

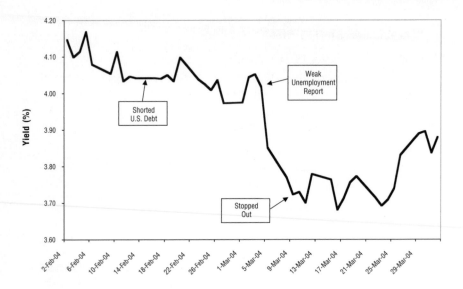

FIGURE 9.4   10-Year U.S. Treasuries, 2004
Source: Bloomberg.

we are living in a normal world, there isn't that much to do in the global macro space. But if you think we are living in a world distorted by the biggest financial bubble ever seen, as we believe, then there are things that are likely to break in very asymmetric ways. That presents enormous opportunities. Clearly, we are in the opportunity camp.

Right now, we are particularly concerned about the amount of financial leverage in the system, from housing to venture capital. Many equities, from tech to financials, seem rather rich. Friends of mine in the Valley report that there is still a huge amount of capital chasing relatively few ideas, so it seems we are still in the grip of speculative fervor.

Do you think we are at an extreme point in venture capital again, five years after the tech stock crash?

Notwithstanding the sell off in 2000 through 2002, we're probably close to where we were in 1999 and 2000. The market averages are obviously much lower but the ratio of money to good ideas is high. In fact, we're probably beyond a 1999 point in places like China and some other emerging markets.

CLARIUM CAPITAL'S PHILOSOPHY

The equity bubble and its collapse have created huge, long-lasting distortions in the markets, which have been exacerbated by pervasive central bank and government manipulations intended to mitigate the damage caused by the deflating bubble. In this environment, Clarium does not attempt to be market-neutral; indeed, it perceives the ubiquity of market-neutral, relative value strategies as one of the prime contributors to the present, overly correlated environment. As relative value styles attempt to maintain returns by using increasing amounts of leverage and risk to extract declining returns from relative value trades, they further correlate markets and inject systemic risk. Clarium believes that high absolute returns with moderate leverage and risk are best achieved in current conditions through directional styles that capitalize on these large, highly correlated distortions, and invests accordingly.

Is this a function of global interest rates being so low?

The level of global interest rates is definitely a contributing factor. But it is primarily a function of the way that governments dealt with the equity bubble. They pumped enormous amounts of extra liquidity into the system, which created a consumer spending bubble and a housing bubble. We have an enormous overhang of capital right now and it turns up in places like Silicon Valley.

What are your views on Alan Greenspan?

I think the Fed made some major mistakes in the 1990s that contributed to the bubble, or at the very least failed to stop its inflation. It will be many years before the Greenspan Fed can be accurately judged, but I don't think history will be kind. Presently, it's not clear how much power he has; on the one hand, his power over interest rates and the yield curve is quite potent, but on the other hand, his actions seem fairly constrained.

Are you still in the deflation camp?

We think there has to be a deleveraging of the world's financial system. Baby boomers are going to start saving soon, which means they are going to shift from equities toward fixed income and other lower-risk products. Regardless of what happens with inflation, real interest rates will come down a lot and nominal rates should come down as well.

Look at the yield on 30-year Treasury inflation-protected securities (TIPS). It got as low as 1.6 percent recently, which is the lowest it has ever been. (*See Figure 9.5.*) That means the risk-free rate of return for the next 30 years is currently being valued at 1.6 percent per year. That rate has been declining every year since the bubble burst, which shows that the bubble unwind process is still going strong.

If TIPS are priced correctly, and we think they are, they're telling us that equity markets are extremely overvalued. U.S. equity market valuations assume a lot of productivity growth, which is not compatible with 1.6 percent real yields.

We think the downtrend in real yields will continue as baby boomers increasingly look to safe places for their savings. The same thing happened

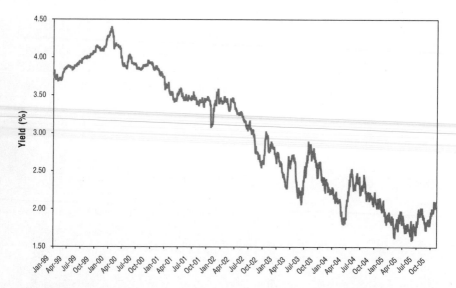

FIGURE 9.5 30-Year U.S. Treasury Inflation-Protected Securities (TIPS), 1999–2005
Source: Bloomberg.

in Japan in the 1990s. Demographically, the United States is 10 to 15 years behind Japan and the same dynamic is playing out.

The path of least resistance for the United States is to go down the deflation path, preferably some mild version where debtors can actually service their debts. Hyperinflation is not a choice. There is no country that has ever inflated its way out of a debt problem with a financial economy as large as the United States'—the 1970s not to the contrary, because the economy wasn't nearly as financialized then.

The debate about Greenspan's policy of extending financial leverage from 2001 to 2005 will center on the issue of whether the ultimate unwinding is that much more deflationary as a result. The path Greenspan has chosen is very different from Japan's in the early 1990s. Japan didn't cut interest rates as aggressively and they ended up with mild deflation.

What was arguably better about the Japanese trajectory was that it created no consumer credit bubbles. American consumers are going to have to retrench the spending that makes up two-thirds of the economy. If these consumer credit bubbles unwind in the United States, deflation is likely to be much stronger than it has been in Japan.

Given your deflation scenario, what advice would you give recent college graduates?

I've thought about that question a lot and it's a tough one to answer. When I was trying to get off the law track and into finance in 1994, I thought about venture capital. I arranged a meeting with a partner at one of the major venture capitalists, whose advice was, "The best way to get into venture capital is to make at least $20 million by starting a company and selling it. Take that money and invest it in other companies as a VC." I would give the same advice today regardless of deflation.

How about advice for someone who wants to be in your shoes, running a large global macro fund?

A career in hedge funds is probably not one that can be aspired to. It is something that is fundamentally nontracked; it almost seems that the people who do the best in hedge funds get into it by accident. They are original, creative, and slightly outside-the-box type people, the kind of people who probably aspire more to doing what suits them than to some specific industry. That will probably still be true in 10 to 15 years.

The worrisome part about being in a hedge fund bubble is the MBA indicator. Every year, the most popular destination for graduating MBAs always turns out to be the sector that is peaking and about to do poorly. And MBAs are rushing to hedge funds now.

When I interview MBAs for analyst positions here at Clarium, my standard question is this: We're a macro fund paid to identify markets that are enormously mispriced. What in the world do you think is incredibly out of kilter right now?

The striking thing is, almost every MBA I talk to simply doesn't have an answer. I tend to hear very qualified things like "Well, X is a *little* bit better than Y," and stuff like that. It's always very intelligent, well-thought-out stuff, but there are no strongly held views.

In summer 2004, our head of research scared our interns a bit by starting off their first day saying, "Anybody who declares that they think markets are efficient will be fired on the spot. If you think markets are efficient, there is nothing for you to do here. But you shouldn't worry about being fired, because if markets are truly efficient, then you won't have any trouble immediately finding an equally attractive job somewhere else."

Nobody said that they thought markets were efficient.

In hiring for Clarium, what skills or background have you found that correlate to success in macro research?

A combination of being good at math, economics, and history is essential. Analysts need to be able to do quantitative modeling, they must understand the economic theory that drives the numbers in the model, and they must have history to provide a sense of context. Analysts who are really successful are the ones who just *like* doing it. They *like* math, they *like* econ, they *like* history. It's something they're just naturally interested in.

What's next on the agenda for Peter Thiel?

I love doing this and am going to follow this route for the foreseeable future. I've enjoyed all the things I've done but I really like the small scale of the fund. We're a small firm and I love the team feel. I love the intellectual diversity and rigor of the work. I'm doing what I really want to be doing. It's a privilege.

CHAPTER 10

THE FLOOR TRADER

Yra Harris
Chicago Mercantile Exchange
Praxis Trading
Chicago

If global macro is a war to generate alpha, or excess return, and take money out of the markets for clients, then the Chicago pits are the trenches where the battles of price discovery take place. Floor traders on the Chicago Board of Trade (CBOT) or the Chicago Mercantile Exchange (CME, or "MERC") fight for every pip and point, shaving razor-thin margins off huge volume and taking bets that often last only seconds. It is a physical job whereby ex-athletes in blue, yellow, or red coats jockey around and box each other out to snap hand signals or scream to clerks for best executions.

Yra Harris has been on the floor of the MERC since 1977, which might explain why he looks slightly older than his years. Yet with years comes a wisdom that could only be gleaned from a lifetime in the pits. Unlike other Chicago floor traders, though, Harris distinguished himself in these markets by having a medium-term view and by understanding how world events impact the financial system and the economy, taking him above the fray of the rough-and-tumble Chicago world.

Many traders look at screens their entire lives, giving them a black and white version of price. Pit traders, however, visually see all sides of price action—the buyers, the sellers, the emotion, the energy—such that price becomes multidimensional. For them, price discovery is the market, and they live and die by taking its pulse. Walking on the floor of the MERC, I could feel the pulse of the markets. It is here where equilibrium levels are found in the markets for interest rates, currencies, stock indexes, and commodities. If macro markets are a zero-sum game, as many attest, there does not seem to be any place to hide from this cruel fact in the trading pits of Chicago.

After spending time on the floor, I went upstairs to Harris's office, a stark, simple room on one of the upper floors of the MERC, where the dull glow of a fluorescent light revealed an old computer monitor; gray, marked-up walls; and a variety of files and papers strewn about. It could easily have been mistaken for a broom closet. It is a strange contrast that despite his obvious intelligence and great talent for trading, Harris seems unimpressed with the trappings that his money could buy. He still goes down to the pit at least once a day, but no longer spends all his time there. The office feels chaotic, but I wonder if that is just the lingering experience of the floor itself, for it is rather calm and quiet except for the constant ringing of the phone by traders seeking Harris's opinion and guidance. Traders from around the world call him, soliciting his thoughts on markets. A prominent trader once told me about Harris, "There is no one better than Yra at deciphering the impact of geopolitical events on the markets."

Like all floor traders, Harris wears a colored jacket, in his case navy blue, and a badge that has three letters to identify him on the floor. Whereas most people have three random letters, Harris's badge reads "Y.R.A.," a testament to his longevity.

Harris trades only his own money now. He walks me through many world events as seen through the eyes of the pits and processed by his blend of classical education and street smarts—something he calls his "middle-class" upbringing, wherein the value of money is never taken for granted and work is valued as a sacred thing. He is never cocky or arrogant, as traders, particularly very successful floor traders, can be. Rather, he is curious. And through his thick Chicago accent and half-finished sentences he recounts his tale of the markets from the trenches, where trading means trading and where the psychology of survival is perhaps at its most pronounced.

How did you wind up on the floor in Chicago?

I was in graduate school for political economy and my main area of focus was multinational corporations. I started looking at how the global flow of money affected them. When the pegs came off with the collapse of Bretton Woods, everyone was writing about the coming collapse of the world financial system. I thought it was all so interesting.

I tried to get jobs at banks but they all said, "What can you do for us without an MBA?" I told them, "Here's the background that I have— you're going to need somebody like me to analyze your loan portfolios when they all blow up." They all laughed, but then about four or five years later there were some major banking debacles.

Meanwhile, an old friend of my father was working on the floor of the Chicago Mercantile Exchange and started talking to me about global markets one night. He asked me what I thought of the deutsche mark, so I wrote three pages and sent it off to him. He said, "This is pretty good, why don't you come down here and work for me?" I told him that I was probably going to Washington to work and didn't have much interest in a trading floor.

He called me again and said, "Look, you little punk, I'm not going to offer again. This is it. Go to f—ing Washington if you want, but I'm telling you this is the chance of a lifetime. The world is changing, you're a young guy, you're not married, c'mon. I'll teach you everything that you don't know, which is a lot."

I was refereeing basketball games at the time and not doing much else. So I went down to the MERC. The guy, Lenny Feldman, taught me about the markets and trading lessons. He had gone broke a few times and there's no greater lesson than failure. I figured I was getting a free ride on his failings.

I went to work in his currency arbitrage business for $200 a week. Little by little, I just took it over and the business grew a lot. We were arbitraging between currency futures and the cash plus forward price. This was all significantly different in 1977. It was as pure an arbitrage as you can get because we were using exact dates—there was no risk. Later, as we got more sophisticated, we started taking small risks here and there by playing with the expiry dates.

By the end, spreads got so narrow it didn't justify the risk. Volume was huge but the edge was minuscule. We were basically just supplying liquidity to the market, paying margin to the exchange if it went against us prior to maturity and running the risk of gambler's ruin in the interim. We eventually closed it down in 1993 and then I focused exclusively on macro trading.

Were you taking proprietary positions while you were running the arbitrage business?

Yes, for myself. I was also managing some money for others and filling orders in the pits from time to time. I've always tried to do as much as I can because I'm a big believer that when the sun is shining, you should make hay. It's a very middle-class approach to life.

Also, I wanted to stay busy and keep the pulse. I knew the currency markets inside-out so people would trust me to fill their big orders. After a while, I had people overseeing the arbitrage business for me so it pretty much ran itself.

What are some of the trading lessons your mentor Lenny Feldman taught you?

How to take a loss—just do it, because you can always get back in. Don't ever put your ego out there where you're afraid to say that you're wrong, because the market is right and you are wrong. Respect that. That was the greatest lesson I learned.

I can't stand it when people say, "Can you believe what the market did?" They better look at what *they* did. Markets aren't wrong. I've seen plenty of traders down here lose enormous sums of money believing they are right. I've seen guys blow upwards of $50 to $60 million in under a year—gone. You can see it happening. They start hanging on to a position too long because they can't get themselves to admit they were wrong. If you're right at the wrong time, you're wrong.

There's a story about one of the very first macro guys that always stuck with me. After sending one of his analysts to Africa to check out the cocoa crop, the analyst came back saying there was no crop so prices should go through the roof. The guy bought some cocoa at 38 cents. It went down to 36 cents and he doubled up. It went down to 34 cents and he doubled up again. It went down to 32 cents and he went broke. A year and a half later, cocoa was trading at $1.50.

He was right, but at the wrong time. You can have this gigantic view of the world but you better pay attention to what the markets are telling you.

There are always bigger factors than you out there. Anybody who thinks they're too big for the market eventually goes down. You're seeing it right now with Pacific Investment Management Company (PIMCO). Bill Gross and those guys are brilliant, but how do they move those massive positions when they're on the wire telling everyone what they're doing? With the consolidation in the banking industry, how many places can you go to move size today? Not many.

At what point did you realize you were good at markets?

I'm still not sure I am!

I grew up in a house of cardplayers. My parents and three older brothers all played cards. I used to get up on Saturday mornings and there'd be 11 guys sitting around the poker table gambling in my basement. I learned how to count with a deck of cards when I was three years old, so odds and probability were drilled into me at an early age.

How have global macro markets changed since you got into the business?

Well, first of all, global macro is really a new term. It used to be called "geopolitics." Secondly, there are so many people chasing it today with so much money. If you would have told me 10 years ago that there would be more than $250 billion allocated to futures trading, I would have laughed at you. I started my first fund with a $1 million investment from Paul Tudor Jones. We got assets up to $7 million and were doing pretty well when Paul wanted to give us another $10 million. I turned it down because I didn't think I could handle the jump in assets. Today $10 million is peanuts.

When people move money into Russia, it comes in such vast numbers. The same with China. When it comes, it comes and it's so fast. Computers have changed the game. In foreign exchange, back in the late 1970s, banks would get a call to sell a billion dollars and were given two weeks to get back with the fill. Now it's a push of a button and it goes down so smooth. It shows you just how vast the markets are and how many people are playing today. I could walk down onto the floor right now and sell a billion dollars of anything. It will make some noise but it will get done quickly. That's a phenomenal change from the old psyche.

It's one of those things where you have to be careful what you wish for—it may just come true. The hedge fund/Commodity Trading Advisor (CTA) game is getting to the point where it's starting to turn in on itself.

In the currency markets, at least you have central banks, corporates, banks, and other anonymous, distant entities to trade against. But the other markets are just full of speculators beating each other up. It's no wonder returns have come down.

What do you mean when you say "the old psyche"?

When somebody said to "take a few weeks" to execute a trade, you didn't have to be so attuned to the market all the time. Now, you have to be on top of it all the time and there's so much more to watch.

Before the Berlin Wall came down, there were only a few places large sums of capital could go. Now, a multitude of places like Brazil, Mexico, Russia, Turkey can absorb serious money.

Money used to flow via bank loans, which is an insignificant game now. If there has been a real major change it's that hedge funds have taken over the role of global financing. Where banks are methodical and slow, hedge funds are fast. Hedge funds don't get themselves invested with clients by doing weeks of credit work, committee meetings, cross-selling, and so on. For them, it's just a question of in or out, then a push of the button.

The real question is what banks actually do in the world today—finance hedge funds? If that is indeed the answer, it means that you and I, the taxpayers, will bear the brunt of any fallout. Every one of these institutions is too big to fail, as we saw with Long Term Capital. And LTCM was a drop in the bucket compared to some of the positions that exist out there today.

When hedge funds start fighting each other for returns, I get scared. Global risk is way out of line right now. There are people biting off some things that they're not going to be able to extricate themselves from when it goes south. And it always goes south at the absolute worst moment possible.

Rich Dennis wrote an article back in 1987 about that phenomenon, called "The Slower Fool Theory." When you look at today's credit markets, that's exactly what they're predicated upon.

How can the credit markets be wrong if markets are always right?

Markets are always right, so maybe there's something else out there on the horizon that we don't know about. Today's bond prices are telling me *I'm* wrong, and I respect that. I worry that there are a lot of people who are

THE SLOWER FOOL THEORY

We are playing a variant of the Greater Fool Theory which should be called the Slower Fool Theory. According to the Greater Fool Theory, investors buy things they know to be worth a lot less than they cost, on the hope that they can find a greater fool to sell to. It is not such a great strategy since there are not enough fools to go around.

Following the Slower Fool Theory, . . . my plan . . . is to be faster than the other fools holding [similar positions] and liquidate before the oncoming economic Armageddon devastates them. . . . To the extent that everyone believes the crisis is sometime in the future and somebody else's crisis, the game is viable.

Unfortunately, the future will arrive and . . . it will be a discontinuous leap for investors specifically and the economy generally into illiquidity, panic, and chaos. I suspect many people's investment strategies are not much different from mine. Keep buying that paper even though it is no good [while preparing] to head for the safe harbor.

So the catastrophe is out there lurking, probably happening sooner than later, and probably nastier than we can understand. . . . Prosperity will last only as long as the Slower Fool Theory of . . . investing lasts. Maybe I will liquidate my investment . . . a little earlier than I planned. . . . The other fools might be a little faster than I thought. I would hate to be caught with the right theory and the wrong position.

Source: Richard Dennis, *New Perspectives Quarterly*, Fall 1987.

just loading up and when the turn comes, like in 1994, it's going to be uglier. One percent interest rates in the United States was such an anomaly, nobody really understands it to this day.

Are macro markets a zero-sum game?

Yes. There are a lot of smart people out there, but not all smart people can do the same thing at the same time. It all just cannibalizes itself at some point. Almost like a black hole where it just sucks into itself. We still haven't figured out alchemy, and you don't create wealth by moving paper around.

What is your biggest worry about markets today?

I've always been nervous about the derivatives market. It is so complex and intertwined that nobody really knows how it all fits together. Greenspan thinks it's a great system for passing off risk, but there's somebody out there sitting on a hell of a lot of risk. And it's socialized risk!

When they repealed the Glass-Steagall Act, it resulted in a consolidated banking industry. Now we have fewer risk takers, so the size of the remaining risk takers is larger. The Fed calls the risk of a systemic blowup a "low probability, high impact event," which the markets aren't built for. There's not enough liquidity to absorb one of these events.

The markets are like water. They will flow to the weakest point that they can push through, and they always do. It's like an omniscient force saying, "F— you, I'm going to teach you a lesson, there's nobody bigger than me." Look at Soros or Tiger. They both got carried out on a stretcher despite years and years of phenomenal performance. There is a point where you become too big. Rich Dennis reached a point where he got too big for his playground. It was the same with the Hunt brothers when they tried to corner the silver market.

Look at their experiences and don't think you know everything, because you don't. The market is smarter than you will ever be, with its combined knowledge of all participants. Pay attention to the signs. Be quick to admit that you're wrong. Don't be afraid to miss something.

How have you adjusted your trading style to adapt to today's market conditions?

I'm much more cautious now. Anytime something is too good to be true, I now recognize that it probably is and that it's there for a reason because somebody knows more than me. Where I used to rush in, I now step back and wait for a move to develop. I don't feel I have to be at the start of every move anymore.

I work off this matrix that I developed 25 years ago based on the flows of money. Money is always going somewhere no matter what, so I just have to stay attuned. But I am more patient in letting moves develop before I get in. As I've gotten older, my patience has improved.

Do you express your views through options?

I don't, but I have a funny story about that. Myron Scholes is on the board of the CME and we went out to dinner one night. I had a couple of drinks in me already and said to him, "Myron, options are for pussies."

Everybody at the table was laughing because here was this idiot floor trader telling a Nobel Prize winner that options are for pussies. But he replied, "I'm not disagreeing with you. Options are slow to pick up a trend because the beginning of a trend is always a grind. If you're a pattern guy, you're looking at the pattern and can see it developing, which is when you're loading up. At the end, when everybody's on it and volatility has been cranked up because it's already been recognized, that's when you are selling."

Tell me about your matrix.

Global macro is the matrix. It's my mental picture of how money flows around the world, the flow of funds on a global basis seeking out the highest risk-adjusted return. Money is always moving somewhere, whether it's from oil to currencies to metals or to stocks. I follow it.

The only time when global money doesn't flow is when it's afraid, like during 1998 or after 9/11, and then it heads to Switzerland. Markets are based on two emotions: fear and greed. The greed part is nice when you're a part of it and are invested, but when fear takes over, it's an unbelievable thing. Money starts running for cover and stops thinking about return. It just wants to save its principal.

Money is always searching, but when it turns in on itself and heads for the exit, those are the really interesting times in global macro. The Asia crisis in 1997 is a great case study. "Let me out of here, I don't care what it costs!" I believe money is fascist. It craves stability more than anything else. Nothing bothers money more than uncertainty.

Where do you get your information for the matrix?

There are certain people in the marketplace I talk to just to bounce ideas off. I read research and things like the *Financial Times* and *The Economist*.

Markets are efficient over a long period of time but there are great inefficiencies on a day-to-day basis, even when the news is out there.

Does your matrix give you price targets or directional biases?

It's directional. I don't like to pick targets. That is what technicians do.
There are certain sayings that all floor traders know: "A market only has
one top and one bottom, go ahead and pick it," or "Pick a bottom, get the
same thing, a handful of shit."

A lot of these floor guys are filled with market wisdom. Like everywhere, there are plenty of guys who are full of crap. But there are also
some real gems down here on the floor.

Can you give me an example of how your matrix has led you to a trade?

A classic one was the Brazilian real devaluation in 1999. My matrix told me
that I should be selling soybeans as a result of the devaluation. Brazilian farmers got paid in dollars as most commodities are priced in dollars, so they made
an astronomical amount of money in their local currency after the devaluation. They started selling as many soybeans as they could and planted fence
post to fence post—supply rocketed and prices collapsed. (*See Figure 10.1.*)

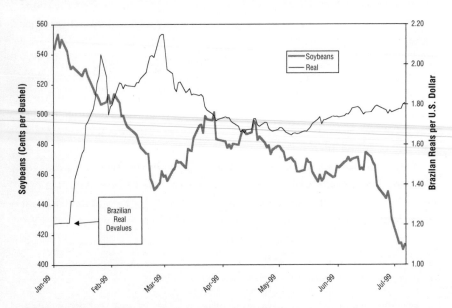

FIGURE 10.1   Brazilian Real and Soybeans, 1999
Source: Bloomberg.

Do you remember the worst trade you ever did?

Yes, and it could have been a whole lot worse.

It was 1989 and I was anticipating that Great Britain was going to enter the European Monetary System at around 2.70 deutsche marks per pound. I figured that if they joined anywhere above that rate, they were screwed economically. Then Maggie Thatcher comes out and announces that Great Britain will join at 2.95 deutsche marks per pound. I couldn't believe they could be that stupid. The market agreed with me and took the rate a lot higher.

My sister Joyce was working for me at the time. I had left her an order to get me out of my fairly large position at 2.95 no matter what. As the cross rate got there, she didn't waver. Had she waited just 10 minutes, it would have cost me a lot more. I got out at around 2.9550 and later in the day it was trading as high as 3.06. You can sit and think all you want, but sometimes it helps to have somebody who is stone cold doing your execution.

By 1992, the Brits realized that I had been right, but they had to go through three years of hell before finally totally pulling out of the euro system. They should build a statue of George Soros in Trafalgar Square because if Soros hadn't forced the pound out of the European Monetary System, England would be in the same poor shape as the rest of Europe right now.

What did you learn from that trade?

The market wasn't agreeing with my view. But rather than listening and being patient, I tried to muscle it. It was a classic case of thinking I knew more than the market.

When the rate ran up there, it told me a lot of people were positioned the same as me. Had I been patient, I could have sold at the top, which was a layup. Instead, I was so badly hurt that all I could do was lick my wounds and get the hell out of there. Not only did I lose a lot of money, I missed a great opportunity, which is always the case.

The worst thing you can do in a trade is try to get back to even. I call that the "prayer trade." I can spot guys on the floor who have it on because they shake back and forth, basically in prayer, mumbling, "Oh, please God, just let it come back to me. Let me break even."

What is that? Break even? That's a loser. I'm not in this business to break even. There's always opportunity in the markets, so forget breaking even. If breaking even is your goal, you're not trading anymore.

Instead of putting on the prayer trade, what is your recommendation to traders when they get sideswiped?

Take a deep breath, step back, clear the books, and start over again. Don't feel that you're missing something, because there is always another train leaving.

I used to think if I went on vacation, I'd be missing some great trades. The "This could be the last good trade" mind-set is a terrible mind-set. There are going to be a million good trades in a lifetime. I go on vacation a lot more now.

Do you trade better after vacations?

I never believed that but now I do. I'm much clearer after a vacation, but I hate the first three or four days back because I've got to catch up.

Do you travel for trade ideas?

No. A lot of times it becomes a distraction. The flows of money are much more important. Jimmy Rogers always says, "Go kick the tires." But I don't know if that's right, because in the same vein, you could lose your perspective being there by just seeing a lot of anecdotal stuff that doesn't really matter. On the other hand, if you're watching the flows, reading, and listening to what the market's telling you, you will know a lot more.

Where does your matrix of flows see the world headed now?

Europe becomes a very interesting story. Will Europe make it as the European Union? I'm not sure. Germany is the motor of Europe but the French have tied up Gulliver for political reasons, not economic ones. Germany is forced to look east so France is screwed. Eastern Europe is their Mexico, where labor is cheap, hungry, and educated. France doesn't want to reform itself. They want the social safety net but who's going to pay for it? The French have a real problem here. With 10 percent unemployment, how much pain can they take from the euro? I'm no lover of the French because their arrogance leads to a lot of problems, but I worry about Europe breaking apart. This to me is the most fascinating part of the world and very important.

The United Kingdom is trying to find itself and could destroy itself in the meantime, which it is prone to do. But there is no way the United Kingdom will join the European Union.

I've always been bullish Russia, even during the devaluation. But Russia has some real problems. The place has a lot of corruption, it's a kleptocracy, they can't steal enough. Putin is trying to right things by going after the oligarchs and taking back some of the wealth to buy off all the pensioners. They will get it and their taxes. They have the best tax system in the world now with their flat tax. The only question is how far Putin goes with respect to property rights. On the positive side, they're unbelievably rich in natural resources and a real comer with an unbelievably educated population. The communists had a great education system.

On the United States, I'm not very positive. That could change if they start cutting these deficits. Everybody says this time it's different, but when the world's biggest debtor is also the world's reserve currency, you have a problem. The only way out of deflation is through the printing press, which is problematic for the whole global financial system.

China will always be an interesting story but it's one of those places where it's probably too good to be true. I won't be surprised if a lot of people lose a fortune in China. The Chinese are going to do what's good for the Chinese. The more you badger them, the more the inscrutable Asians will wait you out. They have their own timetable. Western capitalism is too capricious.

Part of the problem with globalization is the speed of money flows. Malaysia is interesting in that respect. After the Asia crisis, they put blockages on the flows of capital. They let it come in but slapped an exit tax on it prior to leaving. I think you're going to see a lot more of that kind of stuff going on.

Do you think the process of globalization is slowing or reversing?

No, but people have to make adjustments and learn how to live with the bad effects of globalization, one of which is the speed and size of money flows.

If I asked you to put on a trade with a five-year time horizon, what would it be?

Whew! I can't do that. If you forced me, I would be in Eastern Europe. Eastern Europe is my number one place to go for equities and real estate.

It is going to be a fascinating place because of the level of education and the amount of capital that's going to go in there. Europeans like to keep their money close to home and they like stability. Eastern Europe has unbelievable potential to capture that money.

What was your favorite trade of all time?

It was in 1987 when the stock market crashed. I was managing a fund at the time and was positioned long Eurodollar futures and short S&Ps going into the crash. I was already bearish the market because the Germans had raised rates, which threw a monkey wrench into everybody's plan. I actually put the trade on the day before, due to a chart formation, believe it or not, that fit with my bearish bias.

I didn't have on a big position but it was so wicked and wild that I just tried to hang on. I didn't stay for the whole party in the S&Ps but I did in the Eurodollar futures, which opened 200 points higher that day. (*See Figure 10.2.*)

What was it like on the floor on Black Monday?

It was eerie and scary because you just didn't know the extent of everything. People were clearly hurting badly but you just didn't know how

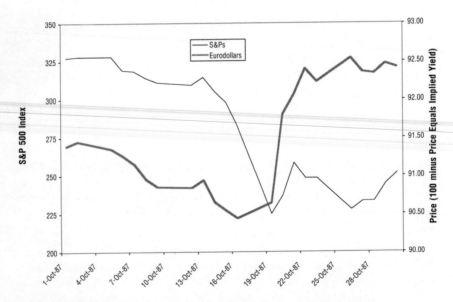

FIGURE 10.2   S&P 500 Index and Eurodollar Futures, October 1987
Source: Bloomberg.

badly. I've traded through a lot of devaluations and debacles but I've never seen as many people pulled off the floor by clearinghouses as I did that day. The pit was practically empty, which actually turned into a great opportunity to trade the S&Ps. I went into the S&P pit and starting making markets because nobody else was. Spreads were so unbelievably wide that it was pretty easy to make money just scalping around. Honestly. I couldn't help it. I remember saying to my wife, "I've had a really good day, but it doesn't mean anything." I wasn't really sure the game was going to come back.

It reminded me a little of September 11. I didn't trade for about three weeks after 9/11 because I had no stomach for it. As soon as it happened, I liquidated everything and bought Swiss francs. It's a classic fascist trade. Money went to stability and that was Switzerland. You know the Swiss won't come under attack because everybody dirty in the world has their money there. Nobody is going to burn their own money.

Have you ever had a losing year?

Oh, yeah! There have been years where I have gotten stubborn and violated my rules. There have been years of chop where I would get beat up, and years in which I thought I knew more than the markets.

I've never gone broke, thank God. I'd like to believe I'm way too cautious, which is also why I don't hit home runs. I hit singles and doubles or the occasional triple. I don't swing for the fences because I don't want to strike out. I have too much respect for money—which, again, comes from that middle-class sensibility.

There are guys around here who'll complain about missing a move and I say, "Let it go. As long as you still know how to take a loss, that's what it's all about." At the end of the day it's 100 percent right. You can't be afraid of losing, because then you may as well disappear. You will have no chance in this business. Also, if you think that you're smarter than the markets, you'll have no chance. Don't be stubborn. Listen to the market. You are going to lose money at times because of unpredictable events such as 9/11.

Do you manage risk differently for yourself than for clients?

You would hope that's not the case, but it is. I'm a mercenary with my own money but with other people's money I'm much more cautious, and it really should be the other way around. The best fund managers are willing to be more of a mercenary with client money.

When you have been successful with your own money first, you become more cautious. Some of the best fund managers have only ever been fund managers, so their paydays have been predicated on how much money they make as a fund. This is different from somebody who has been successful with their own money.

When you build your portfolio, is it well diversified or do you tend to chip away while looking for three or four big trades a year to lever up?

I do a lot of small trades to keep me in the markets, but when I'm focused like radar on three or four things is when I trade best. I'll still be watching other trades—the incidentals, as I call them—but I like to zero in on three or four areas where the matrix is onto something.

When I am not focused or I'm bored, all of a sudden I've accumulated 12 positions, which is not manageable. I wind up losing money in shitty little trades—this is a terrible business to be bored in.

As a global macro guy, why do you trade from the MERC?

I am here because this is where I got my educational background. I am on the floor every day because I can't sit in a room forever. When you just sit in front of your screens all day, you get stale, you do stupid things, or you get involved when you shouldn't. So I go down to the floor, I talk to people, I take the pulse and get some energy from it.

Do you think hedge fund managers sitting in remote offices are at an informational disadvantage?

If they're big enough, they have banks and brokers feeding them information, in which case I would say it's not a disadvantage.

What these new guys don't understand is risk. They come from investment banks and then go to hedge funds. They have the worst trading habits and do not know how to truly manage risk. They sit at desks, look at flows, and manage positions, not risk. There is nothing that teaches trading better than managing your own money. But they create opportunities for people like me. One of the great things about the market is that it's a phenomenally objective force.

Who is the most impressive trader you've ever met?

I would have to say Paul Tudor Jones because he has held on to it. Paul seeded one of my funds, as I mentioned, so I am biased toward him. I was impressed by the way he could maneuver such large positions.

I was also very impressed by Rich Dennis, who was just a phenomenal trader. He could push a position better than anyone. When it was working his way he knew how to add. The big successes know how to push. That has been a weakness in my trading—I am always taking something off.

You must have seen a lot of traders rotate through the floor here. Are there certain qualities that let you know someone is going to be a good trader?

Street smarts and lack of ego. You've got to have enough sense of yourself to be proud of what you do, but if you can't admit that you're wrong, you have no chance in this business. In trading global macro markets, 80 percent of my day is being wrong. I just hope that the returns on the 20 percent that remain, through good trading techniques, far surpass the 80 percent. Most of the trades I put on are wrong because I'm always looking, probing, sending out some soldiers that aren't coming back, like a reconnaissance mission, to see what's going on out there.

Do you think the trading floors of Chicago are going to be around much longer?

Maybe, maybe not. Either way I will adjust. I have been adjusting for years. I love trading global macro markets, it is really the greatest education. So I will keep doing it somewhere, somehow. To be able to test different ideas and theories and then to be rewarded for it is fabulous. Win, lose, or draw, I still find it fascinating.

CHAPTER 11

THE PIONEER

Jim Rogers
New York City

Jim Rogers needs no introduction. He is simply one of the best-known names in global macro. He co-founded the famous Quantum Fund with George Soros in 1969, returning 4,200 percent in a decade when the S&P 500 index returned a mere 47 percent. Never afraid of being a lone wolf, Rogers has consistently found wild, out-of-consensus investment ideas to buck mainstream views, such as investing in Malaysian rubber plantations or the Botswana stock market when most Wall Street practitioners were pitching traditional U.S. companies. In order to uncover the forgotten, neglected, or simply off-the-radar ideas, he has scoured the globe to such an extent that it has landed him in the *Guinness Book of World Records* for the longest continuous car journey—the second such adventure, following on the heels of an earlier motorcycle trip around the world that spawned his first best-seller, *Investment Biker*. *Adventure Capitalist*, his second best-seller, recounted his car trip around the world.

Indeed, with his latest offering, *Hot Commodities*, Rogers is at it again, claiming that despite the recent run-up in commodity prices, we are only at the beginning of a secular bull market in commodities that could last until 2020. He claims that history is on his side, noting that bull markets in the past have lasted for 15 to 23 years, according to his analysis. "One day farmers and lumberjacks may be on the cover of *Fortune* magazine, enrollment at Texas A&M may be greater than Harvard Business School, and CNBC might be a commodities channel," he says.

The Alabama native is accustomed to pitching extremely long-term views such as these, readily admitting his weakness at trading. But that does not mean that he is loath to put his money where his mouth is. He launched the Rogers International Commodity Index in 1998, which has more than doubled since inception, making it one of the top-performing indexes in the world.

Despite his flair for adventure and television appearances, Rogers represents classic global macro in that he is and always has been willing to invest in anything, anywhere around the globe. For him, investing is all about seeking high returns, whether that means being long or short stocks, bonds, currencies, or commodities in Milwaukee or Malawi.

I met Jim at his house, a Victorian mansion overlooking the Hudson River on the Upper West Side of New York that he bought for $105,000 in 1977 after the collapse of the housing market, a then out-of-consensus view, and which has a current value estimated at more than $15 million. I had been familiar with his books and his legendary status in the investment world since my student days and was eager to ask him about the history of the business and some of his vast experiences. His refined southern accent and signature bow tie suggest a mild-mannered gentleman, not the high-energy, obsessive man who was doing at least three different things at any one time during our discussions. As I struggled to take in the myriad artifacts that littered his home—animal pelts, vases, maps, and other objects adorned with Chinese characters were seemingly piled up everywhere—Rogers asked, "Do you mind if I work out during the interview?"

I followed him up to a solarium that serves as his gym. Rogers strapped on an ear-flapped ski cap and then an Indonesian peasant hat, pulled on some gloves and climbed into the seat of a horizontal bike. He fired off e-mails on the laptop bolted in front of him as his face contorted from the high tension of the bike and proceeded to tell me about his investing life, his travels, and his baby girl.

What do you think of the term global macro?

I don't know what *global macro* means, or at least I'm not smart enough to know. I guess *global* means "worldwide" and *macro* means "macroeconomic." So I guess that's what it means, it means a view of the whole world. That sound right? Did I pass?

You were involved in worldwide macroeconomic investing before global macro was a term. How have you seen that style of investing change since you started?

I have always invested worldwide, in all sorts of things, whether it's commodities or currencies, stocks or bonds, long or short. So for me it's just been a way of life. It's the only way to invest, as far as I knew. I didn't know there were all these other things. Ever since my earliest days on Wall Street, I can remember talking about buying things like the Danish krone, to the utter amazement or horror of people on Wall Street.

So has it changed? I guess it's gone from being nonexistent to being a marketing term for people now. I never heard the term until recently—maybe not until I heard you use the term. People who use terms like *global macro* or *small cap specialist* or whatever are using marketing gimmicks, as far as I'm concerned.

Investors, at least my idea of an investor, invested in whatever was appropriate, whether that was long sterling or short wheat or long Australian oil companies. It's just what one did. One didn't sit around saying, "I am global macro" or "This is mid cap growth" or stuff like that. I have never invested that way. These terms will disappear when the next big shakeout comes, which will probably be within this decade.

Do you think terms like global macro or small cap equity are limiting?

Of course they're limiting, but maybe they're doing that because they're a limited person. Maybe they are a limited investor. I would hate for somebody to say to me, "You can only invest in American small cap equity." I wouldn't have much to invest in pretty quickly. I have all kinds of investments in over 30 countries around the world, both long and short. Being limited is nuts.

Is that why we are starting to see a shakeout in the mutual fund industry?

Yes, and also because there are too many mutual funds these days. You have too many people who raced into the investment community in the past 10 years. Whenever there is easy money to be made—whether it's gold in Alaska, land in California, or oil in Texas—people rush into that business.

Everybody goes into it after it's been successful and they soon find out it's not that easy. Then there's a shakeout.

The most recent "gold rush" has been the investment and financial community. There are something like 50,000 mutual funds and 8,000 hedge funds in the world now. There cannot be that many smart 29-year-olds in the world, I promise you. It's just not that easy to make money in the investment business, at least it never has been for me. So for a lot of reasons, we're going to have a shakeout.

You recently said that hedge funds are a bubble; can you explain that?

We have something that is overdone.

But isn't a bubble when money flows into an asset that rises in price, causing people to chase price versus value, which eventually reverses? Hedge funds are not an asset, thus are not rising in price, but rather rising in assets under management.

There have been price increases. Do you know what these guys are charging now? When I was in that business, we charged 1 percent of the assets and 20 percent of the profits. There are guys now who automatically charge 2 or 3 percent of the assets and 30 to 50 percent of the profits. Are you kidding me? There's been a huge price rise. Many of them don't perform yet they still get 2 or 3 percent of the assets.

And bubbles can manifest in more than one way. It has certainly been a way for people to increase their pay and has created a bubble in compensation. All somebody has to do now is say, "I'm a hedge fund," and he gets a whole lot more money. Now everybody's looking for a hedge fund in which to invest. The institutions are frantically trying to find hedge funds, which is crazy. So in that sense it's overdone, whether you call that a bubble or not.

If you were advising an institution—let's say a conservative university endowment—where would you recommend they invest their funds?

Commodities and non–U.S. dollar assets.

Fifty-fifty or how would you split it up?

If I had told the board of trustees of Princeton University to put all its money into an S&P index fund in 1982, they would have run me out of town. But that is what they should have done.

Now, in 2005, a large amount of their assets should go into commodities either via a commodity index fund, which is probably the best way, or via a manager, which traditionally has not been the best way. They should have a large part of their assets in raw materials. At what percentage, I leave that to you, but the rest of the assets, if there are any left over, should go into non–U.S. dollar investments.

Endowments are supposed to last decades. The U.S. dollar is not going to last decades, so anybody putting large sums of their money into U.S. dollar–denominated assets is going to suffer badly over the next several years.

My baby girl is 18 months old. My baby girl has a bank account. She does not have an American bank account; she has a Swiss bank account because she knows the dollar's not going to do her any good when she's 25.

She knows the dollar is a bad investment at 18 months old?

I hope she does. She's got to take care of me someday so I hope she's getting it right.

You have been a well-documented dollar bear for several years now. How much lower can the dollar go from here?

Eventually the dollar is going to go down a lot and there will be exchange controls in America. That's what politicians always resort to. At the moment, American politicians want the dollar to go down, they are encouraging it to go down, and they think it's good. It is a horrible policy that has never worked for any country in the world. I suggest that your American readers be patriotic, help support the government, and sell dollars. Get your money out of the country.

How low will it go? Well, the pound sterling was once the world's reserve currency and it went down 80 percent from top to bottom. The dollar went up 400 percent against it, top to bottom, which is the other side. (*See Figure 11.1.*)

Likewise, the Japanese yen was at 500 to the U.S. dollar after World War II. Now it's at 100, so the yen has gone up 400 percent and the dollar has gone down 80 percent. Yet Japan is still very competitive. (*See Figure 11.2.*)

In my view, the dollar is certainly going to go down another 40 to 50 percent over the next few years. Of course, there are rallies along the way and some of the rallies will be huge. Something always comes along to cause big rallies in multiyear bear markets.

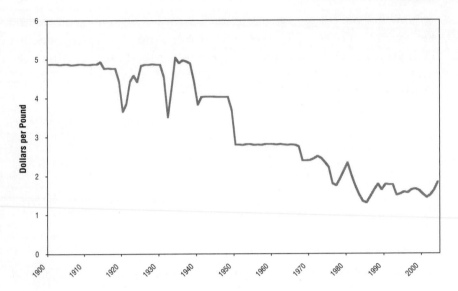

FIGURE 11.1   Pound Sterling, 1900–2004
Source: Lawrence H. Officer, "Exchange rate between the United States dollar and the British pound, 1791–2004." Economic History Services, EH.Net, 2004.

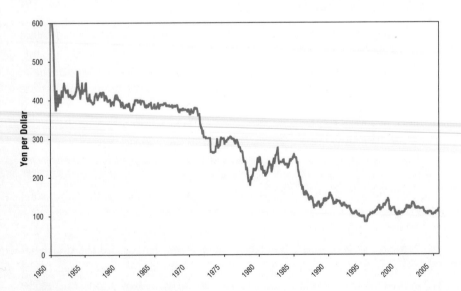

FIGURE 11.2   Yen, 1950–2005
Source: CRB.

Now this doesn't mean we will necessarily be competitive. I gave you the example of Japan. They still have a balance of trade surplus even though the currency appreciated 400 percent against the U.S. dollar.

Could the dollar fall to half the value of the euro?

Oh, certainly. But by then, the euro will be under some serious pressure and will probably disintegrate. I own some euros but I don't expect the euro to survive 15 years from now. I own it, but it has become a political currency rather than an economic currency. Europe has a horrible demographic problem which will be hitting them in the face hard when the dollar declines that much.

Should the European Union admit Turkey to alleviate the demographic problem?

Absolutely. The best thing Europe could do now would be to bring in Turkey. When they recently took 10 new countries, they brought in 10 new problems as those countries have little to contribute.

Turkey has about the same population as those 10 countries, one language, a much more productive labor force, and so on. They could solve many problems by bringing in Turkey. So if I were the European Union, I would bring in Turkey this afternoon. It would be the best thing for the European Union and its survival.

Of course, they are not going to do it because of the dirty little secret they don't like to talk about: The Turks are "not like us" Europeans. "They" got that funny language and that funny religion and that funny skin.

Do you think it would be a good thing for the world if the European Union were to accept a Muslim country?

Well, yeah, but that's a much bigger issue. Unfortunately, throughout history, when things start going wrong, politicians love to use religion and foreigners as a rallying point. They say, "All our problems are because of those foreigners and their infidel religion." That's what's happening now.

There is nothing inherently wrong with Christianity or Islam, and there is no reason that they should be in conflict. It is astonishing. The two have the same God, the same prophets, the same principles for the most part, and just as Christians have been slaughtering each other in the name of Jesus Christ for centuries, Muslims have also been slaughtering each other in the name of Mohammed for centuries. Muslims and Christians have been slaughtering each other in the name of the same God. Muslims, Christians, and Jews all have the same God.

It is not that easy to get people to die for Richard Nixon, but it is possible to get people to die for Mohammed or Jesus. So religion is again being exploited by politicians in various parts of the world. It is a terrible tragedy, but it is happening.

Likewise, whenever there is a war, politicians always say, "You may not like this, this may be hard or whatever, but at least support the troops." Support those good, honest American/German/you-pick-the-country boys at the front, which really means, "Support me" or "Don't criticize me," otherwise "you are not supporting the troops."

Is the pending financial disaster that you allude to being brought forward by U.S. politicians and policies?

Let's hope that we can avoid a disaster; let's hope that it's just a crisis or a semicrisis. But politicians throughout history have gotten things wrong turning a semicrisis into a crisis and then into a disaster, so the odds are against us just having a semicrisis.

American foreign policy at present is making many enemies around the world and is also terribly overextending us financially. It is making us less safe by serving as a recruiting poster for our enemies. It is going to be difficult for us to pull out of this.

We're also extremely overextended geopolitically and militarily. If something else broke out, we couldn't deal with it. If there were some kind of problem in Taiwan or Korea, there is nothing we could do.

How do you see a financial crisis playing out during the next decade?

I am not smart enough to know that. I do know that the currency markets will be a center of whatever happens because of the state of the U.S. dollar. The U.S. dollar has been the world's reserve currency and medium of exchange for 60-odd years and that's in the process of changing. The U.S. dollar is a terribly flawed currency. We are the world's largest debtor nation and our foreign debts are increasing at the rate $1 trillion every 21 months. Do the arithmetic. More and more people will be moving their money out of U.S. dollars. I told you my baby girl doesn't have an American bank account; others will follow.

Why then are 30-year U.S. Treasuries yielding less than 5 percent?

Because of the nuttiness and the inertia of Asian central banks. It's amazing, you can interview those bureaucrats in Japan and ask them why they are buying Treasuries and they will say, "Because it's policy and it's what we have always done." The bond bull market started in 1981 and it ended in 2003, but the mind-set hasn't changed yet.

You are not old enough to remember, but let me tell you about the last shift in bonds from bear to bull market. When bonds hit bottom in 1981, the U.S. government bond was yielding 15 percent. A new long-term bull market had begun and the bear market was over. Yet in 1984, three years later, U.S. government bonds went back to yielding 14 percent. The bear market was long finished and a bull market had begun, but three years later, bonds went back and tested the 1981 low. (*See Figure 11.3.*) That is undoubtedly happening with bonds now, but as far as I can see, bonds are over.

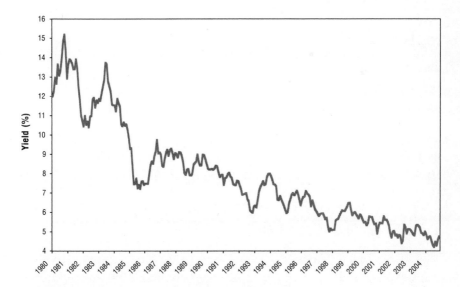

FIGURE 11.3   30-Year U.S. Treasuries, 1980–2005
Source: Bloomberg.

Do markets like to test conviction levels to shake out the weak hands before going where they are inevitably going to go?

I don't know if markets are smart enough to say, "Let's test the weak hands," but history has repeatedly shown that sort of thing happens. It is human nature. Most people have grown up only knowing a bull market in bonds so, like the Japanese central bank, they will continue to buy them—until they cannot take the pain and they acknowledge the change.

You have said before that the markets are almost always wrong.

Correct. I am not the first person to observe that. Whenever everybody is on one side of a market, it has nearly always proven to be wrong. We human beings have not changed in hundreds of years, so we are still guided by the same fears and aspirations.

Usually, when something has a 20-year move up or down, it is wrong and ready to reverse. I am talking about the big picture now—whenever something is at a long-term high and everybody is wildly enthusiastic, it is time to go the other way.

Sell hysteria and buy panic?

Buy panic.

What panic are you buying right now?

As we speak, I am short bonds. I am probably a bit early but something is going to make them go. I am not selling dollars right now, although I plan to sell a lot more dollars sometime in the next year or two. I am buying sugar, cotton, and orange juice.

What are your thoughts on gold?

I own some gold. I expect it to go higher over the next several years, but I expect to make more money in other commodities. You will make a lot more in sugar and cotton than you will in gold over the next five years.

You once said that gold was yesterday's inflation hedge. Has gold changed as an investment tool over your investment career?

Whenever there is a bull market, people become hysterical after a few years. They think, "Gosh, what has happened for the past five years is going to go on forever."

In the 1970s, gold was going up for some very sound supply and demand reasons. As the gold bull market gathered strength, it pulled in everybody so that in the last year or two it tripled. Just like the NASDAQ in 1998 and 1999. Everybody was shrieking that gold always has been, always will be an inflation hedge. Just like in 1998 when people were saying "The dot-com, new-economy revolution will go on forever."

But again, just like the dot-commers, the gold bugs hadn't read their history. We have had new economies and new eras every 30 or 40 years for the past 500 years all over the world. If anybody had gone back to look at gold, they would have seen some very long periods where it has done nothing, and long periods where it has actually gone down during inflationary periods. (*See Figure 11.4.*)

The number of mystics in gold is greatly reduced now, although there

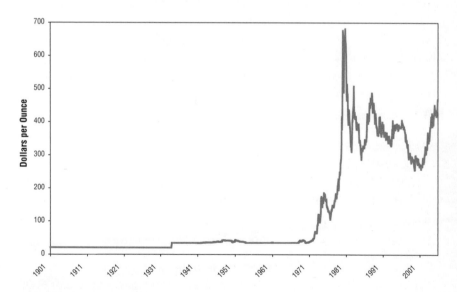

FIGURE 11.4   Gold, 1901–2005
Source: CRB.

are still some who think that gold is holy. As far as gold being the kind of mystical substance it became in the late 1970s, that has definitely changed. Most people now think gold is a wretched place to invest. The realization has sunk into more and more people that gold is subject to the same laws of supply and demand as everything else. So yes, in that sense it's changed.

Does today's investment cycle remind you of the 1970s?

Yes, but it does not just remind me of the 1970s. It reminds me of many other periods in history when supply and demand were out of whack. Go back and you will find that the last 100, 200, 500 years we have had periodic long bull markets in commodities followed by periodic long bear markets in commodities. Likewise, we have had long bear markets in stocks followed by long bull markets in stocks. When you have a bull market in commodities you have a bear market in stocks. I could give you my theory as to why that happens, but who cares about my theory?

I care.

I'll use Kellogg as an example. In the 1980s and 1990s, Kellogg was a great company and a great stock. It went up a lot because it controlled its declining raw material costs, whether it was wheat, rice, paper, corn, or something else. So costs were under control and it could expand margins to make shareholders happy.

When there is a bull market in commodities, the opposite happens. It becomes impossible to control costs. Even if a company tries to hedge, it is on the wrong foot most of the time because the people in the hedging department grew up knowing only a commodity bear market. So in periods of long bull markets in commodities, material prices are fluctuating and rising, squeezing margins, and hurting shareholders.

Now, whether that is correct or not, I don't know. It is my theory, but the fact is that it has always worked that way.

Is history the most important thing to know when investing?

The most important thing in investing is to buy low and sell high.

There are a lot of people in the financial communities who do not even know there is such a thing as history. They think financial markets were invented the day they showed up at Merrill Lynch or Deutsche Bank or wherever, and these people make fortunes.

For me history is important. To be a long-term success in financial markets, you must understand history. The long-term success stories are those who know history either from experience, reading, or just understanding how markets work.

If you want to get a sense of history, look at maps going back 100 years or so from all over the world. You will see how the world is always changing, and whatever we think we know today is not going to be true in 10 years. That thought has helped me enormously in my investments.

I know that bubbles have always happened and they always look the same, it is the damnedest thing. People always say the same things in bubbles: "This new technology is going to change the world," or "You don't understand what is going on, you old fogey." All those same things have been trotted out in every bubble in history, whether it is commodities, tankers, or bonds. People always get just as hysterical. The smart money always loses money shorting them because they cannot comprehend that it could go as high as it does.

Do you always bet against bubbles?

Yes, but like I said it is hard to get the timing right. I remember the Kuwaiti bubble in 1979. I so wanted to short it but thank Allah I could not. They would not let foreigners do anything; fortunately, because I am sure I would have been wiped out at least three times in that bubble. That was one of the great ones of all time.

You once said central bankers are always wrong. Do you like to bet against their policies as well?

They have nearly always been wrong. I mean, remember they are bureaucrats. If they could get a real job, they would not be working for the government. Look at Greenspan, he is a bureaucrat. He has failed at everything he has done. That is why he kept trying to get government jobs. Look at his career history and look at his history as a central banker—it is a mess.

Is moral hazard one of the biggest problems in the world right now?

I do not sit around worrying about moral hazard but it is always a mistake to bail people out. Look at the Japanese—they have been bailing out their people for 14 years and supporting zombie companies. If they had just let them collapse, Japan would have been a great success story the past 10 years.

It is interesting that Greenspan is always going on the circuit saying to the Japanese, "Why don't you clean out your system? Why don't you let the companies go bankrupt? Why don't you stop supporting the banks?" and yet he is doing the same thing here. He cut interest rates down to 1 percent to save everybody and bailed out his pals at Long Term Capital Management.

History is full of examples where you wind up making problems worse by trying to save something with a government mandate. You have to amputate the arm or the whole body dies.

Do you consider yourself of the Austrian school of economics?

To the extent that I put any labels on, I guess it fits.

I have heard you say that you are not a good trader, but you often seem to catch short-term reversals that go against your structural bias. How do you do it?

I have lost enough money being wrong that I have gotten better at it, I guess. If I've gotten better at it, it's because I've made enough mistakes. Whenever something is really pounded or when something is skyrocketing and it is on the front page of the *New York Times*, no matter how much you agree with it in the long term, you have to reverse yourself for a while. The dollar, for instance, was on the front page of the *New York Times* three or four times recently. I am terribly bearish on the dollar, as you have heard, but I have enough sense to know that when it is in the popular press, I should not be selling dollars.

Do you think the same thing is happening in commodities?

No, I don't—just look at some of them. Sugar is 80 percent below its all-time high. Cotton is 60 percent below its all-time high. Silver is 80 percent below its all-time high. Gold is 60 percent below its all-time high. Soybeans are 60 percent below the all-time high. Even oil, if you adjust for inflation, is 50 percent below where it used to be. So it is hard for me to see what's happening in commodities as some kind of bubble. There are pauses and consolidations in every bull market and every bear market. I hope one comes soon for commodities so that I can buy more.

You have said that the time to buy more commodities is when China's hard landing is on the cover of **BusinessWeek.**

That is my plan, but it may not happen that way. I expect a hard landing in China, which will be the next great buying opportunity for commodities and China, perhaps your last great one. There will be some real setbacks along the way, but we are in a big secular bull market and that is how you make big money—that is how I make money.

Do you always plan the trade and trade the plan?

Usually when I try to do something I have a reason for it, although sometimes I wait. Sometimes I anticipate a move and sometimes something happens that I did not consider.

Take airlines, for instance. I'm playing the airlines right now. The bonds are yielding 16 to 20 percent. I bought them over the last two or three months when oil was going sky high. I am bullish oil, too, by the way. When oil was bursting at the seams, airline bonds were collapsing and I bought on the theory that the industry is making a bottom. If I am right, I am going to earn 15 or 20 percent with short maturities. Meanwhile, let's say I am wrong; at least the bondholders are going to be the new owners of the airlines when they are reorganized.

So in that instance, I was not sitting around looking to buy airline bonds. But over a few weeks, I noticed something that I have noticed many times in my investment history: when everybody in an industry is losing money and you have a few bankruptcies, the industry is usually making a bottom. Either it is going to disappear or it is going to turn around.

Where do you get your information for trade ideas?

The *Financial Times*, the *Wall Street Journal*, *Barron's*, *The Economist*, walking down the street. In this case, it was from riding in airplanes, seeing that they are all full, seeing that sometimes it is difficult to get a reservation, knowing they are all losing money, putting two and two together, and thinking this could be a bottom.

So you don't have a magic bullet or a secret formula?

I wish I had a magic bullet! My God, wouldn't life be easy!

How do you structure your portfolio? Are there some modern portfolio techniques that you utilize?

No, no, no, no, no. No, I do not know most of that stuff and do not understand it. My portfolio is organic and changes as opportunities arise, whether planned or unplanned. I just act and if it means I have to close something out, I do. I usually have not had that problem. If I decide to buy airline bonds and do not have enough money, then I sell something. In theory, I close out positions when I think they have matured.

I do not have a committee; I do not have to report my allocation every quarter. In fact, I could not tell you my allocation nor do I want to know my allocation. Anybody who knows how much he is worth does not have enough. I do not sit around figuring out how I did last year, last month, or what percentage I have in various places. I know where something is in my head. I know when it is time to close a position and when it is time to open one. But it is all done with the big picture in mind or the idea that I am going to be long something for several years—in other words, I am not going to have to worry about it or trade it or time it. I am really bad at timing, despite your nice words.

If you are fully invested and some positions start going south because of a market panic and not fundamentals, what do you do?

I am not fully leveraged these days. I do not do that anymore. I can hang with positions and there is always room to put on something new with a little leverage. There was a time when I always was fully leveraged, but now there is always slack somewhere.

How has your portfolio management or trading style changed from when you were at Quantum?

We used to be fully leveraged. Totally leveraged! We had leverage that I look back on now and say, "What the hell was wrong with us?" Yet we did not have any trouble sleeping at night. Looking back, the main thing that was wrong is that we always thought we were right.

I was more on top of things back then. If I owned airline bonds, I would have visited all the airlines, I would have spreadsheets on all the airlines, I would have been to the trade associations, I would have been to see Boeing, would have been to see Airbus. I would have done an enormous amount more work and have been sitting on top of it every day. I would have been watching every tick, every trade—not trading them, but just so that I would know what is happening. Those days are long gone. Is that because I have more knowledge or more experience, or because I am lazier or sloppier? Probably all of them.

What lessons did you take away from working with George Soros?

I did not learn anything from him except that there are great traders and there are great investors in the world. I learned that I am not a great trader. Whatever success I have had has come from finding things that are cheap where a fundamental change is taking place and buying. I have always done that, then and now.

Do you think long-term success stories in markets are lucky?

If somebody flips a coin a hundred times, somebody is going to come out on top. But there are enough people who have made investment decisions and have explained *why* they made them and have turned out to be right, to know that they were not just flipping coins. If a guy says, "I'm going to buy X for these reasons" and it goes up for 10 years for those reasons, I hardly call that flipping a coin.

Who in the investment community do you admire?

Anybody who is successful.

The guys who built Merrill Lynch were astonishingly successful guys. In the 1920s they said, "We're going to focus on retail investors," and everybody scoffed. Well, that was a stroke of genius and they have built a big company.

Mike Steinhardt has been phenomenally successful. The way he has been successful is totally 100 percent different from the way I have been, but one has to admire him.

Look at Roy Neuberger. He is over 100 years old and he still goes down to his office every day, buys and sells, and goes home. I once worked for Roy Neuberger for a short period of time. I remember him sitting there reading the *Journal* and the tape would be going by and he would say, "There's 100,000 shares of IBM for sale on the floor. Bid 379 1/2," and the trade would print at 379 1/2. The guy had developed such a sixth sense for the ticker, it was unbelievable. I could not even comprehend what he was doing, but you have to admire somebody who does that well.

I admire people who can run the 100-meter dash in record time, but I cannot do that, either.

One of the beauties of the investment community is that it is very simple. It is not like working for a big company like General Motors where you go to work every day, wear the right suits, say the right things, and join the right clubs. There, you either make it or you don't make it, but you never know why.

The investment community is like the track and field people. If your stocks go up, they went up, period. It does not matter whether you went to high school, wear the right suit, or play golf well. It is the same way with the 100-meter dash. If you run it faster than anybody else, no one cares anything about you except that you ran it faster than everyone else.

So you prefer investing to trading?

Trading is not my idea of fun. My idea of fun is to track these great "macro" events, or secular trends, as I used to call them. I remember we wrote something in the early 1970s that the way to make money was to buy a secular trend. People would call us up and ask, "Do you mean God?" *Secular* was not a word that people used in that context. I guess *secular* is the word I used to use and now I should be calling it *macro*. Worldwide secular.

What worldwide secular trend have you caught that you would consider your favorite?

I don't know, there have been some nice ones. When you ask about favorites, that implies success. I usually prefer talking more about the things I have gotten wrong, because I learned from them.

The best one, the one I loved the most, was defense stocks in the 1970s. After the Vietnam War, defense went into the tanks—everybody hated defense, nobody was spending money on defense, so these were dollar stocks at best. I bought a lot of them.

Back then I was 32 years old and I got invited to one of those dinners where the hotshots sit around and say, "I'm doing this" and "I'm doing that." I remember saying to the table, "I'm buying Lockheed and these are the reasons," when a more knowledgeable, famous guy at the other end of the table said in a loud stage whisper, "Who the hell buys stocks like that?"

It was my first time to this kind of event. There I was with the big boys and this guy crushed me. Meanwhile, everyone was talking about companies that were trading at 50 to 100 times earnings, and I was talking about this industry which was bankrupt. Lockheed went up about 100 times, by the way, over the next few years.

After that, a guy who heard about what I had said called me up. I said, "Now you don't want to buy Lockheed, you want to buy Loral." Loral was selling at $2 at the time. The guy said, "I cannot buy stocks under $10."

ROGERS: "The stock is going to go to 30."

GUY: "Well, when it gets to 10, call me up and I will buy."

ROGERS: "But it would have quintupled by then!"

GUY: "That's fine, I will buy it when it has quintupled."

And he did! It was the goddamnedest thing I ever saw in my life. He waited for the stock to quintuple and then bought the story. I remember those two vignettes extremely well because they partly explain the madness of the investment community.

There seem to be a lot of artificial opportunities in the investment world because money management companies have rules such as "You can't buy a stock below ten dollars."

Absolutely. Another favorite of mine, obviously, is commodities. It was the end of 1998 when I started this commodities index fund because I was convinced that the 20-year bear market in commodities was coming to an end. You cannot believe the ridicule I used to get on CNBC. They were all giggling and drooling and talking about dot-com this and dot-com that, while I was sitting there saying, "I am starting a commodities index fund and China is a great place to invest." Well, you know the rest of that story. That has been a nice one. There are many mistakes I could tell you about, but you asked about my favorites.

I'd love to hear about some of your mistakes and what you learned from them.

The first one that pops into mind is when I shorted oil in 1980. Literally the Friday afternoon that Iraq invaded Iran. It was sloppiness or I just hadn't been doing enough homework. If I had really been doing it I would have realized that the Iraqi army was moving in on the Iranian border.

It was six months or so after I had retired and I was not doing what I used to. A little hubris, a little whatever, and it reminded me with full force, "You better do your homework." Markets know more than you.

But aren't markets always wrong?

Even if they are wrong, they are still going to slap you in the face every once in a while just to remind you who is boss.

Another bad trading experience you might enjoy was from the early 1970s when I first started in the business. I was tripling my money when everybody else was going bankrupt, and then I lost it all in a few months because I thought I knew what I was doing and I didn't.

I took all my money and bought puts on the stock market. I figured it was all about to collapse, and it did. In May 1970 the market had the worst collapse since 1937, and I tripled my money again. I thought I was so smart and thought, "This is easy."

Then I thought the market was going to rally, so I sold my puts and went flat. The market rallied, just as I thought it would, so I started to think I knew a little bit about trading. After the rally was over, I wanted to buy puts again. The premiums were pretty high by then, however, so I took all the money I had and went outright short. Two months later I was wiped out. The hell of it is, most of the companies I had sold short went bankrupt, but it didn't matter because I didn't have the staying power as the rally had its final run.

I learned that I did not know anything about trading even though I was supposedly smarter than everybody around me. I still had an enormous amount to learn.

What are some of your current big-picture views?

I am very bullish on Africa. It will be another great secular kind of play. I still own every share I ever owned in Botswana. Whenever I get dividends, they are automatically reinvested into more.

After my first trip around the world, I came back very bullish on Africa because I could see that nobody wanted to be there. The Berlin Wall had just fallen, so the last thing anyone wanted to be was a socialist. All those African leaders who espoused Communism and socialism quickly got the message and were changing their tune.

So I went back to Africa on my second trip with great enthusiasm. The first time I had gone down the center of Africa. This time I did more of the perimeter and stopped in 32 countries. The reasons I spent more time there this time were (1) I love Africa and (2) I was going to see if I was right.

I came away realizing that a lot of the guys in whom I had such confidence turned out to be just as bad and power-corrupt as their predecessors. They were thieves, crooks, and criminals. There are some good stories in Africa, but there are others that I thought would be good but turned out to be the opposite. Uganda turned out to be a good story, but not what I would have hoped. Ethiopia is fine, Angola has got a wonderful future, and Tanzania is a great story.

The wars in Africa are winding down now because nobody supports them anymore. During the Cold War, the CIA and the KGB poured money down there. Nobody wants to be a Communist anymore, and even if someone did, the KGB does not have any money.

So there are several reasons why I like Africa. There are plenty of great stories, but the major theme of Africa is that they have a lot of natural resources and I'm bullish on raw materials. They do not have an automobile industry, they do not make a lot of laptops, but they have a lot of raw materials. If I am right, the raw material bull market will last another 15 years or so, so there are going to be some great fortunes coming out of Africa. A lot of those stories are going to be spectacular but will not last because the bull market in Africa will not last. When the bear market in commodities comes again, Africa will suffer.

It is interesting that you brought up the KGB. The investment community seems worried that Putin is taking Russia back to its KGB roots. Also, you say they do not have any money, but the recent oil move is making Russia a lot of money.

Sure, there is a lot of money being made from oil, but most of it is being sucked out of the country. Putin is getting what he can but he is not wasting it on African dictators. He has better sense than that.

Putin took power in a silent coup. I don't know if you have read about Yeltsin's last days, but he says, "When they came to see me . . ." and talks about the group that removed him from power. So it wasn't just Putin. It was a group takeover and it was silent because they knew if it was public, the West would take all its money out. So he did it very cleverly, but it is definitely the KGB back in control.

When Communism collapsed, the brave and opportunistic guys in places of power grabbed what they could. If you were running the vodka factory and had your wits about you, you said, "This is my vodka factory."

There was nobody to stop you. The workers had always been working for you and suddenly it was your vodka factory. If you were really big-time, you said, "This is my chemical plant" or "This is my oil company" and it was. These were mainly young guys in their 20s or 30s, maybe 40s, and they just grabbed it. Putin is now trying to grab some of it back.

The ones who grabbed it and thought they were smart are suffering now. The ones who knew it was just a one-off opportunity are skipping town and buying football teams in London. They are not sitting around saying, "I was some great genius." They know they were in the right place at the right time, and now they have their money in Liechtenstein or Panama. The ones who thought they were some kind of genius are in jail and are going to lose everything.

You could say a similar thing happened in the United States during the tech bubble. Right-place, right-time guys like Mark Cuban sold out and bought basketball teams.

Exactly. Mark Cuban at least knew he was lucky and got out while he still could. Whether he is going to make it with his basketball team or not, I don't know. A lot of those guys did not have the smarts to get out and lost it all. I know a few guys who sold their companies and put a billion dollars in their pocket and then the companies disappeared. Completely gone! In fact, there was never anything there to begin with, but now they have a billion dollars in their pocket and that is real. It is astonishing to me.

Should I assume you are not positive on Russia, or are you short?

I was short the ruble, but that was back in 1998. I talked about it during the *Barron's* midyear round table in June or July. The first thing I said was, "I am short the ruble and you should be too." I guess you know the rest of that story.

You must have been selling to Soros, a well-known Russia bull.

I will let you get into that. All I know is that somebody bought it.

Russia is still in the process of collapsing. Russia is going to deteriorate into a catastrophe and will continue to break up and disintegrate. Yes, there will be some nice fortunes to be made, but you better have your feet on the ground and be one of those guys who is nimble and quick, because it is outlaw capitalism.

How long do you think the oil/commodity/raw material boom will last?

The bull market will last until sometime between 2014 and 2022. This is not a prediction; history shows that bull markets in commodities last 15 to 23 years. You can look it up.

Do you own commodity country currencies?

I own some. The Canadian dollar is probably the soundest currency in the world right now. I own 12 or 15 currencies around the world. Not that I have great confidence in each of them, because politicians all over the world have learned how to buy votes. Even the Swiss have learned to buy votes, but at least the Swiss franc is less flawed than the U.S. dollar. I own the Australian dollar but mainly because of the commodity component, not because of the politicians who are not doing anybody any good.

Do you own Latin America currencies on the same rationale?

Yes, I own some Peru, Chile, and Brazil. Brazil is going to do a lot better in the next 10 years than it has in the past. The problem is that the Brazilians like to say, "Brazil is the next great country in the world—it always has been and always will be." Ha! So I do not have any great confidence that they are going to get it right, but for the next 10 or 15 years, it is going to be easier for them with the commodity wind at their back.

What are your thoughts on India?

There is a whole section in my book *Hot Commodities* about why I would not put a nickel into India.

Where do you see the world in a decade?

Africa is much more prosperous. China will have had a hard landing but it will be on the rise again. Oil will be at $150 a barrel and they will be drilling for it on the White House lawn. Cotton will be at $4 and they will be planting it in Central Park. The commodities boom will be in great shape.

CHAPTER 12

THE COMMODITY SPECIALIST

Dwight Anderson
Ospraie Management
New York City

At the beginning of our meeting, the big, smiley, affable guy that is Dwight Anderson explained that he was slightly reticent to conduct this interview. The ex–Tiger Management star and commodities/basic industries specialist elaborated that, of late, others have been trying to copy his style. Although Anderson is no longer working for a $20 billion-plus mega-fund, his reputation and stellar returns have the market gunning for any and all information they can get about the reigning king of commodities.

Anderson's clout in the markets has grown rapidly since founding Ospraie Management in 1999, a multibillion-dollar hedge fund complex that seeks to exploit Anderson's talent for analyzing commodity markets. "Dwight is our secret weapon," his head trader and longtime friend, Jason Mraz, confides to me. What he means is that no one can quite do what Anderson does, despite the fact that many are trying. What does Anderson do that is so special? Mountains of primary, bottom-up, traditional supply and demand research. Where some traders take directional positions based on top-down analysis, Anderson starts by drilling down and ripping apart the numbers inside every commodity market and related equity. He flies around the world to gather and compile endless data, building very sophisticated financial models in search of solid risk versus reward opportunities.

What makes him unique is not merely his stellar performance at Ospraie. Before going to work for hedge fund legend Julian Robertson, Anderson actually worked in industry, consulting for various manufacturing companies all over America and becoming a full-time employee of a printing company in upstate New York. While many traders come up through the ranks of investment banks, looking at computer screens in offices, or on Wall Street trading floors, Anderson trained on factory floors before moving to the hedge fund world.

Anderson is a guy everyone seems to like, and it is not hard to imagine him in his school days at Princeton kicking back with friends, joking around, and enjoying life. He exudes this type of demeanor and is known for taking groups of friends and colleagues helicopter skiing in Alaska or running with the bulls in Pamplona. But this demeanor changes abruptly when he begins to talk about his business. He leans forward in his chair and squints intensely, asking me pointedly if I am following his explanation of why commodities are inherently mean reverting or his strategies around his various value plays in basic industry equities. I nod in agreement as Anderson drills down level after level, comfortably explaining in excruciating detail what he does best. He is at home in minutiae, which he synthesizes and then filters for noise. Then he takes a position, which he takes in size—something he claims to have learned from Robertson.

I first met Anderson in March 2003 when he gave a presentation at a Drobny Global Conference that articulated his view that owning U.S. housing stocks would be a winning trade. The audience of top hedge fund managers peppered him with scorn and skepticism. At the time, many were bearish the U.S. economy in the post-bubble world and were particularly bearish real estate. Anderson methodically refuted every single attack against his theme, to the point that one participant finally conceded, "Dwight, you turned me from a massive housing bear to a convinced housing bull—I am going to go out and buy a huge house." Anderson responded, "I am actually bearish high-end real estate. I rent."

In other words, Anderson's view was that the top end of the property market was overvalued but that home builder stocks were cheap. He focused on the low- to medium-end segment of the market, which he believed was poised to consolidate and grow. The home building companies were pushing out the mom-and-pop shops that had dominated the building industry for years, changing the dynamics of the market. When another participant asked how he would hedge this trade, Anderson replied off-the-cuff, "Go short auto stocks."

Home builders, despite having outperformed the S&P for the two prior years, ran up another 50 percent in the two months following his presentation, while auto stocks fell. It was yet another home run for Anderson and the investors in Ospraie.

How did you get into this game?

I'll give you the long answer. I was a history major at Princeton and blindly headed to law school because that's what liberal arts majors did. I woke up in a panic in the middle of my senior year thinking, "I don't want to be a lawyer!"

So I started interviewing for every job out there and got job offers for all kinds of different stuff. I accepted a job offer from a computer software and consulting company called Pansophic which had a division that dealt with manufacturing companies. They really came after me because they needed someone with a different background from all of the engineers they had hired.

This was back in the 1980s when all the talk was about Japan kicking ass and America being hollowed out. It was when *Say Anything* was the big movie where John Cusak says, "I don't want to buy anything processed or sold or process anything." The thought that I could actually do something was attractive to me, so I took the job.

> **SAY ANYTHING**
>
> I don't want to sell anything, buy anything, or process anything as a career. I don't want to sell anything bought or processed, or buy anything sold or processed, or process anything sold, bought, or processed, or repair anything sold, bought, or processed. You know, as a career, I don't want to do that.
>
> *Source:* Lloyd Dobler (played by John Cusack) in *Say Anything* (1989).

At Pansophic I dealt with a fruit company in Eugene, Oregon; a golf club manufacturer in Fort Worth, Texas; a valve company in Little Rock, Arkansas; a truck/trailer company in Parkersburg, West Virginia; a dairy company in New Jersey; a shrimp company outside of Boston; and finally a paper company in upstate New York. The paper company, Amsterdam Printing and Litho, was the largest employer in a town called Amsterdam, New York. It was a very tough town with huge unemployment, illiteracy, and drug use.

I'd been there for a while when I was made an offer to come on full-time as a project manager to help implement our recommended changes. As a consultant, you tend to roll in, offer your advice, and leave. I actually wanted to implement some ideas and see if there was any value. So I took the job and was there for about two years helping to change shop floor operations. While there, I also studied and took the exams for Certification in Production Inventory Management, which is the manufacturing equivalent of the CFA (Chartered Financial Analyst) or CPA (Certified Public Accountant) exams.

It was a great experience dealing with a private, traditional, old company and managing people much older than me in that sort of environment. It was also interesting to me that the company realized the purchase price of something but not the cost. For example, it had a massive employee turnover issue. If someone left after three years because he or she could get 25 cents more an hour, the company would hire another person at the same original wage. It viewed this transaction as costless but, in truth, it just lost three years of hard-earned experience, which has value. There were also the classic management mistakes, such as having parking slots for the officers of the company but not the workers.

After a while, I started thinking, "Is this what I want to do with my life?" I looked at my friends' careers, and the people who liked their lives the most were the proprietary traders. I started spending my spare time in upstate New York reading finance stuff: *Reminiscences of a Stock Operator*, *Bonfire of the Vanities*, *Market Wizards*, *Money Masters*—anything I could get my hands on.

My game plan was to go to business school; get a job in proprietary trading; work 10 years on the sell side developing my knowledge, experience, contacts, and track record; and then make a move to the buy side.

I applied to a bunch of business schools and was offered a fellowship at the University of North Carolina (UNC). It paid full tuition, full expenses, plus a $10,000-a-year stipend. That was too good to pass up. The fellowship was in the name of Julian Robertson because it was funded by one of Tiger Management's early investors for whom Julian had made a fortune. I found out later that one of the guys on the selection board saw my application and said, "Julian would love that manufacturing guy."

So Julian Robertson had his eyes on you even before he met you?

Yeah. I got the Tiger fellowship because of my manufacturing background, but at that point I had no idea who Julian Robertson was. I'd been reading about the guys of the 1980s, at which point he hadn't yet achieved his prominence. But I soon learned.

That fall he got a "Distinguished Alumni" award at UNC and I was asked to pick him and his wife up from the airport. I had to borrow a car to do it and actually had to spread a blanket over the back seat. The owner had just used it to take his dogs out hunting and the seats were all covered with mud. The Robertsons were very gracious about it.

Did you work at Tiger during your summer internship?

No. I worked at Goldman Sachs in the J. Aron division, the commodities and foreign exchange area. I had gone up to New York the previous fall on a UNC finance trip. Although the human resources person at Goldman told my class that UNC grads had almost no chance of getting a summer internship, I ran into a friend from Princeton who was working there and actually got offered an internship that same day.

Apparently, that same morning, Robert Rubin, co-head of Goldman at the time, had rounded up all the J. Aron partners and said, "Look at you— you are a bunch of old men. You need to hire people out of business school and start morphing into the Goldman Sachs culture. Bring yourselves into the modern world."

As I am hanging out with my Princeton buddy, one of the partners asks, "Who the hell are you?"

My friend says, "A friend of ours who is on a business school trip visiting investment banks."

The partner goes, "Awesome. You got a job. Done!"

It was the easiest Goldman Sachs interview ever and a huge relief to have my summer internship nailed so quickly. The rest of my first year at business school became a lot more relaxed.

J. Aron had never had a summer associate so they didn't really know what to do with me. I set up my own rotation program, going to all the different commodity and foreign exchange desks. I also sat in on the fixed income and equities training programs if they were doing something interesting.

It was the summer of 1993. I was on the gold desk when gold got ramped up to $410 by Soros and Sir James Goldsmith, and on the FX desk when a confrontation was forced between Germany and France, breaking the control levels on the European Exchange Rate Mechanism (ERM). It was a fun summer and I learned a lot.

I ended up spending the largest chunk of my time on the coffee, cocoa, and sugar desk. They had me build a financial model that would automatically show whether it was possible to arbitrage between the exchanges in London and New York. The London contract was Ivory Coast cocoa priced in pounds while the New York contract was Indonesian cocoa priced in U.S. dollars. I had to calculate all the costs: insurance, freight, warehousing, and so on. It was ideal because I had everything I needed to create a real commodity market. There were different grades, various costs, and different currencies, so it was possible to create the whole curve. I was also given a small dollar amount to prop trade cocoa as long as I closed out my positions at the end of the day.

At the end of the summer I was made a nice offer to join the cocoa desk. I appreciated it, but it was just too specific—I didn't want to just do cocoa. I was offered another job at Goldman to prop trade equities as well, but the guy who made the offer left soon after to start a hedge fund.

Here's one funny story from my interviews with Goldman equities. After the guy who made the offer left, I was brought up to New York to have lunch with the head of equities to discuss other jobs. He took me out for sushi and I'd never used chopsticks before. I had a piece of sushi precariously balanced between my chopsticks and proceeded to drop it from a good height right into the soy sauce. The soy sauce splashed all over him, ruining his shirt and tie. He was literally covered in soy sauce, and this was the head of equities at Goldman! All attempts to keep me ended precipitously after that.

I had a few other offers, including one on the night desk at Tiger, but I went to JP Morgan to trade in their derivatives and commodities area. I joined the energy trading group and was there for a couple of weeks, going through the training program, when I got a call from Julian, asking me to join him for breakfast.

I thought it would just be a friendly "Welcome to New York, how you doing?" breakfast, but I got grilled by a bunch of people from Tiger. They were grilling me about cocoa: how I think about it, what the market's going to do, and so on. I thought I got roasted, but by the time I got back to my desk, there was already another message inviting me to another breakfast.

Julian had started trading commodities in 1993 with good performance and wanted to expand this area because he was excited by it and it fit the Tiger investing style. What must have happened is that he opened his Rolodex, flipped to commodities, and it was empty except for me.

Had you developed your thought processes and trading theories in commodities yet or were you still pretty green?

There's no question I was green, and I had strong opinions but I didn't know anything—I shouldn't have had strong opinions. When I look back now at those opinions and how superficial my knowledge and experience were, I'm scared witless by some things I said and did.

So I had another breakfast with Julian and team and another grilling. At this point I knew they were interviewing me. I was ecstatic at the prospect of being able to skip 10 years of my plan and go directly to the buy side at a place like Tiger. It was exactly what I wanted to do.

I joined Tiger in October of 1994 and my direct report left soon thereafter. Julian said, "Dwight, I like how things are going so far, so we'll have you run the commodity group. If you do well, you stay, and if you do poorly, you go." As of January 1995 I was running commodities for Tiger, and I'd only been in New York for five months!

How big was Tiger at that point and how big was the commodity allocation?

Tiger had a little over $4 billion in assets. The commodity allocation was either nothing or billions because it was almost all done over-the-counter (OTC), which didn't require margin.

What do you hear from Robertson in the back of your mind today?

Julian was a great coach. He focused on the fundamentals and never cared about technicals. He only asked, "What are the economics here?" He believed that prices eventually have to go to the economics.

Julian would always ask, "Are we right in this situation? If so, we should be bigger. It doesn't matter that prices moved against us." He just focused on the conclusions and then had the conviction they were right. Julian always wanted to get to a really simple conclusion. It might be months of work and data to prove and support that conclusion, but it had to be simple.

A good example of that would be palladium, where we lost money being long for three years in a row in the mid-1990s. But we had done an enormous amount of primary research and knew we were right, so we held on. We attended conferences, surveyed users, and met with suppliers in order to amass information. I even went to mines in Siberia and South Africa to check on supply.

Our sole focus remained, "Are we right that there is a deficit?" In a six-million-ounce production market, the deficit of supply was over two million ounces and growing dramatically. We figured prices could more than double before substitution would occur. Julian was great through those years. He kept saying, "Are you sure your numbers are right? You're sure this is in deficit? If so, then we should be bigger."

You went all the way to Siberia to answer that question?

Yep. Sixty percent of the world's production of palladium comes from a big set of mines in Norilsk, Siberia. A couple of months after I'd gotten to Tiger, Julian sent me to visit them.

Welcome to Tiger, off to Siberia you go?

Yeah, and not only that, it was in the wintertime and this was north of the Arctic circle, not southern Siberia!

What we found and what eventually played out was that the Russians got into an internal greed struggle. Between Norilsk, the export company, the ministry of finance, and the central bank, a massive turf war ensued over control of the sales of palladium and platinum externally. No one wanted to let the others sell palladium externally because each worried it would prevent them from selling, so all action stopped. The price of palladium eventually exploded from $120 per ounce to over $1,000 per ounce. (*See Figure 12.1.*)

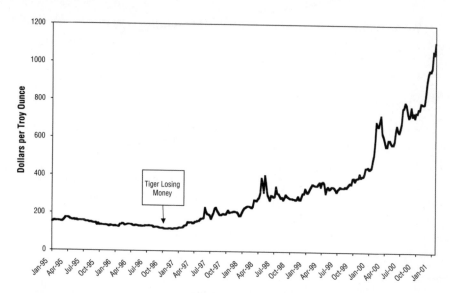

FIGURE 12.1   Palladium, 1995–2001
Source: Bloomberg.

Do you find yourself treating your analysts in the same manner that Robertson treated you?

Julian had a number of catchphrases. It was either, "This is the best idea I've ever seen" or "This is the dumbest idea I've ever heard." I was constantly setting new records for the dumbest idea he'd ever heard. And he hated the expression, "The market is telling me." He'd always reply, "The market isn't telling you anything—how come it's never talked to me?"

Julian just had this simple focus on fundamentals that is embedded in my approach. His philosophy on fundamentals was, "It's trading here now but that can't go on forever. It has to reprice, so I'm going to be there and I'm going to be there in size."

I find myself annoying my analysts all the time, saying, "Just give me the economics, the numbers, the math on this. I don't want to hear random chatter or talk of rumors or what's going on in the market." I don't care about the day-to-day. I care about the economics. If we have the economics correct, we're going to be right and we're going to get paid.

What's the limit to that philosophy? There is a limit, right?

Yes. The problem is sizing and concentration. At Tiger, I never had to worry about my positions being too big. In fact, the key at Tiger was to manage internal expectations because Julian would always take positions up to whatever size he was told was the maximum possible. Julian used to ask, "How much can I lose on that?" And often his reply was, "Okay, then we're not big enough because I'd be willing to lose twice that, so increase the position."

Julian would size it based on how much his analyst thought could be lost, which was a huge amount of trust. In stocks, Julian had enough experience to have a great filter, but in commodities and macro, because he didn't have 40 years of experience, he relied more on his analysts to guide him.

At Ospraie we do it from position size and ask, "How much money am I willing to risk? How much could I lose?" We also use a subjective limit of "If this happens, we get out." We manage all of our position sizes individually, then aggregate them based on worst-case moves. We look at value at risk (VAR), but if there's a very high VAR I know I have much larger risk on because VAR is dampening.

In a concentrated portfolio, like a lot of commodities portfolios, I think it's incredibly dangerous to manage off a VAR number. If you have a thousand traders, like a Goldman Sachs, a VAR calculation can make sense because you have enough diversification to give you something statistically significant.

VAR assumes that there is some positive/negative correlation between commodities. If I am long $100 of aluminum and short $100 of copper, and copper is more volatile, it would show me that I have a net risk of, say, $20 from the copper, choosing an arbitrary dollar amount. Here, we would say we have $200 dollars at risk.

Take a look at copper during the stock market crash of 1987. You can see huge daily swings up and down over a couple of days. If you weren't managing off a max loss there, somewhere during the course of that week, you would have blown up. (*See Figure 12.2.*)

Do you have a preference for running long or short positions?

I don't care. I am not biased either way. I only focus on the economics.

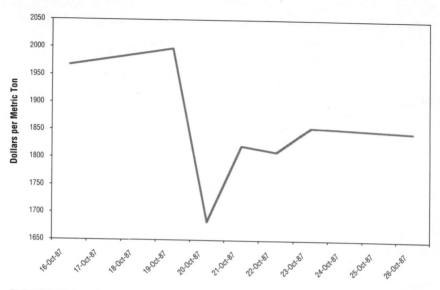

FIGURE 12.2   Copper, October 1987
Source: Bloomberg.

Besides commodities and basic industry equities, is there anything else that you trade?

We will trade bonds if they offer a high enough, equity-like return. We would never trade government bonds but we do look at the corporate debt of industries we know, such as a distressed bond or high yield credit in an energy company.

We're not doing that much in this space right now because there's not much there. Junk spreads have collapsed so it's difficult to get paid for the risk assumed. Also, our industries have done so well over the past two years that there aren't that many distressed people out there at the moment.

Another risk control you seem to have implemented is managing your asset base. Is that another lesson you took away from your experience at Tiger?

I'd come out of an environment where we had arguably gotten too big and I didn't want to repeat the same mistake. As Tiger got to be upwards of $25 billion, positions had to be massive to be meaningful. For example, $250 million was only 1 percent of the fund. As the basic industries guy, due to liquidity constraints, the entire universe of stocks that I could invest in had collapsed to about 20 names.

When we sat down with prospective investors in Ospraie in 1999 and 2000, we decided, given our style, liquidity constraints, and the size of our analyst team, we would close at $750 million and could end up taking assets up to $2 billion. We actually ended up closing at $550 million and have only taken strategic investors since then. We are now at $2 billion and I think we could take more.

Why do you think you can manage more capital now?

For one, the dollar is weaker. In simple terms, I could ramp up my assets by the amount the dollar has weakened without affecting our style. Also, because the world is much more profitable, market capitalizations are bigger. Take a look at BHP Billiton. It has a market cap of about $80 billion and it's just one mining/oil company. With assets under management of $2 billion, I could lever up two times and have only one position on of 5 percent of just that company. Then you add in ExxonMobil, which has a $400 billion market cap. Newmont Mining trades $200 million a day and is a $25 billion company. You get my point.

In commodities, take a look at something like crude oil. When we started, oil was $15 to $18. Today, it's more than double that, so I can manage twice the capital just from that. When your inventory doubles, you need twice as much capital to carry it.

In the beginning, we were actually too conservative about what we thought our capacity could be. We do commodities, home builders, mining, energy, tankers, and oil service, and use the exact same investment discipline methodology across all these comparable industries. There's actually much more capacity out there than I had originally thought.

Did you leave Tiger because of the asset base and its effect on your area?

I wasn't enjoying it as much, partly because my investment universe had collapsed. Also, as the firm grew, the culture changed into that of a less entrepreneurial operation. A couple of the analysts were leaving Tiger to form Viking, and they approached me to do basic industry equities and a separate commodity fund that would be optional for investors. That was the catalyst to start thinking about leaving.

After four and a half years, I figured I'd given Julian the time I owed him. I wanted to go off and start my own fund, but I also wanted to be able to focus on investment management and minimize as much of the business management issues as possible. The economics of hedge funds are so robust that my plan was to maximize the probability of succeeding by teaming up with an established firm and giving up some of the short-term gains.

I spoke with Moore, SAC, and Tudor about running money for them in a new vehicle and all three made bids. Tudor made the lowest payout offer with the least amount of capital, but didn't require any long-term owner-ship of the fund, so we went with them.

What was it like working at Tudor Investment Corp.?

It was a good partnership. The operations people were top-notch. It was a phenomenal support organization but on the investment side, we were on our own. Paul Tudor Jones is a great guy and a phenomenal trader, but our investing styles are just so different that we had very little interaction. We trade off fundamentals and are very long duration while Paul is much shorter duration. He manages off technicals and is one of the best risk managers out there. He cuts his losses better than anyone I know.

When you started, were you nervous being on your own and having your own P&L for the first time?

I was completely nervous. You don't fully know what you're doing until you do it, and I was very worried I was not going to be good at it. I had a friend who'd been working at JP Morgan for 10 years who had a pregnant wife and a new home—he quit his job to come work for me. I had friends and peers who entrusted me with their money. I sat here at my desk and thought, "Holy cow, what are these people thinking?" It was a very ner-vous time period.

I questioned if I was a good analyst but a bad portfolio manager. I didn't know, and I was worried. Everyone at Tiger besides Julian was really just an analyst—Julian was the only portfolio manager. Each analyst had a nomi-nal P&L tied to his name, but that represented the trade ideas that Julian allowed to go into the portfolio. That was a good thing, because I had all sorts of bad ideas that didn't make it into the portfolio, but it wasn't a true representation of my portfolio management style.

Also, the size and length of time that positions stayed in the portfolio were at best a confrontational negotiation with Julian. Sometimes he'd want to be much bigger or the analyst would want to be bigger and there would be back-and-forth to work on that. So it was P&L, but I was an analyst, not a portfolio manager. As an analyst at Tiger, you just had to be right, but you didn't have to be right today.

Given the increased interest in commodities today, your timing for launching a commodities and basic industries fund in 1999 seems quite fortuitous.

Well, we had an equity bear market right after the equity bubble collapse of 2000. The economy was weak and copper, steel, and other base metals didn't hit their lows until October or November 2001. We actually started two or more years before the bottom in commodities. We made money the first two years by running shorts in commodities and equities.

The reason I started the fund at that time, though, was not prescient market-timing but personal timing. And the reason we do basic industries and commodities is because it's what we know. It's where we have some competitive advantage from the experience, information, and resources we've built up.

It was definitely countertrend setting up a hedge fund at that time, though. My mom was nervous when I left JP Morgan for Tiger because she had heard of JP Morgan but not a "stockbroker" named Tiger. Likewise, she was nervous when I was leaving Tiger to start my own "stockbroker."

MOM: "How much do you think you can make?"

ANDERSON: "We hope we can make 25 to 30 percent a year."

MOM: "People will give you money if that's all you're planning on making?"

This was 1999, remember. The NASDAQ was putting up 50 to 100 percent years and a lot of people's return expectations had just exploded. We were lucky to have a number of experienced investors who had seen multiple cycles. They understood that delivering a 25 percent return over multiple years was actually a very competitive return.

We tell our investors, "We're here to give you a competitive risk-adjusted return, whether commodities are going up or going down." Our portfolio doesn't correlate on a daily, weekly, or monthly basis to either equity indexes or commodity indexes because we're both long and short in both commodities and equities. We want to be judged by the absolute return, not anything relative.

How did the launch of Ospraie go?

We started during the fourth quarter of 1999 with only Tudor's capital. The idea was to start up with a smaller dollar amount and no external money. Tudor understands risk, and we wanted to be prudent by making sure the systems, risk reports, and everything else was working properly without endangering external investors' money.

Our first week we had a report that showed a purchase of a million shares of Alcoa, a $35 stock at the time. We had decided to not have more than 5 percent in any one stock, yet my report showed a $35 million position in Alcoa, which was well over our limit. It turned out to be just a decimal error, so it was okay, but it proved wise to start off slow.

For the fourth quarter in 1999 we returned about 9 percent on the Tudor money, and then we started taking outside investor capital on February 1, 2000. We started off with a bang by losing 4.57 percent during our first month.

We had told people that there's a cost of putting money to work. People often think that you can trade things at the prices you see on the screens. What they miss are all kinds of costs related to first putting capital to work. There is breakage, commissions, and the expense of entering a position by moving the market while putting it on. We lost 1 percent on our first day as we tried to put all of our money to work right away. That was a tough opening gambit.

What was going through your head after your first month managing client money where you lost almost 5 percent?

It was stressful, but we had told Tudor and other investors that we had no idea if we could make money in any one month, let alone a week, a day, or even a quarter. But we did know that over a one- to two-year time period we should be able to make money. That's the duration for our investments and that's what we focus on.

There was also the benefit of youth, inexperience, and just plain ignorance. We asked the same question we asked at Tiger: "Are we right?" and we thought we were. We weren't too big so we stuck with our positions. As an epilogue, in December of our first year, thankfully or luckily, we made 18.5 percent to finish our first full year up 23 percent.

How did you start off your second year?

We came out of the gate down 8.5 percent and I could have sworn it was much worse. We lost money on all four of our largest positions and I think we only had three profitable days in the month. We didn't have any really bad days, we just lost a little bit of money every day.

We were long energy stocks, some oil service names, some exploration and producers (E&Ps), and some oil and gas companies. We were short copper, the calendar strip for 2002 natural gas, and we were long corn.

These were noncorrelated positions. If anything, long E&P service companies and short forward natural gas should hedge each other. It's illogical to lose money on both positions. But in any one month, anything can happen—that's why we disregard correlations. Correlations can really get separated, especially between equities and commodities.

So again, right out of the gate, we were down 8.5 percent. We lost money in everything. Another epilogue, we made 27 percent that year.

Do you lock up your investors' capital for a couple of years for their own benefit so as to match your investment duration?

We lock up capital for everyone's benefit, including the other investors'. The withdrawal of investor capital can sometimes be debilitating and costly. At Tiger we had investors who would trade the funds, essentially taking money in and out on a monthly basis. We had to grow and shrink the portfolio regularly. As I said, there's a cost to putting money to work, and that's especially true when people are redeeming and you are in a drawdown.

You have said that 90 percent of your time is figuring out what you're doing wrong. Do you think insecurity helps drive your investment process?

Yes, very much so. I'm constantly worried that I'm wrong and I'm constantly asking, "What am I missing?" I like to call it "insecure confidence." Because we react to fundamentals and not price, large price moves against us in an individual position without a change in the fundamentals can be painful, but as long as there is not a change in the fundamentals, we are not worried. We try to invest in things that are microeconomically inevitable.

What we do is not the vision of your classic global macro guy. We come to our decisions after a tremendous amount of work. It takes multiple financial models, a lot of primary research, and a lot of contacts built up over the years to get the information necessary to reach our investment conclusions.

How has global macro changed since when you started?

There are probably more players in the macro space today, but what we do hasn't changed. We are global micro, not global macro. What we do is pure Microeconomics 101: supply and demand, identifying which companies are low cost, which have cash, and so on. We are constantly striving to understand the changes in our industries: how the composition of demand is changing, how the cost curve is changing, what currencies are doing to change the cost curve, and who the competitive players are.

We want to make sure that our thesis and assumptions are so robust that we can withstand macroeconomic assumptions that are aggressively forecast against us. When we're short, we assume great growth, and when we're long, we assume very low growth. Conservative but realistic macro assumptions.

In other words, when a classic macro guy really likes the world economy and buys base metals, he is assuming that the economy is going to be stronger than everyone expects and that base metals should benefit from that. When we buy a base metal, we assume that the economy is going to be worse than people expect, but despite this, the fundamentals are robust enough that prices will still go up. This way, if we actually get a strong economy, it's an extra bonus.

Was Tiger global micro?

Tiger allowed me to operate that way, but Julian would superimpose his macro view on what we were doing. He would say something like, "If you think copper is a good short even with good economic growth and I think the world's going to hell and Asia is going to implode, we should be short five times your amount." He would look at trades as we did and then superimpose his macro views on our micro thesis.

Is there anything else of note that you learned from Robertson?

One thing that Julian did very well, which we do poorly, is pay up when the fundamentals start to develop as anticipated. A trade he used to like to talk about was Citibank in 1990 and 1991. He bought it at 10 and it went to 20. When one of his analysts wanted to sell the position, he doubled it instead, because he felt it was cheaper at 20 then than it was at 10. When he first bought it, there were real estate problems that were resolved by the time it got to 20, so it was clear that Citi wasn't going bankrupt. It ended up going to 100, split adjusted.

In commodities, it is tough to get used to paying up because you have mean reversion versus huge open-ended trends. When I say mean reversion, I am saying that margins revert to the mean. People often get it wrong and think it's price that reverts to the mean, but that is not the case in commodities. It is margins that revert to the mean, so paying up is something you need to do.

Adding to a position that is going your way has always been a tough one for fundamental discretionary traders but a hallmark of systematic black box Commodity Trading Advisors (CTAs). Has the huge increase in capital allocated to CTAs (see **Figure 12.3**) *forced you to change your style?*

It's changed a little bit in the way we size our positions.

Because all these CTAs tend to be shorter duration, their money flows can change the short-term volatility. They can cause dislocations and inef-

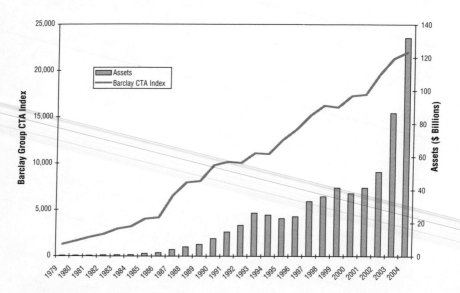

FIGURE 12.3   Barclay Group CTA Index and CTA Assets under Management, 1979–2004
Reprinted courtesy of Sol Waksman and The Barclay Group.

ficiencies in the market as a result of large speculative positions one way or another. They can dramatically change the short-term volatility but, over any three-month time period, they tend to have bought and sold with zero net effect on the market.

Normal investors are trained to ask about leverage as opposed to volatility. Volatility is what one should really look at—risk based on volatility. Being long $100 million of gold with a volatility of 8 to 16 percent is dramatically different from being long $100 million of natural gas with a volatility of 35 to 135 percent.

With more money being managed by CTAs, there is more short-term volatility. We've adjusted by running slightly smaller positions, but we have more positions more often. It has brought down our average duration as well because CTAs move commodities to price points that are interesting to us more often.

To stay on top of ever-changing market conditions, do you monitor your competitors?

We pay attention to the composition of the market. We don't look at the moving averages or technicals except to understand when there might be a huge position out there or to figure out what price level would trigger an exodus by short-term players. In some instances, we adjust our position size down if we think it is a crowded position, especially if it is crowded by CTAs. We will still be involved, but not in the same size that we would have been had the CTAs not been involved.

If changes in market conditions do not dramatically alter what you do, then what is the key to longevity?

Everyone is taught lessons over time, expensive lessons. The key is to learn from them and reduce mistakes.

Can you discuss some of the expensive lessons that you learned over the course of your career?

I have two good ones. The first one happened in my personal account. At Tiger, we were allowed to trade our personal accounts as long as they were in areas outside of our own. As a value investor, I was attracted like a moth to a flame by the apparent high multiples and valuations of tech stocks in the late 1990s. I got short a number of the higher profile names such as the Amazons, Yahoo!s, and eBays of the world, but especially Amazon.

Were you influenced by Robertson's negative tech stock view?

Tiger did not have any material short tech positions in the portfolio. Julian was known to be a nonbeliever, but he wasn't materially short. He just didn't get it, so Tiger wasn't involved.

To be honest, it was my own mistake, but it's a comparable mind-set and I learned the mind-set from Julian. So I shorted a bunch of tech stocks and went off on a research trip to South America to visit aluminum and nickel mines. A couple of days later, Henry Blodgett came out with his famous Amazon price target of $400 that sent all of the tech stocks flying. Amazon had been trading at $240 and immediately jumped to $290 after Blodgett's call. Soon thereafter it went as high as $600. I was in Colombia at the time and got a call in my hotel room from my assistant informing me that I had received a margin call. I did not think it was possible and asked my assistant to verify it. Not only had I received a margin call on my short position, but to add insult to injury, I had also sold a bunch of calls on Amazon with strikes way out-of-the-money. The options were now in-the-money, exacerbating the margin call.

It was a traumatic lesson in learning how to manage a portfolio—in this case my personal net worth, which immediately went down by 20 percent—but it was also a great lesson about the timing of a view. You can be right, but your timing can be totally wrong.

The most expensive lesson we have had at Ospraie was when we bought into a private, high-cost refining and marketing company. There is a business adage that says it makes sense to open a gas station at an intersection. Similarly, in the refinery world, it helps to have the biggest refinery, but our investment was in the smallest. We had invested in the gas station in the middle of the street, not at the intersection. To make matters worse, our refinery was across the tracks from a school. Any emissions flowed right into the school, creating legal and political risk.

We invested in this refinery because the company was buying another huge, high-quality refinery that was being divested from ExxonMobil after its merger. They didn't have the capital so we put up the money to allow them to buy the refinery. We now had one good asset and one bad asset, plus a bad balance sheet, poor financial management, and terrible operations management.

We bought shares at 128 and sold them at 95. It was a great sale, actually, because it ended up getting restructured and the bondholders got it. What I learned was that you can't buy a high-cost asset cheap enough. We paid five cents on the dollar and sold it for four. When you have a high-cost asset, you have to get the price and the timing right. After that experience, we will only invest in low-cost companies because we don't have to get the timing right.

Another thing I learned is that management has to have at least mediocre competence, from operations, costs, and shareholder returns perspectives. Because our industries have huge cash flows, it's very important how management handles the cash. Do they reinvest those cash flows or buy a shiny new toy that interests their engineers or do they focus on generating the best returns for their shareholders? A management that focuses on what is best for their shareholders is mandatory.

When you meet management at manufacturing companies, are they surprised by your knowledge of their operations and industry, given that they are probably expecting you to be Mr. Wall Street hedge fund guy?

They are surprised, but in a good way. It allows a more meaningful relationship to develop, because there is mutual respect. It opens up communication and allows a deeper conversation about business, strategy, and industry, such that a real dialogue can develop. Ideally the relationship develops over time, enabling opinions to come out about their industry, other companies, or other management teams.

With whom do you spend the majority of your time talking?

We get the best information from the people in the industry. They know their economics, they know their businesses, and they know what's going on. It is extremely important to visit a plant to see how it's run or visit a company at its headquarters to get a sense of its culture.

There is a dramatic difference in the knowledge and information picked up on the ground. That's why in the past 12 months, my people have been to Africa, Australia, Mongolia, Siberia, Brazil, Mexico, Argentina, and other countries, while I personally have been to Vietnam, Hong Kong, Korea, China, Japan, Australia, Brazil, and a few places I am probably forgetting.

So I get the most value from talking to the people in the different industries we invest in. After that, whether it's industry-specific consultants, sell-side analysts, salespeople, whoever, we are here to plagiarize the best ideas we can and we'll take them from any source.

Is traveling a critical requirement for what you do?

Spending time on the ground is very important. For example, we spend a decent amount of time in China even though we rarely invest there directly. China has huge impact on our different industries. Whether it's property law, corporate governance, or real honest, accurate accounting, we have not yet gotten to a conviction level that justifies material investments in China. But we do a huge amount of research and spend a lot of time there because of its effect outside of China.

At what point will you stop visiting Siberia, China, or wherever because you can send someone else and can't be bothered to go yourself?

I love the intellectual challenge of what I do. I am in a seat where almost everyone in the world is incented to teach me, whether it is a company, because it might want us to invest, or sell-side research staff, because it wants us to buy shares through its firm. I am constantly learning. The economics of a hedge fund are such that I can have the best research services in the world—all these people and experts who focus on our industries send us research and teach us.

I went into proprietary trading to assemble information into a coherent thesis and test it. I will always do that, whether it's with Ospraie or my own personal account. That learning process is what's fun, exciting, and challenging.

Although this is an incredibly rewarding job in terms of the intellectual satisfaction, it is also very stressful. Lately it hasn't been as much fun as it used to be. When I worked at Tiger, I could take the afternoon off to go golfing because it was Julian's firm, not mine. Now, as the head portfolio manager, I create much more of an example for others.

The stress of having other people's livelihoods and life savings entrusted to you is something that is constantly worrying, as well. I met people at Tiger who had invested with Julian in the early days and I got to see how he was able to change their lives for the better. I have investors who would see a real difference in their lives if we failed them. That responsibility means a lot to me.

How valuable is your network and your strategic investors? If I put you in a room with no phones and just screens with price action, how much would you be handicapped?

In the very short term, I could still do it because of the residual of my 15 years of experience, but that would quickly decline. Somewhere between 6 and 24 months, I'd be materially handicapped. Keeping abreast of what's going on in the industry in terms of the economics, the changes in demand, and everything else is mandatory. This job requires constant reinvestment and that reinvestment takes time.

If you had to put on just one trade for the next five years and drop out, what would it be?

We'd be long forward energy. Energy is on the cusp of losing its ability to grow production. Therefore, demand has to be priced out of the market. That price is multiples of where we are today, so prices could double or triple.

I'm not saying production is going to fall off or the world is going to run out of energy. If production flatlines, demand can't grow. You've seen it happen in natural gas in North America. You're going to see that happen in crude oil. Crude oil and natural gas are completely tied. With the marginal incremental costs of carry going up, you get rising oil service cost. Each marginal extra calorie of energy is costing more and more.

Look at some statistics. The average natural gas field in North America is 30 percent smaller than it was 10 years ago. Even if costs are the same, it's spread over 30 percent fewer barrels. Also, because of net present value, the cash flows you get in the beginning matter the most and they are plummeting.

So you've got higher decline rates, smaller fuel sources, and usually they are located in more difficult areas, deeper or farther offshore, and therefore more expensive to get to. That is somewhat balanced by improvements in productivity from oil service technology and better methods. But the combination of all of these factors means you have rising capital costs. The result is an overall slowing to flattening out of production growth for energy.

What would change your thesis? What's the risk to the trade?

One problem with your parameters is that I can't exit the trade for five years, so there is event risk along the way. Say, for example, Saudi Arabia blows up via a revolution. That would have a significant effect on the world energy markets.

It would help my trade if it happened close to the end of the five-year time frame. But if it happened the day after I put it on, oil could go to, say, $100 and then there would be time for supply and demand to adjust. Demand would get killed while alternative energy sources would be incentivized to develop and come to market.

So by the time five years rolls around, there will be a balanced market again. In the meantime, there will have been $100 crude; a recession; massive investment in conservational, alternative energy; and a fall in the demand for crude oil. Long-dated energy contracts could actually sell off. There's the old saying, "The cure for high oil prices is higher oil prices."

It seems that in order to properly trade the commodity markets, one really needs a deep understanding of the internal dynamics and cost structures of each micro commodity market.

Yep. I often find it amazing how people trade things that they really have no clue about. When I worked on the energy desk after business school, a sheet called *The Oil Daily* had a headline one day that read, "Shell to Spud New Well." I asked the other traders what *spud* meant and no one on the entire desk could answer. These guys had been trading oil for years and

MASLOW'S HIERARCHY OF NEEDS

Maslow's Hierarchy of Needs is a theory proposed by Abraham Maslow in his 1943 paper entitled "A Theory of Human Motivation." The hierarchy can be depicted as a pyramid consisting of five levels: The four lower levels are grouped together as "deficiency needs," while the top level is referred to as "being needs." The basic concept is that the higher needs in the hierarchy only come into focus once all the preceding needs (lower down in the pyramid) are mainly or entirely satisfied. The highest or "being" needs are also referred to as self-actualization, a description that Maslow applied to humans' instinctual need to make the most of their innate or unique abilities. In other words, he tried to capture the idea that at some level painters are driven to paint, writers to write, (traders to trade) and so forth. (*See Figure 12.4.*)

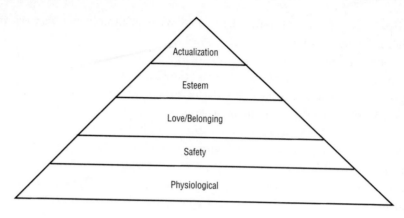

FIGURE 12.4   Maslow's Hierarchy of Needs

years and the firm was trading tens of millions of dollars of oil every single day. I couldn't believe it.

Besides energy, what else do you see as the major trends in your world over the next 5 to 10 years?

We are watching the Asian miracle. The largest populations in the world are getting to an economic level where the gross domestic product (GDP) per capita is moving into the materials-intensive phase of economic growth. When a country first gets household income or per capita GDP to around $3,000, it starts to move up on Maslow's Hierarchy of Needs pyramid.

People first worry about food, warmth, shelter, and then move on to the higher-quality stuff. In Asia, we are seeing formerly rural, agrarian populations with incredibly low consumption and income levels starting to move up the economic chain. When people move out of the subsistence level to a more self-sustaining level, it leads to an explosion in the consumption of raw materials.

What is happening in China and Asia, where people are trying to improve themselves and the lives of their children, is a great thing. How the world handles this from a pollution and global warming perspective is another story. Asia largely uses coal for heat because it is very cheap and available, but coal is the worst commodity for the environment. There's a cost to be environmentally clean.

There will be massive ripple effects on a number of our industries as these masses of people make marginal changes in their lives. There are going to be massive booms and busts with huge drains on the world's natural resources. This is going to be one of the major drivers in many of the world's markets going forward. We saw the first phase of this move over the past two years in the commodity markets and we're going to have a couple more moves like this over the next decade.

Look at Vietnam as a good example. Milk consumption is growing 30 percent per year there. Dairy is a growth industry in the first phase of economic growth because people start drinking pasteurized milk and their diet changes. The next move from dairy is to electricity, TVs, consumer appliances, then cars, and so on. You can watch the cycle unfold in every emerging market.

Bigger picture, the global growth rate is going to be slowing, but there needs to be a distinction between the short-term and long-term. Five years is long-term, but I actually don't think people have the ability to see well beyond two years. Too many things change.

There are two main drivers for world growth right now: the U.S. consumer and the industrial and capital investment side of Asia. Asia and China's growth rate has to slow in order to satisfy their internal resource needs. The U.S. consumer also has to slow. We are cautious as to whether this can be done smoothly and we worry about how it will unfold in the medium term, which we consider to be 6 to 24 months.

I also worry about event risk in the Middle East because there isn't enough spare capacity in oil. The world cannot afford to lose any refineries for a material time period. If one of them goes, we'll see $100 crude very quickly.

Meanwhile, I spend most of my time worrying about what's going on with supply and demand in our individual industries. As I have explained, we tend to make our macroeconomic assumptions against us, so we have some cushion on that front.

What worries you about the hedge fund industry?

I'm not worried because there will always be alpha for someone with vision, someone who can employ the data points and details to create and substantiate that vision in order to have a better probability of being right.

Here at Ospraie, our style requires a lot of work to stay on top because there is a massive amount of information to assimilate. There will come a time when I will need to transfer that workload over to other people who don't have a lot of kids or do have a high energy level or whatever else. It means building a culture where we can attract, train, and retain the best so that the baton can be handed over to them. It is part of my job to position the organization for this time.

If I retire and the firm is still flourishing, the people I'm with are flourishing, and I have had a positive impact on my family, friends, community, and everyone around me, I will consider that to have been a good life. That is success. I want to see the people that I am with doing well and the people whose money I have been entrusted with doing well. Then I will have lived up to my responsibility and will have created an environment that will keep going. But you don't know until the end.

What do you look for when hiring?

We look for intelligence first and foremost. We don't need brilliance but a minimum amount of intelligence is required. We look for a combination of work ethic, pride, ability, passion, and interest. This is something that's going to take a tremendous amount of time and if you don't enjoy what you're doing, it's tough to be good at it. Communication skills and interpersonal skills are huge because we are constantly trying to assemble information from varied sources. I find that the toughest quality to gauge during an interview is judgment and common sense, which is extremely important in markets.

One of my favorite headlines in the commodity section of the *Wall Street Journal* was "Corn Prices Plummet on Rumors of Chinese Buying." What probably happened was a reporter had a deadline so he called some trader and they quickly rattled off, "Rumors of Chinese buying caused prices to fall, gotta hop." We all know that if the Chinese were buying, prices should go up, but the poor guy didn't stop to think that his headline drew an illogical connection. It's not really surprising though, given that the commodities section has been a neglected area of late.

What's the funniest thing that's happened since you've been on your own at Ospraie?

We were just starting up in 1999 with Tudor and I was over in London at the annual metal producers get-together. I am walking back to my hotel from a late dinner, and I see this guy in an orange shirt stumbling around on the street. He is obviously completely loaded, so I go to help him out.

ANDERSON: "Excuse me, sir, can I help you?"

ORANGE SHIRT GUY: "Oh, you're an American? I'm looking for the entrance of the hotel."

ANDERSON: "Well, you just come around here."

ORANGE SHIRT GUY: "Oh, thank you so much. What do you do?"

ANDERSON: "I'm starting up a hedge fund."

ORANGE SHIRT GUY: "Well, you've helped me out so now I want to help you out. I work for Soros and I've got something to tell you. Don't be long gold next week. We're going to do something. Just don't be long gold. It's the only advice I can give you."

This was right when Ashanti was blowing up and gold had moved from $250 to $325. We were long some gold at the time, so I was thinking that this guy was saving our skin. I was totally expecting that Soros was going to come into the gold market the following week and dump a whole bunch. I covered our long position as soon as I could and waited.

Here I was two weeks after the inception of my new fund and I was still very nervous. I had a long gold position and a drunk guy who supposedly works for the biggest macro hedge fund in the world telling me not to be long gold. I was thinking that a good deed was getting rewarded, that this was the way life was supposed to work.

Nothing happened. To make matters worse, I had told my partners that the reason we covered our long gold position was the orange shirt guy. Meanwhile gold just continued to go up.

I learned a great lesson, which is to ignore tips and random rumors. It was the last time I did such a thing and was such a perfect way to learn a lesson. To this day, we still laugh about the man in the orange shirt. I would love to find that guy. Maybe this interview will help me find him. Mr. Orange Shirt from Soros—please get in touch with me!

CHAPTER 13

THE STOCK OPERATOR

Scott Bessent
Bessent Capital
New York City

Scott Bessent has trained under some of the best-known traders, including George Soros, Stanley Druckenmiller, Nick Roditi, Jim Rogers, and Jim Chanos. He has traded through some seminal periods in the evolution of global markets and the hedge fund business, perhaps most notably the transition from a few dominating mega-funds such as Soros and Tiger to the launch of a myriad of smaller funds like his own. While he manages exclusively his own money now, he is able to address a worrying trend in hedge funds: giving investors what they want as opposed to sticking to what one does best. After he left Soros Fund Management in 2000, Bessent did not heed the advice he received at the time from hedge fund legend Robert Wilson. Wilson advised Bessent against taking any outside capital because in order to be up 100 percent, you have to be willing to be down 20 percent, and it's not possible to go down 20 with other people's money.

Still, Bessent launched his own fund with $1 billion of investor capital in the fall of 2000. After his first real drawdown, he had to confront the exit of hot money and all the difficulties that entails. He has since heeded the advice of Wilson and returned all outside investor capital. Pressure to give investors what they want can compromise any trading style.

I interviewed Bessent on a cold New York winter afternoon. Inside the steel and glass tower on Fifth Avenue in midtown Manhattan one could hear a pin drop, which is a starkly different scene from that of rough-and-tumble traders shouting over screens that blink with thousands of market prices. Bessent reads, he claims. Indeed, he and his team were sitting around reading the entire time that I spent with them. The cerebral, Ivy League demeanor of the place could not have been more diametrically opposed to the Chicago pits or the trading floors of major New York and London banks.

Books, newsletters, magazines, and newspapers were everywhere, giving them ample material. Bessent's reading must have been keeping him up at night because during the interview his eyes were blood red and he appeared to have had many sleepless nights.

"I have been up for days," he acknowledged. "Something is happening in China."

Bessent rubbed his eyes and looked at his screens as he discussed what it was like running the London office of Soros Fund Management when George Soros became known as "the man who broke the Bank of England." He apologized profusely for his fatigue, saying he was sorry to be such a poor interview subject. But while he may be unassuming and prefer reading to talking, Bessent's wealth of experience speaks for itself. Having cut his teeth at Soros Fund Management, Bessent comes from the equity stream of global macro. As Bessent explains it, "My style differentiates itself from other macro managers because I express a lot of macro views in equities."

While his style may require a lot of reading and research on individual companies before finally selecting the stocks he will use to express his larger macro views, one particular story drives home the point that he is not a classic equity fund manager, but rather a trader first and foremost.

While at golf school in Florida shortly after the meltdown of Long Term Capital Management in 1998, Bessent found himself teamed up with John Meriwether of LTCM infamy. The golf coach paired the two, reasoning, "You guys do the same thing." Bessent replied, "No we don't—when a trade goes against John, he adds. When a trade goes against me, I cut."

How did you become a global macro hedge fund manager?

I was a liberal arts major at Yale and wanted to become a journalist. In between my junior and senior year, I did an internship for Jim Rogers, one

of the founders of the Quantum Fund. I had met Jim through an investment club for which he had donated the seed capital. The first thing he
said was, "You're probably going to lose it all, which is the best thing you
could do. If you want to learn about investing, go short some wheat and
see how it feels."

Jim had an office on the Upper West Side, next door to his townhouse,
where he managed his own money. I worked for him for a couple of
weeks, and thought, "I like this. It's just like journalism—you gather a lot
of information and make a decision, but instead of writing a story with an
angle, you make an investment with an angle."

What did you learn from Jim Rogers?

I learned about doing primary research. To just keep digging and look
where nobody else is looking. He used to have me do these spreadsheets
before there was Excel. *Barron's* had an issue that ranked the stocks of industry groups and we'd flip it upside-down to look at the worst performers to buy and the best performers to short.

What did you do after graduation from Yale?

I went to work at Brown Brothers because they were one of the few places
that would let you do equity research right out of college. I worked there
for six months and absolutely hated it because it was basically "Are we going to buy GM or Ford?"

An opportunity came along to work with a Middle Eastern family,
helping to manage their money, and I jumped. They had about $600 mil-
lion, which in 1985 was a lot of money. There were five of us with a big
concentrated portfolio of stocks and commodities. We managed the portfolio as a group along with one of the family members and had good lee-
way to take some big bets.

What did you learn specifically about how a wealthy family managed their own money and how they viewed risk?

They liked to know the management of the stocks they bought and only
invested in businesses they understood. Their approach was colored by
their first real equity investment in 1975 in Donaldson, Lufkin & Jenrette
(DLJ). The stock had gone from 30 to 2 and American Express was selling
its 25 percent stake. The father of the family was friends with one of the

founders of DLJ, and he asked him, "If you think it's a good buy, I'll buy the whole thing," and he did. Seven years later they sold it to Equitable for $30 a share. So a lot of their investing philosophy was built on trusting the management.

The other thing that was important to them was keeping their powder dry. They used leverage but they always kept a segregated pile of money in case there was a problem or they needed buying power. This paid off in spades on the day of the 1987 crash. I thought we were wiped out when all of a sudden I found out that there was a large cash hoard stashed away for a day like October 19, 1987.

I can still remember every stock on my screen, and I'm probably still traumatized by it. I couldn't believe how calm they were, considering the amount of money we lost. It was an out-of-control hit but because of the spare capital, we weren't backed into a corner and were never forced sellers. They were able to be rational about it and actually bought more shares. It turned out to be a great buying opportunity.

What was your next job?

I went to work with Jim Chanos, who just did short selling. It was interesting going to work with him after the family, who were always optimistic and incredibly bullish. Jim was always trying to go against the crowd. He constantly picked things apart and looked for what "the market" had wrong.

One thing Jim was never great at was figuring out why it would end. He never really looked for the catalyst that would change the market's focus. He was usually right, but what I've learned since is that it's more important to be there when a mania ends, than spotting it early.

What I came away with from my time with Chanos was that you don't have to be skeptical about everything. Maybe the guys at Starbucks really are good managers and it really is one of the greatest concepts ever. Maybe eBay is the perfect business model. Short sellers can't think that way. Short selling is a unique and specific mind-set. According to them, every Internet stock had to go bankrupt. Jim's always betting against the house but, working with him, I learned that the house usually wins. That's part of the short seller's problem. Another problem is that it's harder now because there are a lot more people doing it.

There are also other inherent problems with shorting. There is a difference between investing or buying stocks and shorting. If you are a long/short player and one of your longs goes down 10 or 20 percent, you'll buy more. If one of your shorts goes up 10 or 20 percent, you'll get out. Knowing that you can lose multiples on your position in a short but only your investment with a long makes it more difficult to hold a short position. Also, when a short goes against you, it becomes a bigger percentage of your portfolio, but when it's working, it becomes a smaller percentage. So with a short, your risk increases as its goes against you.

What distinguishes Jim Chanos as a short seller?

Jim has been very successful and has caught some great shorts, like Enron recently. The great thing about Jim is that he is the presentable, educated face of short selling. He'd gone to Yale and is very articulate and thoughtful. He wasn't one of these guys from a strange religion who crawled out from under a rock. We weren't squeezing little trades and constantly fighting with the Vancouver Stock Exchange to borrow stocks. A lot of what he did was to catch the big shorts. He actually sat there and did a lot of homework.

When I was there, the firm went from $20 million in assets under management to $500 million. What was exciting about that period was that while the averages didn't do much, some of the industry groups got crushed.

In 1991 I said to Jim, "I can't find anything to short," and he said, "Well, that's what we do. We're a dedicated short fund so we have to be short." I didn't really want to short Citibank at 12.

Our biggest client was Soros and the people there said, "If you're going to leave Chanos, come work for us, but only if you're definitely going to leave." In retrospect it was the best market call that I ever made, not to mention career call. I didn't know that I was making a market call at the time but it turned out to be the bottom. (*See Figure 13.1.*)

I took a couple of months off to travel the world and then started at Soros Fund Management in New York as an analyst. It was November 1991 and the portfolio manager in Europe wasn't doing very well. It was just after German reunification and he had a big bullish bet on in Germany that wasn't working. I was literally the only one in the New York office who knew anything about European stocks from my days working for the family office, so I was sent over to the London office to report back.

I was only over there for two weeks when George couldn't take it anymore and fired everyone in London. I was sitting by myself with a portfolio of $300 million, mostly in one stock, when all of Quantum was $1 billion.

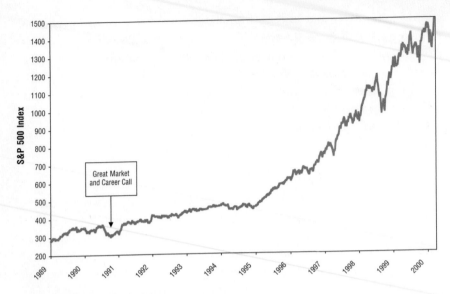

FIGURE 13.1   S&P 500 Index, 1989–2000
Source: Bloomberg.

I started helping manage the European book with the help of Stan Druckenmiller, the chief investment officer (CIO) of Soros Fund Management at the time, who was in New York. He and George said, "Just stay there until we find a high-powered European guy to take over." Then I got lucky, my performance was pretty good, and they said, "Why don't you stay?" I ran Soros's London office for another seven years.

So you were running the Soros London office when the pound fell out of the ERM. Can you talk a bit about what happened on that famous trade?

We'd been thinking about it for a while. The trade is a good example of what made Soros a different sort of macro fund in that we did a lot of bottom-up research. Stan and George believed that if you can find out what's going on at a micro level, you can figure out the big picture.

My very minor contribution to the breaking of the pound was an analysis I had done on the UK housing and property market. In the United Kingdom at the time, about 90 percent of mortgages were linked to the overnight rate. If the Bank of England raised rates on Wednesday, mortgages went up on Friday.

I had been short UK housing stocks for a while and George was chewing on me to cover the position because they were going up. I said, "George, I have done my work. These property stocks are going under." George likes it when you argue with him if you're right, which is why I think I did well there.

Anyway, the housing stock trade was overshadowed by the pound trade, and rightly so. What is most interesting to me about the breaking of the pound was the combination of Stan Druckenmiller's gamesmanship—Stan really understands risk/reward—and George's ability to size trades. Make no mistake about it, shorting the pound was Stan Druckenmiller's idea. Soros's contribution was pushing him to take a gigantic position.

With the pound, we realized that we could push the Bank of England up against the trading band where they had to buy an unlimited amount of pounds from us. The plan was to trade the fund's profits and leverage up at the band's boundary. The fund was up about 12 percent for the year at the time, so we levered the trade up to the point where if they pushed us back up against the other side of the trading band, we would lose the year's P&L but not more.

The UK economy was already weak, so when they raised interest rates to defend the currency, the average person's mortgage went up. They basically squeezed everyone in the United Kingdom with a mortgage. When they raised rates from 7 percent to 12 percent with the stated goal of defending the pound, we knew it was unsustainable and that they were finished.

As the Soros rep in London, did you take any heat as a result of Black Wednesday?

Oh yeah. After that, a lot of companies wouldn't meet with me. At first, it was a matter of national pride for the Brits, but as they saw interest rates come down and the economy improving, they softened their stance.

Interestingly, no one had ever heard of George Soros before this. I remember going to play tennis with him at his London house on the Saturday after it happened. It was as if he were a rock star, with cameramen and paparazzi waiting out front.

A lot of credit should go to the UK officials, though; they knew to fold their hand quickly. UK Chancellor Norman Lamont and Prime Minister John Major suffered short-term humiliation for long-term good. I mean, look at the muddle France and Germany are still in.

What do you think is going to happen with the whole euro currency project?

It's going to force structural reform eventually. The euro's current strength reminds me of what George always used to say to us: "I'd fire you, but the others are worse." Whenever anyone asks me, "Why are you long the euro?" I say it's because everything else is worse.

There might be a very large policy mistake brewing right now, not dissimilar to Japan's mistakes in the 1990s. There are all the elements for a real policy problem, especially with a very academic central bank. I get the feeling that the European Central Bank (ECB) is like a bunch of clueless college professors. The woman from Finland, who is the most hawkish central banker I've ever met, comes in and all she cares about is core consumer price index (CPI). All the president of the Bank of Spain cares about is that real estate is out of control, and so on and so on. They aren't paying attention to the two largest economies that still have serious problems and the fact that Western Europe gets a minuscule amount of foreign direct investment. The euro can muddle through but, again, if the dollar weren't in such a predicament, it wouldn't look so good.

Let's talk about another crisis where Soros took some criticism, Malaysia in 1997. What was that like, to see a country change its currency policy and then publicly blame Soros for it?

That was slightly worrying. It was the first time that someone had actually stopped paying lip service and actually shut down an economic system. Fortunately, no one else followed their example. I can honestly say I don't understand Malaysia from an economic perspective.

There have been numerous instances where policy makers have blamed speculators for their country's problems. What is your view on money managers forcing policy change versus policy mistakes attracting capital?

Occasionally, there can be short-term moves as a result of speculators, but I don't think they can drive underlying fundamentals. On the other hand, when locals want to get out and you see capital flight, there is a fundamental problem—Russia being a classic example of locals getting out. So as long as the locals maintain faith, the speculators usually can't break a system.

The problem is, with the amount of capital out there today, a small currency block can get pushed around temporarily. In general, though, if you have the proper policies, speculators can't do anything over the medium term.

A good example of this was the Hungarian forint currency band recently when there was a big speculative push to actually strengthen the currency. The Hungarian central bank started printing forints and pushed it all the way back. It was a wide band so speculators got cleaned out.

Speaking of Russia, Soros made the headlines again but this time for being on the wrong side of a big trade and losing $2 billion in a day.

It was actually between $1 billion and $2 billion, and it was nerve-wracking. We lost most of our profits for the year when it happened. It was totally unexpected because Economics 101 will tell you that a country will never default on its local currency denominated sovereign debt. There's absolutely no reason to, because you can always print more money. Literally, it was a zero-probability risk event.

Going into that, we were up 24 percent on the year and lost 15 percent that day, so we still had some performance cushion. Stan's whole thing was to never get backed into a corner, so we started liquidating our other positions. We wanted to be able to add to the trades we liked so we trimmed the ideas where we had the least conviction.

Let's talk about the technology boom/bust of 1999 to 2000. Both Soros and Julian Robertson were famous naysayers on tech shares and the "new economy" but were clearly hurting toward the end of the move. I remember reading about Druckenmiller flipping the portfolio from short to long, a reversal that saved Quantum in 1999 but then hurt it a few months later in 2000.

Stan's better at changing his mind than anybody I've ever seen. Maybe he stayed with it a little too long, but one of the great things about Stan is that he can and does turn on a dime. To paraphrase John Maynard Keynes, when the facts change, he changes his positions.

In fairness to Stan, he finished 2000 up for the year. He went from down 12 percent in March to up 15 percent for the year in his own portfolio, Duquesne Capital, which he ran alongside Soros. If you remember, the NASDAQ dumped in March 2000 but then almost made a marginal new high in September at which point he changed his mind again, went from net long to net short, and caught that whole move down from September to December in 2000.

Is Stan Druckenmiller the money manager you most admire?

Stan and Nick Roditi would top my list.

Stan Druckenmiller may be the greatest moneymaking machine in history. He has Jim Rogers's analytical ability, George Soros's trading ability, and the stomach of a riverboat gambler when it comes to placing his bets. His lack of volatility is unbelievable. I think he's had something like five down quarters in 25 years and never a down year. The Quantum record from 1989 to 2000 is really his. The assets grew from $1 billion to $20 billion over that time and the performance never suffered. Soros's record was made on a smaller amount of money at a time when there were fewer hedge funds to compete against.

Nick Roditi, who managed the Quota Fund at Soros Fund Management, is the other fund manager I admire. He knows how to find two or three investment themes, take enormous positions, and stick with them for multiyear periods. His intuition for a trend change in the currency or bond markets is unmatched, as is his ability to withstand short-term movements against him. Interestingly, Nick works alone and visits over 100 companies per year.

Aside from their trading acumen, Stan and Nick are the class acts of the hedge fund business. Their word is their bond, they eschew publicity, and they are dedicated family men.

George Soros, on the other hand, is much more volatile than Stan and Nick. He is the opposite of Warren Buffett. Buffett has a high batting average. George has a terrible batting average—it's below 50 percent and possibly even below 30 percent—but when he wins it's a grand slam. He's like Babe Ruth in that respect. George used to say, "If you're right in a position, you can never be big enough."

Having worked with both Soros and Jim Rogers, what differences did you note between former partners?

Rogers is an analyst while Soros is a trader. That's why George and Jim were such a great combination. Jim is thoughtful and analytical but can't really trade. George can take information and jump on it like nobody I've ever seen.

Do you have any other anecdotes from your time at Soros?

Soros used to give out a lot of money for other people to manage. George wasn't bothered when people started losing money, but he was always worried that they weren't feeling the pain properly because it was his money and not theirs. If people managing his money were down in November or December and he saw their trades getting bigger, he'd pull the money immediately. Also, if the manager was down and their trading volume picked up dramatically, he'd pull it. The worst thing you can do when you're having a hard time is flail. In trading, when there is nothing to do, the best thing to do is nothing.

How did your run at Soros Fund Management finally end?

When the NASDAQ cracked in March 2000, we had a big drawdown. George wanted less risk in his life at the time so most of the senior people decided to leave.

I then set up my own fund in the fall of 2000. When I was raising money, I actually gave the market what it wanted instead of what I wanted to do or was good at. Initially, we had no macro because at the time, *global macro* was a dirty word. We had big diversified positions because everybody wanted diversification. We had a lot of analysts because people wanted to see bodies.

The biggest mistake I made was not taking the advice of this guy who was a hedge fund legend from the 1970s, Robert Wilson. He was a huge guy back then but now runs his own money almost exclusively. When I was starting, he had a mutual friend arrange for us to have lunch, where he leaned across the table and said, "If you have as much money as I've read you do in the paper, you're an asshole if you manage anybody's money except your own. To go up 100 percent, you've got to be willing to go down 20, and you can't go down 20 with other people's money."

I learned that it's very difficult to run a business and a fund. After my first big drawdown, I had a lot of investors pull and it was a nightmare. So I told the remaining investors, "This is what I'm going to do with my money. If you want to come along, fine; if you don't, that's fine, too." Then I went back to my global macro style with mostly my own money. There's more volatility but much better returns.

That's what was so great about working at Soros. Most of the capital was the partners' and all we cared about was making money. We weren't worried about monthly volatility or drawdowns if we believed in the position.

I find it difficult to foresee the day when global macro won't matter. There may be periods of time where there are no major moves, but unless we go to

*a global currency block, those periods are unlikely to last long. And even if
we do go to a global currency block, it will create other imbalances—and
opportunities for global macro funds.*

Exactly. Again, I was just giving the market what it wanted because in
2000, as far as investors were concerned, global macro was dead.

When David Swensen, who allocates capital for the Yale endowment,
comes in and says, "If you do macro, I will never give you a penny," then
you say you don't do macro. But even Swensen is doing macro. When he's
got X percent of Yale's portfolio in venture capital, he's doing macro.
When he's got Y percent in oil, gas, and timber, he's making macro calls.

Recently, I was at a money manager round table dinner where everyone
was talking about "my stocks this" and "my stocks that." Their attitude was
that it doesn't matter what is going to happen in the world because their
favorite stock is generating free cash flow, buying back shares, and doing
XYZ. People always forget that 50 percent of a stock's move is the overall
market, 30 percent is the industry group, and then maybe 20 percent is the
extra alpha from stock picking. And stock picking is full of macro bets.
When an equity guy is playing airlines, he's making an embedded macro
call on oil. I honestly think that people forget what a macro trend is.

How has global macro investing changed since you started?

Back then they didn't call it global macro. Basically anything where you
could go short was a hedge fund. Nowadays, I'm astounded at (1) the size
of the leverage, (2) what people are arbitraging versus other things, and
(3) the esoteric things people are doing. Also, it used to be much more
directional.

The leverage in the system shows up in the intraday moves. Look at the
currencies now—the intraday moves are huge but on a weekly basis they
don't go anywhere. There's a lot of noise around the trend.

Also, look at the prime brokerage business. The first thing any of them
say when they visit is, "We can give you more leverage than the other guy.
We can do this offshore, we can get around that, and we'll repo out these
Russian corporates for 95 percent." It's insane.

In a low volatility, low return environment, people mistake low volatility for low risk. We're setting up for another perfect storm and it's going to
be because we haven't had much movement and everyone is leveraging to
get returns. What's different now is it's at every single level.

The hedge funds are leveraged, and the biggest investors in the hedge funds are the funds of funds, who are also leveraged. A lot of the fund of funds guys are leveraged five to one, which doesn't include the leverage of the hedge funds they invest in, so you can see how the whole thing can unwind.

I'm not sure where the pressure point is. I'm not sure whether it's in corporate spreads, which is where everyone is, or whether it's in emerging markets, but it's somewhere. (*See Figure 13.2.*)

If I told you every fund of funds investor is going to redeem tomorrow because their investors redeemed them, where would you position your portfolio?

I'd be short corporate spreads. They'll blow out. We are not in the position yet because you get killed while waiting, but we will be in it at some point.

It reminds me of being short a Janus stock during the Internet bubble. There was this fund called the Janus 20 and the only reason the stocks went up was because of asset inflows. The mutual fund was taking in $50 million a day and they just kept jamming it into those 20 stocks. It's the same thing now with corporate spreads. There are these big hedge fund complexes that are taking in a huge amount of money every quarter and they just keep putting on the same trades, bigger and bigger.

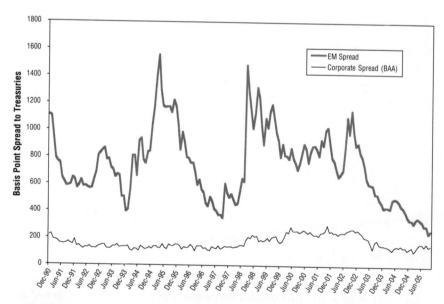

FIGURE 13.2 Corporate and Emerging Market Spreads, 1990–2005
Source: Bloomberg.

In general, people aren't trying to make money nowadays. A lot of these guys have huge asset bases, so they're running a business, not a hedge fund. Hedge funds used to be about making outsized returns.

The fund of funds guys are shooting themselves in their own feet. They want low volatility and low risk, so you see hedge funds stopping out of positions much quicker than they normally would. Managers can't risk the volatility. If you're running a $10 billion fund, your 2 percent management fee is $200 million in the door every year, so why fool with that? Up 10 percent is respectable and that's another $200 million. Big managers are disincentivized to make money.

Again, that's what was interesting about Soros, he never cared about the business. The reason he's worth $8 billion is because if he was up 20 percent in June, he would try to be up 100 percent by December. Most people today will close out their positions and take the rest of the year off if they're up 10 percent in June and that's what their investors want them to do! Most people are so gun-shy now that they'll take profit quickly on the good trades.

I recently had an investor call me up after a good month and say, "We would normally like to invest with you, but you must be doing something very risky if you had a 6 percent up month."

That's a signal that investors are all afraid of their own shadows now. Eventually, it will be just like venture capital. People will start to question what they are getting for their fees. Hedge funds recently underperformed the S&P 500, and if that keeps happening, people are eventually going to ask, "What's so great about these hedge fund guys?"

Do you think hedge funds should be benchmarked against the S&P?

No, but that's the way most people do it mentally. Most hedge funds should just tell you what they think they can make, and then see if they can do what they say.

Do you think part of the problem in hedge funds is all of the equity long-only fund managers who are suddenly calling themselves equity long/short hedge funds and charging higher fees, while their returns remain remarkably correlated to the stock market?

Oh yeah. Even the best ones are routinely 150 percent long, 85 percent short, and they just hope that the beta on the shorts will save them on the way down. You'd be surprised at how many of them have never actually been net short.

A friend of mine recently gave a speech at Yale on hedge fund investing about who will survive the bear market. He showed the returns of hedge funds in the bear market of the 1970s and it was unbelievable in terms of the losses. The average loss was 40 percent. Steinhardt and Soros were up and one other guy was flat and that was it on the positive side. His theory now is that it will take a systemic problem to wipe everybody out.

The catalyst will probably come from somewhere people aren't looking as well, like a clearing broker problem or something. JP Morgan, Fannie Mae, or one of the finance subs of a major corporate is probably the pressure point now. Maybe it's a big continental European hedge fund. I am not sure who is regulating those guys. No one seems to know if it's the ECB, the Bank for International Settlements (BIS), or who.

Would your portfolio withstand a systemic shock right now?

We actually have very few positions on right now, so yes. I'm having trouble finding ideas. When I have a position on that I don't like or have trouble finding good trades, I can't sleep. George Soros used to have this thing that when his back hurt, he had to get out of a position. With investors, I can actually make up an intellectual reason for why I got out of some trade, but normally it's just because I can't sleep. The way we're set up now is that if there's nothing to do, we do nothing.

Let's talk about portfolio construction. How do you structure your portfolio in normal times?

We'll have 8 to 14 positions on at a time but they're usually big positions and not necessarily equally weighted. From January until April 2004, for example, we probably had 80 percent of net asset value in Japanese equities, half of that in Japanese banks and half of that in one bank.

We do lever up the portfolio, but there is no set formula or cap. The Japan position is beta adjusted and a volatile, large position. We could be 200 or 300 percent in G5 currencies, but in theory they aren't going to move more than 2 or 3 percent in a day. I'm never quite sure how you measure your leverage anyway.

What was the logic behind the Japan banks trade?

It reminded me of 1991 when everyone thought Citigroup was going bankrupt, but this time you had a catalyst. (*See Figure 13.3.*) Japanese stocks

FIGURE 13.3 Japanese Banks, 2002–2005, and Citigroup, 1989–1993
Source: Bloomberg.

and especially the bank stocks were incredibly cheap, and then Goldman Sachs came in and bought Sumitomo. Meanwhile, the sentiment was terrible and everyone thought it was the worst idea they'd ever heard which are often the best times to put on a trade. Although, sometimes the best trades are when everyone thinks it's a good idea but nobody has it on.

When you put on a position, what kind of time horizon are you looking at?

It depends. Optimally, when I start thinking about a trade, it is with a 6- to 18-month horizon. With the Japanese banks, I thought there was a chance that I was going to own them for several years, but it worked much quicker and the outlook has now changed. I'm worried about China slowing now, so our position is much smaller because clearly a lot of the economic growth in Japan is coming from China.

Take Russia right now. I'm dying to buy the bonds of these Russian oil companies ex Yukos. They're yielding 9 or 10 percent in dollars and the coupon is covered five times with oil at $35. My dream scenario would be that they never move in price so I can just sit and collect that coupon leveraged up a few times for the next five years.

When you initiate a trade, do you have profit targets and stop-loss levels?

I don't usually have stop-losses. One of the things that I learned from Stan Druckenmiller is how to enter a trade. The great thing about Stan is that he can be wrong but he rarely loses money because his entry point is so good. He has an incredible constitution. So I try to make sure that my entry point is good enough that I rarely stop myself out of a trade.

Profit targets change with more information. I have a plan that "If this happens, I'll sit with it; if that happens, I'll buy more," and so on. I visualize what might happen and what would get me out, what would make me buy more, what will keep me in.

What is your favorite trade at the moment?

I love UK Gilts. There is a slightly inverted yield curve, and the Bank of England is the second best central bank in the world, after the Bank of Canada. They've taken their medicine early, jacked interest rates, and effectively killed the housing bubble, or at least they've taken the froth off of it. The pound is very strong on a trade-weighted basis and the United Kingdom is much more sensitive to currency movements than the United States. Sterling is a small currency, so as people move out of the dollar, if you don't like the euro and you can get 4.5 percent overnight rates in the United Kingdom, you buy the pound. Currency strength is bullish for interest rates.

Do interest rates matter once again for currencies? What the market focuses on in foreign exchange seems to be constantly changing.

Soros used to say, "Don't try to play the game better, try to figure out when the game has changed."

We are in the midst of a paradigm shift with the USD. The dollar used to trade off the current account back in the late 1970s into 1980. Then when Volker started jacking up rates, it became interest rate differentials that mattered. Now, there's a very good chance that we've had a paradigm shift again and we're going back to the focus being the current account. Catching a paradigm shift is where you make a lot of money because everyone is still focusing on what mattered.

Do you remember your worst trade?

Being short the Internet stocks too early in 1999. Right trade, wrong time. It taught me the lesson that you can be right and lose all your money. Also, if a stock is going to zero it doesn't matter where you short it, you're still going to make 100 percent because you can short on the way down. You made just as much money shorting $100 million of Enron at $25 as you did shorting $100 million of Enron at $50. It's better to have more conviction and do twice as much.

I'm waiting on this trade in short-term Japanese rates now, which may be the trade of the decade when Japan's zero interest rate policy ends. I don't need to be early on that and I may even wait until they raise rates for the first time, because once they move, this thing will be in motion.

Have you become more patient with experience?

Yes, and also more willing to miss things. If you were to ask me my biggest mistakes over the past two or three years, two of them have been misses.

In the summer of 2002, I should have gotten on a plane and gone to Argentina—the opportunity of a lifetime, and I missed it. This year I was long the Mexican peso instead of the Canadian dollar, but you miss things.

Take Russia—I thought the Yukos affair would create a down wave in the Russian markets, both for debt and for equities, that would be a buying opportunity. Definitely five years ago I would have been buying now. Instead, I'm just waiting and assuming that probably the day Yukos is finally at zero will be the bottom and then I will buy up all the Russia I can.

Do you find that it helps to visit places where you have a trade on or are considering putting a trade on?

I'm not sure there's any value to that, especially as it pertains to Russia. There's more value in talking to other managers about it because they've whooped themselves up to a fairly hysterical level now. That's the other thing that's changed about the hedge fund business: Your biggest risk can be how your competitor is positioned.

The hedge fund business is like whale watching in that the biggest risk isn't a whale hitting the boat. It is that everyone sees a whale, runs to that side, and tips the boat. That is what is happening in the hedge fund business today. Everything gets too far to one side and the boat tilts. I want to be on the other side of the boat or not on it at all.

Do you think the market likes to test conviction in crowded trades?

Yes, and more so now. It's always looking for the pain trade. What's interesting, if you follow technical analysis, is that you never know why a market is going to do what it's going to do, but it usually does. Technical analysis shows you what the crowd is thinking.

Do you use technical analysis as a behavioral analysis tool?

Yes and we also use it to keep us on top of things we might not be seeing. We have a system that screens about 1,400 stocks and commodities around the world every week. We never trade based on it, but if all of a sudden 10 stocks in Indonesia show up, then we'll look at Indonesia.

Where else do you get your information to decide what to trade?

A lot of newsletters, thought pieces, magazines. We get very few ideas talking. We basically just sit around here and read. We probably get four or five thought pieces that provoke an idea on which we keep files. At any one time we have 20 hot idea files going so we know what we want to buy and wait for good entry points.

For example, we've been thinking about India for a long time. I thought I'd missed it and then—again, the unpredictable event—you get a surprise election and their stock market is down 18 percent in a day. With India, I got too greedy and we didn't buy very much.

Coming from Soros, you must have a tremendously valuable network.

I only speak with a few people. Being able to get some primary information about what's really going on is very helpful, but in general it's much better to just sit back, watch the world, and do my own thing.

In each country or region, I have one brokerage firm that I deal with, but that's more to get a flavor of the local consensus. Take Turkey, for example—it looks so obvious to me, so I ask my local broker there, "Why aren't you recommending the Turkish treasury bills?" and then I work from there. Turkey is fascinating to me right now because it is to the European Union what NAFTA was to the United States. No one in the United States realized what a favor Mexico was doing us, nor does anyone in Europe realize what a favor the Turks are doing them. Basically, the Turks are going to provide cheap labor and a growing, young population to counterbalance the aging, negative European growth rate.

What is your long-range view of the world?

At some point, we will have had The Big One. It's out there.

I don't know whether it's a financial asset depression or a real depression. The thing that I'm sure about is that financial assets can't keep doing what they're doing, or that so many people can be rewarded for being imprudent.

I have a friend who, unbelievably, actually puts away money every month to buy a house. She's getting squeezed because the $500 she puts away every month to save for her vacation house is getting 1 percent. All of our other friends who have gone out and bought houses all leveraged up when they really couldn't afford them are being rewarded. So the house that she's saving up for now costs 20 percent more, the person who borrowed the max has made multiples of 20 percent, depending on their leverage, but yet she's made 1 percent. Over the long term, that's not sustainable.

Longer term, we'll have a problem with crude. I wouldn't be surprised if in three to five years it hits $100 a barrel. The pull from Asia is just gigantic. There are eight million nongovernmental cars in China versus 120 million in the United States and China has five times the population. I'm not one of these "China is the be-all and end-all" types—and again, it's like the Internet, I'm not sure if there's going to be any return—but it's definitely going to change the world.

Another big-picture view is that we're going to be in an arms race with China at some point. We will know it's really under way when Japan rearms, which I suspect will start happening in the next two to three years. This is the beginning of China's decade. We're beginning to see China flexing its muscles, and the United States is probably where the United Kingdom was around World War I in terms of world dominance.

CHAPTER 14

THE EMERGING MARKET SPECIALIST

Marko Dimitrijević
Everest Capital
Miami

arko Dimitrijević has been investing in emerging markets (EM) since he was 19 years old. He put on his first EM trade in 1978 and started his own firm, Everest Capital, in 1990, making it one of the oldest hedge funds still operational.

The hedge fund business has changed over the last 15 years, and EM investing is drastically different today than it was in the early 1990s. For one thing, former "emerging markets" such as Portugal or Greece have developed, thereby dropping from the radar screen of managers seeking frontier markets. Today Uruguay, Mongolia, and Pakistan qualify as emerging markets plays, but in another 15 years they may not. So emerging markets investing evolves with the world around it, a world rife with volatility that most EM managers, Dimitrijević included, are not immune to. Everest experienced a significant drawdown in 1998 on the heels of the simultaneous Russian devaluation and default. Although, unlike many other emerging markets players who got burned in Russia, he did not close the fund, but instead carried on and has since surpassed his high-water mark, meaning that his investors have more than recovered their losses. Quite an admirable feat.

Having persevered, Dimitrijević's Everest Capital is now expanding beyond emerging markets and global macro. He is launching funds specializing in China and Japan, as well as other strategies such as event-driven. Meanwhile, the lines have blurred between what is considered global macro and traditional EM investing, and the evolution of Everest epitomizes this change. If true global macro managers will seek opportunities in any market or asset class, anywhere in the world, this would include all so-called emerging markets. Yet there are many intricacies to fringe markets that can only be known through experience, local market contacts, and on-the-ground due diligence, all things that Dimitrijević and Everest have acquired over the past few decades.

Everest now manages over $1.5 billion in assets and is based in Miami, Florida, far from the major world financial centers. In a gleaming, lone office tower complex with a view of the ocean and port of Miami, I sat down with Dimitrijević to talk about his ups and downs in the volatile world of emerging markets. When I first contacted him about conducting this interview, his response was, "I don't know why I would be interesting to include in a book, other than the fact that I have been around for 15 years." But staying power in emerging markets, and in the hedge fund business in general, speaks volumes. Dimitrijević survived some monumental emerging market crises, including Mexico in 1995, Southeast Asia in 1997, Russia in 1998, Brazil in 1999, and Argentina in 2002, not to mention less abrupt sea changes such as the transformation of Eastern Europe from communism to capitalism and the emergence of China as a world power.

Dimitrijević himself grew up in Switzerland but comes from what he terms a Yugoslavian family, a claim perhaps testament to the world changes he has witnessed. He is intense but mild-mannered, with angular facial features and a penetrating gaze. His answers are almost always short, giving the impression that he has more pressing issues to attend to, like uncovering the next big emerging markets opportunity.

How did you get into markets?

When I was in college, I had a few hundred dollars in savings that wasn't yielding much so I went to the bank and asked what else I could do. They introduced me to stocks and that is when I got hooked.

The first stock I bought was a real estate investment trust (REIT), which went up 10 percent in three months. The second was an Argentine oil company called Astra (Compania Argentina de Petroleo), which doubled in about a week. Right then I thought, "This is it, this is what I'm going to do the rest of my life."

I was 19 at the time. My family is from Yugoslavia but I grew up in Switzerland. When I finished my economics degree in college, the logical move was to go into portfolio management. I joined a small Swiss bank that, in typical Swiss fashion, invested globally. That's how I got into global investments and that's what I've done ever since.

Why did you start your own hedge fund?

That was more of an accident. I was working for a group called Triangle which was run by two very smart New York financiers who had moved to Florida. After a while, they decided to move to London and I was not enamored with the idea. I wanted to stay in Florida, so I decided to manage my own money and anybody else's if they were interested. I started in 1990 with $8 million.

How have markets changed since you started?

In general, markets are made up of human reactions. To the extent that human nature hasn't changed in the past few hundred years, and certainly not in the past decade, I don't think the markets have changed. Look at what happened with the NASDAQ in 2000 and you see that human nature is still the same. There are booms, busts, greed, fear. That won't change.

How has the global macro hedge fund space changed?

When I started, there were only 150 to 200 hedge funds in existence and even then, people thought there were too many. Throughout the years, the main question has always been—to what extent performance is sacrificed as more players enter the fray.

Today, you have to differentiate between global macro or directional type strategies and arbitrage type strategies. In the past couple of years, the arbitrage strategies have become overcrowded. With 8,000 to 10,000 hedge funds, there is not enough supply, in terms of things that you can arbitrage, to meet the demand. That's why returns have come down.

In global macro, whether it is 1990 or 2005, if you get a trend right, the markets are so big that it doesn't matter how many hedge funds there are. The difficulty then and now is catching that trend. Recently, you could have put tens of billions of dollars to work in the oil market and you would have made a fortune. From that standpoint, nothing has really changed. You just need to be right.

Information circulates a bit faster now. We didn't have the Internet back in 1990, but that's not a big difference. Some of the best opportunities are when it takes weeks, sometimes months, for the investment idea to gel.

Do you think that all the arbitrage strategies are creating opportunities for global macro funds or taking them away? For example, do you blame RV and arbitrage funds for the decline in volatility over the last couple of years?

They are certainly a factor but low volatility tends to be a temporary phenomenon. We had the same thing between 1993 and 1995, and then volatility shot back up. Volatility levels have more to do with the fact that there hasn't been an external shock for the past couple of years, calming human emotions, so we just have to wait.

Every investor in hedge funds these days seems to want that 1-percent-a-month strategy. The problem is, when everyone wants that, it becomes more like half a percent a month. Investors often trade smoothness for returns.

We're big believers in what Warren Buffett said: "I'd rather have a lumpy 15 percent than a smooth 12 percent." Everest has generated 15 percent net to investors, albeit in a lumpy manner at times, for 15 years.

I don't think the alternative is a smooth 12 percent anymore but more like 6 to 8 percent a year. It's all about investor preference and clearly, for our own consumption, in a macro fund we much prefer a lumpier, higher return.

In terms of your portfolio construction, do you normally have on a lot of small, hopefully uncorrelated positions or a few big bets?

The former. It is something we have changed over the years. We don't have heavily concentrated risk in the portfolio anymore. Before 1998, we would take concentrated positions at the country level but would be diversified at the individual stock or bond level. We were very concentrated in Russia back in 1998 and were hurt, so we've changed our approach.

Clearly 1998 was a mistake because any instrument that traded in Russia collapsed after their dual default and devaluation. Stocks, currency, local bonds, foreign currency-denominated bonds, it didn't matter.

We learned that when a country implodes, it acts like a company where management is discovered to have committed fraud. Owning Russia in 1998 was like owning Enron in 2001 where Enron stock, Enron bonds, Enron receivables, and Enron pensions all suffered. Everything related to Enron collapsed. Since then, Everest has put strict limits on how much exposure we can have to a single emerging market, and we look at an emerging country in aggregate like a company.

After 1998, we revamped our risk controls. We had risk controls before but we learned some lessons and really tightened them. In particular, we set very strict exposure limits to any single emerging market country. In the global macro fund, it is 10 percent. In the emerging markets fund, it is 15 percent.

If you look back at the Russia episode with these new limits, we would have been hurt but it would have been much more limited. The other Eastern European countries like Poland, Czech, and Hungary didn't default and, despite selling off in sympathy with Russia, came back strong.

I understand that you liquidated your Russia position before the 1998 meltdown but then reentered just before they devalued and defaulted. What happened there?

We had invested successfully in Russian debt instruments for several years prior to 1998, including MinFin domestic dollar-denominated bonds of the Russian Republic, the former Soviet Vneshekonombank debt, and S-Account GKOs. By the spring of 1998 we were not completely out of Russian debt but we had reduced our position significantly. Then in July, when yields really started to rise, we thought it was a very good opportunity. We thought there was a decent probability that they would devalue, but in a controlled fashion. A currency devaluation of 10 to 15 percent was manageable.

What we didn't expect was a devaluation and a default at the same time. It doesn't make economic sense. It was the first time a country had devalued and defaulted at the same time, so it created a real panic. It was unprecedented that a government would do that, as you always got either one or the other.

From their own prosperity standpoint, it was not the right thing to do. Russia really suffered from its action. Recently, they have gotten lucky because oil prices have skyrocketed, but if that hadn't happened, Russia would still be suffering from those actions. They should have done what a lot of the Asian countries did in 1997, which was devalue but not default. I have yet to hear a convincing rationale for why they did it. Yeltsin was not the sharpest economic mind that has ruled a large country.

In the fall of 1998, you lost over half of the value of your emerging markets fund but didn't close down like several other funds at the time. Why not?

Staying in business was the right thing to do. We had investors who wanted to stay with us and I felt it was not fair to them to close, only to reopen a few months later. It was a very difficult period because we didn't know how many investors or employees would stick with us. Many investors had confidence and stayed with us, and several added to their investments as well, which was terrific.

Did you use panic as an opportunity and get back into Russia in 1999?

We put on some positions, not big, but yes. It turned out to be a great trade.

We try to look at things as unemotionally as possible. You have to forget where something was yesterday or a month ago or a year ago and figure out if it makes sense now, here. Part of our job is to ask ourselves, if we had a clean sheet of paper, would we or wouldn't we consider this investment at the current price? If the answer is yes, then even if the fund just lost money in it in the past, we should be in it.

Do you have an annual return target in mind or does it depend on what the market offers?

We look at each position individually rather than a portfolio target. We start with positions where we know going in that the return is going to be low but with a high probability of success. Then we'll look for some more aggressive positions, size them accordingly, and accept the fact that they will exhibit more volatility.

Meanwhile, our time horizon varies. There are some trades that are very short-term plays, where we are looking for a catalyst or an event and we expect something to happen within a predetermined time frame. Then, there are other, more long-term positions where we see fundamentals driving the trade over several years. There are some positions that we have held for three or four years.

Can you give me an example of one of the more aggressive positions that you have on right now?

We believe emerging market equities are very attractive. It is our core theme.

Taking it down to the country level and then the sector level, we like Brazil and especially Brazilian banks. Brazil is interesting because they're probably nearly finished raising interest rates, which helps the banks. Also, there is a good probability that a global bank could acquire one of the remaining independent Brazilian banks.

How exactly do you manage the high-risk positions?

We start by looking at how much we think the position can lose and adjust the size to the point where we are comfortable with the risk. Once we've done that, we'll try to see if there is a hedge to the position, either directly through options or indirectly, through something that we think would correlate with the instrument.

In the case of Brazilian banks or Brazilian equities in general, we think the Brazilian bond market is mispriced relative to the equity market. Brazilian debt is too rich versus equities, so the fund is short some Brazilian fixed income as a hedge to its equity view. From a macro standpoint, if Brazil continues to look good the debt will continue to tighten, but we think the equities would do even better in that scenario. In a sell-off scenario in Brazil, the bond short should serve as a good hedge to the equities.

It seems as if some emerging market debt currently prices in your bullish EM thesis while the equities do not. Is hedging your equity view with related debt instruments a strategy that Everest is running throughout its portfolio?

We look for those types of opportunities. In some cases, the bonds are already so far into the investment grade process that even if something bad happens to the country, it's not going to act as a good hedge.

Do you use stop-losses?

Stop-losses work in continuous markets and we use them there. When you move into distressed debt or value plays where markets aren't continuous, they don't work well and can be dangerous. Our stop-loss levels are always internal. If you give stops to counterparties, they invariably get hit. If our internal stops get hit, we then have a one-month cool-off period where the fund will not reenter a trade.

What has been your favorite trade since you launched Everest?

Buying Brady bonds in early 1995 was a very compelling trade. The contagion from the *tequila effect* created some terrific opportunities.

In 1994, there was a lot of money going into Mexico because its currency had a crawling peg to the U.S. dollar so it was deemed a very safe investment. The stable exchange rate caused a lot of money to go into local debts called *Tesobonos* (fixed income securities issued by the Mexican government, denominated in U.S. dollars), which were yielding higher rates than U.S. Treasuries. The interest rate differential was pretty much free money if the peg held.

When Mexico devalued at the end of 1994, it came as a complete surprise. A lot of investors were leveraged in Mexican and other Latin American debt, so the devaluation created the fear of further devaluations or the so-called *tequila effect*. Venezuela, Argentina, and Brazil saw their bonds sell off massively, but the economic reality of the situation in each of those countries was very different.

We thought that their Brady bonds were trading at ridiculously low levels. Brady bonds have their principal backed by U.S. Treasuries so when you buy one of those bonds, you basically get two securities: The principal is a U.S. Treasury zero coupon bond, which is easy to price, and the coupon stream, which is represented by local sovereign risk.

When the other Latin American Brady bonds sold off in sympathy with Mexico, once you stripped out the zeroes, you were left with sovereign risk for next to nothing. The implied interest rates embedded in these coupons were so high that we felt it was a terrific risk/reward opportunity. The sovereign spread to Treasuries ended up moving from over 1,900 basis points in early 1995 to 400 basis points by early 1997. (*See Figure 14.1.*)

Again, talking about the ability to trade size in directional opportunities, you could have put tens of billions of dollars to work on this trade and made a killing.

Are the best opportunities in emerging markets always after panics and natural disasters?

For sure. There's no doubt about it, but we obviously never wish bad things on anyone.

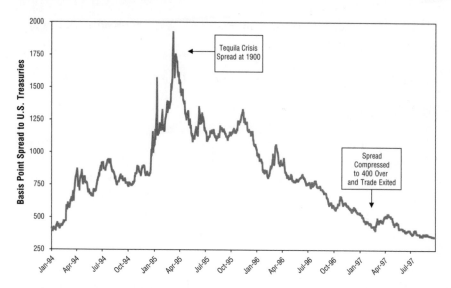

FIGURE 14.1   JP Morgan All Brady Index (EMBI Spread), 1994–1997
Source: JP Morgan.

Actually, we've made a lot of money in times with no crises. Sometimes, it is those long, quiet spells where momentum has a chance to develop. It's when momentum investors take things from undervalued levels to fair levels and eventually overvalued levels when you can generate some spectacular returns.

That being said, we like contrarian investments. Whether it's a natural disaster or human action that creates a market sell-off, we will always examine it to determine if it is a buying opportunity. For example, after the U.S. invasion of Afghanistan in response to the September 11 events, we felt that Pakistan would be a large beneficiary of U.S. and international aid. We looked at their markets, felt their currency and equities were very cheap, and took positions that have done very, very well since. There are three or four Pakistani stocks that trade in fairly large volumes, which we bought and held in the local currency. (*See Figure 14.2.*)

Have investors in emerging markets become better informed such that unwarranted contagion is less of a risk today than it was in the 1990s?

A lot of emerging markets have become deeper and more liquid due to the number of people who are now investing in them. One of the most important changes in a lot of these markets is the number of locals

FIGURE 14.2   Karachi Stock Exchange Index (KSE100) and Pakistani Rupee, 2001–2005
Source: Bloomberg.

involved in their own markets. People globally and in emerging coun-tries especially are richer. As they create wealth, they save more and start to invest. Their first investments tend to be in their home country, which is why we have the *home country bias*. This helps to decrease the correlations or the contagion effect between markets that we've seen in the past.

As recently as six or seven years ago, a few big funds and bank prop

HOME COUNTRY BIAS

Home country bias is an empirically proven behavioral phenomenon whereby investors tend to hold a substantial portion, if not all, of their assets in their home country. This overweighting goes against the no-tion of diversification and implies that investors believe that foreign markets are several times riskier than their home market. This behavior tends to create inefficiencies and anomalies in the relative valuation of assets and instruments across countries.

desks were by far the largest players in emerging markets. Now, the markets are a lot deeper with many more participants. No longer is it just a few guys in London or New York driving what's happening in emerging markets.

Take a look at the most recent EM crisis, which was the Argentine devaluation and default. Argentina was the one of the largest borrowers in emerging markets, and tens of billions of debts were defaulted on. Given past experiences, you'd have thought the impact on other emerging markets would have been as big or bigger than the Russian default. Yet it wasn't. Investors learned from the experience of 1998 where corollary markets sold off even when they shouldn't have. Again, the fact that these markets are now much more domestically driven is key.

When locals investing in Central Europe saw the Argentine default, they knew that it had no bearing on them. Their countries don't trade with Argentina, their banks don't have exposure to Argentina, and their companies don't have anything to do with Argentina. Therefore, they knew their markets shouldn't be affected by Argentina. (*See Figure 14.3.*)

In Argentina, unfortunately, we didn't get short the currency or bonds because it was very expensive and we didn't have a crystal ball in

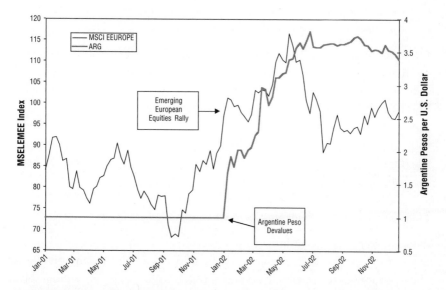

FIGURE 14.3 Argentine Peso and MSCI Emerging Markets Eastern Europe (Local Currency) Index, 2001–2002
Source: Bloomberg.

terms of timing. Meanwhile, our experience in Russia prevented us from going long interest rates as they were increased as it was clearly unsustainable.

Are there any other trading lessons that you picked up along the way?

In terms of valuation, no matter how cheap you think something is, it can always get cheaper. Vice versa, no matter how much you think something's overvalued, it can become more overvalued.

You also have to be very careful of strategies that rely on historicals. When people say things like, "This has never traded above X" or "This has never happened before" or "It's never moved more than three standard deviations," it often does just that.

Are there certain variables that you look for that signal a great emerging market trade?

There is no template. It really is different every time.

Your major thesis right now is that emerging market stocks, which you collectively call Emerging Markets Inc., are attractive. One of your reasons is the underinvestment by mutual funds in emerging market equities. Why focus on mutual funds and not hedge funds?

Until recently, hedge funds in emerging markets were mostly involved on the debt side where they could lever up. Hedge funds getting involved in EM equities is not really good or bad. What's going to make this trade work is if long-only, traditional investors (pensions, endowments, mutual funds, and other long-term investors) around the world shift some of their portfolio into EM equities. It also helps if local money shifts into its own equity markets. In places like Korea, for instance, most locals have their savings in bonds.

How important are demographics to emerging markets trades?

They are very important but a slow force. We are looking at this trade on a three- to five-year basis, which won't be affected much by demographics. If you go longer term, which a pension fund should, then yes, demographics are extremely important. With the exception of the United States, most of the developed world has a demographics problem, whereas most emerging markets have the benefit of growing populations entering the workforce at the outset of their consumption stage.

Another positive factor you cite for the emerging market equity thesis is structural reforms. How do you measure structural reforms in emerging markets?

You just have to see where things were, where they are now, and where they're going. We've seen a lot of markets making it easier for investors to buy and control assets. Takeover laws are being introduced; reduction of taxation is being introduced in a lot of places to the extent that a lot of emerging markets now have much better tax regimes than developed markets, including the United States. These are the types of trends we are looking for.

Given the pace of technological advancement, do you think developing countries have an advantage over developed countries in some ways?

Oh, undoubtedly. It's good to see developing countries leapfrogging. In telecom, developing countries are passing over wire lines and going straight to cellular. It requires much less investment in terms of the infrastructure and it's much faster. So you see whole populations getting cell phones, which speeds everything up. They don't have to wait for weeks for their neighborhood, their streets, and their houses to get wired.

The Internet is the same story. People in very poor countries have access to Internet cafés and suddenly they can correspond with people all over the world for almost no cost. Companies in developing countries have web sites that allow them to sell their wares all over the world at very low cost just because people can now know they exist. There's undoubtedly an advantage there.

How much has the downtrend in the U.S. dollar the past few years helped the long emerging market equities theme?

It depends. We always look at the currency independently, and if Everest has a negative view toward it, it will be hedged. In many cases, the reason why emerging market equities are so attractive now is because their currencies are undervalued as well. Currently, most of Everest's equity portfolio is currency unhedged, so on the margin it has helped.

The weak dollar is not a required ingredient to our thesis, though. It has helped to the extent that some commodities may be stronger because of the weak dollar and some emerging countries are commodity exporters. If we had a stable dollar at this point, it would not necessarily invalidate our thesis, because some commodity prices will remain strong due to supply constraints even with a strong dollar.

Do you think the world is moving away from a U.S. dollar standard?

The euro is becoming an alternative to the dollar, so at the margin that is the case. The question is, how much of the fact that people are considering it as an alternative is as a result of the euro being up 30 percent over three years? If the euro were to reverse, would people be so eager for an alternative?

If there is a big sell-off in U.S. Treasuries, can emerging markets still perform?

Again, it depends. If inflation is under control and a Treasury sell-off is due to growth, then the emerging market story can continue as equities and direct investment in a growth environment offer good alternatives to fixed income.

It also depends on what a Treasury sell-off does to the U.S. equity market. If U.S. stocks and bonds really sell off, given how big they are in the world's portfolios, emerging markets will probably go down as well, although they might go down less. In terms of absolute performance, I have a hard time imagining emerging markets up if U.S. equities are down by 20 percent.

Given that China is one of the big question marks in emerging market land, what are your views there?

Investors are oversimplifying China. The whole debate about a soft landing or hard landing for China is not the right question. China, like the United States, has a lot of different regions and a lot of different sectors that each have their own dynamics and their own stories.

Take their automobile industry. There are 17 different car manufacturers in China with a lot of capacity, all keen on establishing market share in the belief that it's going to translate into profits later. In the meantime, none of them is making any money. So I would say that the Chinese auto industry is in for a hard landing.

Meanwhile, leisure and tourism is a sector that's going to have no landing even if China slows down dramatically. There are so many people there who are getting to the stage where they have enough discretionary income to take a vacation. There is so much pent-up demand that you won't see a slowdown in the Chinese tourism sector for a long time.

By the same token, everybody talks about a real estate bubble in Shanghai, but that doesn't mean there's a real estate bubble in all of China. That would be akin to saying there's a housing bubble in Kansas because real estate prices in the Hamptons or Palm Beach are going through the roof. There are regions in China where there's actually a housing shortage. In some regions, house prices have gone up by 40 percent in the last seven years while incomes have gone up by 70 percent. Hence the affordability factor has gone up in some areas rather than down.

We spend a lot of time in China because it's a very large place that's very different across regions and businesses. No one can say China is one place.

One of the market's conventional wisdoms about China is that Westerners get killed when they try to invest there because they will never understand it. The Everest Capital China Opportunity fund invests more in other countries that benefit from China than China itself. Is that how you avoid getting hurt as a Westerner?

We believe that a lot of the winners and losers from what is happening in China are outside China. The China fund is structured to take advantage, globally, of who we think those winners and losers will be. Only about 20 percent of the fund is invested in Chinese shares, while the great majority is invested outside China's borders.

We look for companies exporting to China or companies that are reducing their manufacturing costs by opening factories in China. Companies that are winning from what's happening in China are often easier to find, or it's easier to see how they're benefiting from what's happening in China, than is the case with Chinese companies per se. So yes, it's not easy investing in China directly, which is why it is only about a quarter or less of what the fund is doing there.

*Can you give me some examples of investments that Everest has
made directly in China and how you got over the lack of
transparency hurdle?*

Everest is invested in Shanghai Zhenhua, which is a manufacturer of
container cranes. Given the expansion we are seeing in world shipping,
a lot of ports are adding to capacity and will need more cranes. This Chinese company is the world leader in that sector.

Everest has invested in A shares, the B shares, and the H shares, so we are
very familiar with this market. We have four people who speak Mandarin,
one of whom is a Chinese national formerly from Shanghai, so we know a
lot of people and companies there.

*Are there any U.S. companies in your China fund that benefit
from the China story?*

YUM Brands is a U.S. company that benefits from China. YUM Brands is
the parent of KFC (Kentucky Fried Chicken) and Pizza Hut. A lot of their
earnings growth is coming from China.

One of the hurdles to finding a company that benefits from China is
that you have to find ones where China is a large enough percentage of
their growth to make a difference. If a company's business with China is
booming but its share of the company's revenues go from 0.5 percent to 1
percent, it's not enough of a reason to invest.

One sector with strong earnings growth from China is European lux-
ury goods companies. We expect that upwards of half of their earnings
growth for the foreseeable future will come from sales in China and to
Chinese tourists. These companies are a great way to express our positive
view on Chinese disposable income and tourism.

*What do you see as the major risks to your emerging market
equity thesis?*

Terrorism is an obvious short-term risk because of the detrimental effect it
has on economic growth, but I don't think it derails the story.

We see two main risks over the next three to five years. One is China
and Taiwan. We think there is a probability that is nonzero that China takes
over Taiwan with force. You can start to see things going in that direction.

The consensus is that China will not do anything before 2008 because they don't want to endanger the Beijing Olympic Games. We think Taiwan is much more important to the Chinese leadership than hosting the Games at a certain date. They have a long-term view so they could easily say, "Let's take Taiwan now and we'll have our Games in 2016 or 2020."

China's military is much stronger than it was and the United States is tied up in the Middle East, so there's a window of opportunity for them. Taiwan is very important to the Chinese as it is part of the whole national psyche and it would be a very strong display of strength on the world stage.

The other risk is North Korea flexing their nuclear muscles. There is a chance they could use them out of desperation. One of the things Everest uses to hedge these low-probability but nonnegligible events is credit default swaps on China and Korea which, interestingly, are extremely cheap.

Do you think markets underprice tail risk?

Yes. We've seen it time and again. Things happen that nobody thought possible. The crash of 1987, the Mexican devaluation of 1994, the Asian devaluations of 1997, and September 11 all were unimaginable.

Do you foresee a day when the term emerging markets ceases to exist? In other words, all markets emerge to become first world or developed countries.

It's a very interesting question. We've already seen it happen in Europe. You see it with countries like Portugal and Greece, and you'll probably see three Central European countries moving to developed status soon. Korea and Taiwan are two big ones in Asia that have emerged.

Many countries are going to move to the developed bucket, but we'll have a lot of other countries opening up to take their place. There are a lot of small countries out there that don't have anything right now in terms of capital markets. But yes, at some point, the whole world will be developed. We're a long way off from that right now.

In this vein, what is your view on Turkey?

We like Turkey, and the Everest funds are invested in some of their equities. Turkey is benefiting from the fact that its currency is cheap versus the euro, which brings a lot of money in from Europe in the form of invest-ment and tourism. Turkish bank stocks, in particular, are interesting to us. You see it time and again with emerging market countries: When interest rates come down, pent-up demand for consumer loans explodes. That benefits the banks, because people start buying their houses with loans or mortgages instead of paying cash.

What are some of Everest's more exotic emerging market plays right now?

Cyprus, Mongolia, and Uruguay are some of the smaller markets that Everest has invested in recently.

Where do you get your information to find these far-flung opportunities?

Traveling, talking to people on the ground, reading the local newspapers. Traveling is important and a serendipitous way of acquiring information that you can't get from reading. Just walking around a city, looking at the level of construction, looking at what people are doing in stores, talking to people in hotels, trying to get a feeling of what kind of people are coming to visit, where they are coming from. Are locals bullish or bearish on their own market? How has their perception changed over time?

We look at the price levels and do anecdotal purchasing power parity studies. None of these things necessarily has an immediate impact on things. We're not necessarily going to make money from those observa-tions, but often it gives you a good pulse, especially when you come back to a place over and over again and see how things change.

I've been going to Eastern Europe and Latin America for the past 20 years. I have people who work with me who have been traveling consis-tently to, or have been living in, Asia for the last 15 years. My partners, col-leagues, and I travel, then come back and talk among ourselves about what we saw going on.

Do you also meet with government officials when you travel?

No. We found it to be pretty limited in value. For example, I met with Hugo Chavez a few years ago and I thought the guy would be terrific for Venezuela. After a while, actions speak much louder than words.

Everest doesn't have any offices in New York or London—only Miami, Geneva, and Bermuda. Is that by design in that being removed from the major financial centers helps you be contrarian?

I don't know if it's an advantage, but Everest has operated that way since the beginning and it hasn't hurt us. Everest just opened a Singapore office two years ago to give it an Asian presence. Longer term, we see a bipolar world between China and the United States, so we need to be there.

When Everest opens a new office, what type of skill sets do you look for in new hires that denote success in emerging markets?

It's really a variety of ingredients. We like people who have emerging markets experience and curious minds. Typically, they don't have the background that people here have, which is being able to look at debt, equity, and currency markets. They usually come from one of those specialties, so Everest will train them and hope that they'll be curious enough and agile enough intellectually to start looking at all asset classes. That's the best way to approach emerging markets.

What advice would you give to someone who would like to run a billion-dollar emerging market fund someday?

You have to love investing and looking at new things every day. Particularly in emerging markets, you have so many things that are changing and unpredictable, so you have to be comfortable with that. Just be curious, go to those places, try to think on your own about where you think things are going to grow, what's going to suffer, and how you can make money from it.

What keeps you energized?

The fact that it's fun. It's like a puzzle. Every day the pieces are moving and you have to try to put them together. You're judged every year on how well you're able to put the pieces together, and it's really hard to find something that's as much fun and as challenging at the same time.

If I weren't doing what I'm doing for the Everest funds, I would be doing the same thing with my own money. That's how I started. When I started the fund, I didn't know if I would have any investors; I was ready to do it just with my own money. Maybe that is because I was cocky at the time and thought I could compound at 15 percent per year and live off that. Fortunately, that's what we've done.

It seems like a number of hedge fund strategies out there are getting crowded. What's exciting and fun about global macro and emerging markets in particular is that the playing field is so large, while the number of players willing to do the work and put real money behind their convictions is relatively small. We think this bodes well for our approach and our investors for many years to come.

CHAPTER 15

THE FIXED INCOME SPECIALISTS

David Gorton and Rob Standing
London Diversified Fund Management
London

David Gorton and Rob Standing of London Diversified Fund Management (LDFM) represent another evolutionary trend in the hedge fund world: the convergence of fixed income relative value and traditional global macro strategies. But while the rest of the investment universe is just catching on, the unassuming British pair have been on this trend for some time, quietly racking up astounding performance numbers since launching their fund within the confines of JP Morgan in 1995. For their first 10 years, they posted an average annual return of over 15 percent with a standard deviation of 5.5 percent, compared to just over 7 percent return and 6.6 percent standard deviation for the 10-year U.S. Treasury Index. In other words, versus an index of investible securities deemed virtually riskless, Gorton and Standing have given investors twice the return with less volatility.

These two 40-somethings generally eschew publicity, and neither is a household name in Britain or anywhere else. Indeed, they personally are little-known in the hedge fund world, although most are aware of their firm. Both men operate in a rather esoteric world where advanced mathematics, cerebral cunning, and superior analytics are the required tools of the trade. Gorton and Standing operate in the quantitative model–driven world of relative value, where simultaneous long and short positions are taken in similar securities to exploit subtle anomalies and inefficiencies primarily in global bond markets. What makes them unique is that they overlay their relative value trades with global macro strategies. Both are quick to cite this combination as having saved them during times of extreme market stress. During the 1998 crisis precipitated by the Russian crisis and subsequent implosion of Long Term Capital Management (another relative value/arbitrage fund), many relative value players were wiped out. LDFM, on the other hand, posted a positive 10 percent return for the year, which allowed them to capture the wider spreads that were available in relative value trades when most of their competitors were licking their wounds or closing up shop.

I went to see Gorton and Standing at their London offices which inconspicuously occupy the fifth floor of a Mayfair townhouse. Talking to each of these gentlemen, I was struck by the impression that I was just another meeting in a very long day, executed in a very methodical manner with the utmost efficiency and attention to detail. There were few jokes, little banter, but many courtesies and an utter lack of extremes. They seem to conduct their lives and their business in the same manner in which they approach the markets, exacting an executioner's precision and carving out mountains of cash for clients in a mundane way that they describe as "bloody arcane rubbish."

Do you classify what you do as a relative value (RV) or global macro hedge fund?

Gorton: We are an RV stroke macro fund. Traditionally, we have had about two-thirds of our risk in RV and one-third in macro, although at any given time, it could be 100 percent either way.

When we first launched as an RV/macro fund back in the mid-1990s, it was extremely difficult to market to investors because it didn't fit into any particular box. We tried to explain to them that running a pure RV strategy on its own is very dangerous.

After Long Term Capital blew up, people woke up and realized how dangerous pure RV is. Getting out of RV trades during the LTCM unwind was near impossible, and the best hedges were classic macro trades like Eurodollar futures and out-of-the money options.

What is your definition of global macro?

Gorton: Global macro is about trying to find imbalances within or between the major asset classes, which are equities, commodities, fixed income, and foreign exchange. Macro is at the top of the hill looking down, trying to find which of those four big chess pieces is about to move.

One difference between a pure global macro fund and LDFM is that hopefully we have enough attention to detail to grind out money during the slow periods for macro. Our analysts and PhDs spend a lot of time analyzing detail in the marketplaces through a variety of models. While we will not be as leveraged in the great macro trades as a pure global macro manager, we should be outperforming in the slower periods and, on average, outperform.

Standing: Also, our global macro view is an important input for all of our RV and micro strategies. If our macro view is flawed, a lot of our other strategies won't work. All investment methodologies have a macro component no matter how RV or quantitative they get. Even RV modeling has an important global macro element in the calculation of models concerning views on interest rates, volatility, and curve shapes.

The advantage of global macro is that it is very easy to allocate big sums of capital to trades because there are less liquidity constraints. Global macro markets are all so deep that you can put all the capital you want into the views you have.

How do you define relative value?

Gorton: Relative value is a very difficult concept to define. Some funds have very strict parameters as to what they would consider an RV trade while we have a much looser definition.

To us, it is a trade that exploits an inefficiency, typically in the yield curve or the volatility surface. These inefficiencies are not pure arbitrages, which is why you need a macro or structured reason as to why they are there. Once you know the reason for the inefficiency, then you have to decide if doing something simple such as buying short sterling or selling U.S. Treasuries is a better way to exploit it.

Are there still pure arbitrages out there in the risk-free sense of the word?

Gorton: If there are, we would love to find them, and we look every day.

Has the relative value space become more difficult?

Gorton: You never know if the game is harder or if it has just changed.

A few years ago, you could buy Italian bonds at euribor (Europe interbank offer rate) plus 100, so it was pretty easy. Then again, there were not many of us who had the knowledge, risk capability, or experience to put those positions on in the kind of scale you should have done then. As our knowledge base has grown, the markets have become more efficient.

When I started trading, I really didn't know an interest rate from a frozen pea. Back then it was the Wild West, but it is completely different now. Trading is a bit like an explorer going off in the jungle. The first guy through has to spend a really long time hacking away, but once he is there, it is easy for others to follow. Clearly, there are not as many no-brainer trades around, but we do find them occasionally. The problem is, they usually go from looking really good to looking extraordinarily good. The key then becomes putting positions on in the right size relative to your account.

At the same time, central bank management of markets has become much more adept. Core consumer price index (CPI) in the States has been between 1 and 2 percent in the last eight years. That is an extraordinarily stable number. We just had a year with 4.5 percent growth and core CPI went from 1.3 to 1.6, which also points to fewer opportunities.

Has the inflow of capital to relative value hedge funds or hedge funds in general altered your space?

Standing: From the global macro perspective, I do not think the amount of capital being allocated to it is being noticed at all. Let's take the U.S. fixed income market, for example. Growth in central bank assets is greater than growth of hedge fund assets, so hedge funds, as a percentage of that market, are shrinking rather than growing. Also, some macro imbalances are at their worst level ever, so while you have stability in some places, the imbalances in the world economy are likely to have an impact on foreign exchange or interest rates in the near future.

If you look at certain narrow, quantitative strategies, we might be at the point where there is more capital than risk available, but in general, growth in financial markets has been as fast as the growth in hedge funds. So will opportunities disappear because of the growth of hedge funds? Possibly, but we haven't reached that point yet.

Gorton: We notice the presence of more players in the markets we trade than we used to. More people, such as macro funds, now understand RV better so they are better able to express their trades in the right part of the yield curve, which is less anomalous as a result. In general, people in the markets have also become much better at attention to detail. When I go to manager roundtables now, the understanding of detailed economics is much greater. I think all of us are being pushed by the rise in competition.

Do you think the "shortage of ideas" you hear so much about today is more a function of good central bank management, growing expertise in the market, or the growth in hedge fund assets?

Gorton: I would say it is a function of all three, the least of which is the amount of money that is being allocated to hedge funds.

Standing: I would argue that the decline of volatility and thus opportunities in financial markets is partly due to the shift of risk assets from the banking sector to the asset management industry.

Banks used to take a lot more market risk. Because they guarantee their depositors' money back at par, they are not well equipped to withstand shocks. Hedge funds and asset managers are now taking on a larger percentage of risk around the world, and because they do not guarantee investors their money back at par, they are better suited to handle that risk. That is why the system absorbs shocks quite effectively these days.

A prime example of this shift in risk can be seen in the credit markets. Banks now have a lot less credit exposure on their balance sheet relative to their capital, which makes the financial system more averse to shocks than it was in the past. The growth in credit derivatives and various hedging products makes this possible. It all makes perfect sense because the participants who want risk can have it, while those who do not want it are not overly exposed.

How do you approach risk management for your fund?

Standing: We run two different funds. We have the London Diversified Fund which, by definition, has a number of diversified themes in it, and the London Select Fund, which is more concentrated and riskier. Investors can then choose which profile they want. The partners here have a higher percentage of our own capital in the Select Fund, but we have money in both.

In our Diversified Fund, we are always looking at a broad number of themes in a number of different currencies simultaneously. We will not allocate more than 20 percent of our capital to any one particular trading strategy, in order to maintain diversity.

The Select Fund, on the other hand, is designed to be more aggressive and more macro biased than the Diversified Fund. We will have fewer trades and could have as much as half of the risk in one trade where we have a very strong view. *Ex post*, you would expect the Select Fund to be more volatile and have higher returns than the Diversified Fund.

When you say no more than 20 percent allocated to one trading strategy, how do you define a strategy?

Standing: A strategy would be an RV structure or a macro theme. If two strategies are in the same market, say different parts of the U.S. yield curve, but are not correlated, we would be very comfortable allocating the maximum of risk to each one independently.

Gorton: One of the restrictions of our fund being sold as an RV/macro fund is that we have a very low risk tolerance. We tell people that we will never lose more than 5 percent. To date, touch wood, we have never drawn down more than 3.5 percent. That means that even when we see outstanding opportunities, we cannot concentrate risk in that trade and we will underperform a bit. The portfolio effect of running RV and macro strategies has been quite strong but it also tends to skew performance to the middle of the range. Our average annualized return has been over 15 percent since we started in 1995, but if we had been more concentrated in the great trades, it would have been upwards of 25 percent.

I would argue that 15 percent annualized returns (after fees) and a worst case drawdown of 3.5 percent is pretty damn good.

Gorton: It is not bad. Our original investors are now worth four times their initial investment after 10 years, so we have asked them to move some of those gains over to the Select Fund to push up their average. With the Select Fund, we have a vehicle ready and waiting for when those great trades and near arbitrage opportunities arise.

Being RV and macro, does your portfolio volatility position tend to net out?

Gorton: We are very rarely net short volatility. We constantly run stress tests on our portfolio to see what would happen in a financial market accident, and generally we make money.

Standing: In concept, a lot of RV trades are inherently short volatility. If we have on a lot of RV structures that have short vol characteristics leaving us net short vol, we would be very conscious of that and look for ways to balance that out. As David said, it is very unusual for us to be short vol.

In a portfolio sense, we feel more comfortable with a long vol position. We get long vol through a combination of macro strategies and some RV strategies that are uncorrelated with short vol RV strategies.

Are there any risk management lessons that you learned the hard way?

Gorton: I was the first trader at Chemical Bank worldwide to make $2 million in a month, which happened to be September 1987. I was short bonds, which was a disaster during the following month when the stock market crashed. The lesson I learned there was: when a disaster is happening, just get out. Chop all ropes. Trust your instincts on what is winning and recognize what trades are not working, so you can cut them before they suck too much energy and money from you.

If you were launching today with a blank slate, how would you go about building out your portfolio?

Standing: There are a number of RV strategies that work very effectively in certain environments. These RV trades are consistently structured and are easily implemented, so we would start with that. The next stage would be to identify the opportunities in the global macro markets and structure our macro view. Macro themes might be whether the USD is overvalued, if oil prices are going to go up and stay there, where U.S. interest rates are going, whether the U.S. yield curve is going to flatten or steepen, whether the European Central Bank is going to tighten or ease. These are the types of themes that we form views on.

If our macro view is very clear, we look for strategies that work effectively in that environment. Then we start allocating capital to micro strategies within our macro themes, whereby if our macro views are right, we produce excess returns, but if our macro views are wrong, we have very small losses.

If our macro view is not clear, in other words, saying "This could happen or that could happen," then we start looking for opportunities in a more relative value sense and start building up our portfolio from that.

Where do you get your ideas?

Gorton: I am a total whore when it comes to ideas. I have never had an original idea in my life. I get the germs of ideas just by talking to people. I talk to salespeople, economists, other traders, and so on.

If a bank sales guy calls you up with a good idea, will you go ahead and put it on?

Gorton: Not immediately, but yes. If I hear something of interest, I will explore further and dig a lot deeper.

A typical trade filtering process from recent experience was where I heard some guy tell me that all emerging currencies entering Europe have strengthened except for Poland, which has weakened. This piqued my curiosity, so I asked a few people why and nobody had a sensible explanation. I started talking to more people, having conference calls with economists, bringing in Poland and Eastern Europe research guys, and so on. I found that the fundamentals in Poland were very different due to some fiscal problems that caused the currency to weaken and interest rates to remain a bit higher than they should have. From that, I started thinking about how to express a trade. After some more work, it became clear that the best way to get exposure to Poland was through the currency. Foreign exchange (FX) is not our forte, but it was obviously the right place to be. In FX, we were able to combine our views on the Polish yield curve, volatility, and spot to fit our macro view.

When you identify an interesting opportunity like Poland, do you normally express the trade with just one instrument that you deem optimal or through several instruments?

Gorton: Normally, we will put two-thirds of the risk allocated to the trade into the instrument we like best and split the other third between two or more trades.

For example, in the fourth quarter of 2004 we recognized the growing imbalances in the United States and the need for a higher savings rate and thus a weaker dollar. We looked at those macro factors and positioned ourselves through foreign exchange and bonds. Foreign exchange was clearly the best trade, but again, we're not really a global macro fund so it's hard for us to have all of our risk in foreign exchange.

In this example, we put a total of 2 percent of our value at risk (VAR) into that macro view, with 60 basis points of VAR going toward short USD, long euro FX, and 70 basis points each in long European bonds and short U.S. bonds. This trade structure captured the idea of slow domestic demand in Europe, higher short rates in the United States, and a weaker dollar. We expressed quite a lot of the bond side through options because European interest rate volatility was very cheap. We ended up buying almost twice as many options in Europe than we sold in the United States for the same premium, so we got real leverage out of it when the position went our way.

We like adding leverage to our winning trades. So many people in this business take their profit when they have a good trade on and end up missing a lot of the move. That is such a limiting mentality. When you are up a percent or so on a good trade, that is when you really need to push.

What is the average time horizon for your trades?

Standing: Generally, it's between two to three months, although there are some positions we've had on for several years and some we've had on for three minutes.

Gorton: The really good trades last for a long, long time. Sometimes you want trades to happen quickly, sometimes you do not. I would be delighted if TIPS (Treasury Inflation Protected Securities) still yielded 4.25 percent and the price never changed.

Was TIPS the best trade of your career?

Gorton: I have seen about four or five great trades.

TIPS at 3.25 percent was a great one. Back in 1998, yields on TIPS were well north of 3 percent and clearly anomalous. It is outrageous that you can get paid what is perceived to be trend growth plus inflation while taking no risk. We figured that, in light of productivity growth, they should be yielding around 1.5 percent.

We started buying TIPS with a 3.4 percent yield and they traded up to 4.25 percent, at which point it was getting a bit hairy as we got close to our stop-loss. We were able to stay in, though, and over the years, we have kept most of our capital invested in TIPS. We learned various ways to hedge them with time by looking at what their correlations were with the underlying marketplace, what the likely response was to any given rate level, how they should respond to volatility, and so on. Back when we bought them, all we knew was that they were completely the wrong price. Since then, the market has also learned and adjusted. We finally got completely out of TIPS in July 2003 at our original target of 1.5 percent yield. (*See Figure 15.1.*)

A 15-year, 15-year forward sterling versus euros trade at a 225 basis point spread back in 1998 was another great trade. We knew then that clearly it was the absolute wrong price and we felt strongly that, over a reasonable holding period, the spread would come in. We had the trade on in the Diversified Fund for a good six years, but it would have been nice to have had a larger position.

Another one was the Japanese yield curve, which again we started trading around 1999 or 2000 when you could do a 5-year, 5-year forward against a 20-year, 10-year forward steepener. Like the TIPS trade, it started totally wrong and we lost money on it every single working day for nine months. It was a disaster and we had to fight just to stay still, but the carry on it was just unbelievable. Also, all the macro factors lined up such that if anything, the Bank of Japan was going to ease, not tighten. After that first nine months, we made money every single day for the next two years. It was an outstanding trade.

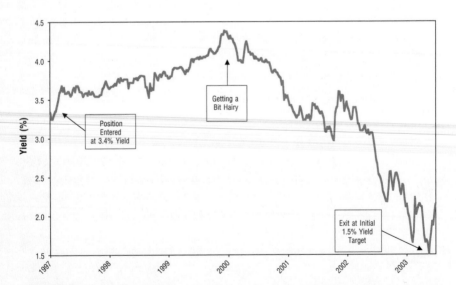

FIGURE 15.1   10-Year Treasury Inflation-Protected Securities (TIPS), 1997–2003
Source: Bloomberg.

Were you able to hold on to the position because you were running a broadly diversified portfolio?

Gorton: Exactly. We had other trades on that were doing well. We also hung on to that trade for so long because it was so outstandingly good. I have never seen a yield curve that was as mispriced as the yen curve at that time.

Other great trades over the years were curvature and conditional steepener type trades on the U.S. yield curve back in 2001 when nobody understood them. Now everyone understands them so there is not much juice left in it.

The trade is where you buy a receiver swaption or a call on the one-year interest rate one-year forward, and sell the same on the 10-year interest rate. There is a slight macro bias to this trade as it is a pure curve trade, which I consider more macro than RV.

We built models of the whole yield curve out to 30 years to see what we thought the shape of the curve would be at any given rate level, how convex we thought the curve should be, why it should be that convex, and so on. We determined that the market was mispricing these trades. Ten-year volatility was bid way too high due to hedging by the agencies (Fannie Mae, Freddie Mac) to protect their portfolio convexity issues.

Standing: After September 11, the Fed was cutting rates, which created a very, very steep yield curve in the United States. The market consensus was that long rates were also going to come down, so implied volatility was very high in the 10-year sector when compared to the short end. Our macro view was that Greenspan was going to keep cutting rates until things were proven to be better.

There were a number of things that pushed an RV surface to very attractive levels, such as the shape of the yield curve, which was in our favor, and mortgage guys hedging the long end pushed vol up, among other things. It was one of the few occasions where all the variables came perfectly into line, giving us the confidence to put on a big position. Since it was structured with options, if we were wrong, we were not likely to lose much. That was an exceptional trade.

Gorton: Due to the interest rate and volatility skew in the market, we actually got paid 25 basis points for the privilege of having on the trade we wanted. It was extraordinary. When I first stumbled onto this, I could not believe it and kept thinking, "What is wrong with this?" That was probably the best trade we have ever had. It was the first time we made over $200 million, real dollars and cents, from one position.

A couple of the best trades you talked about originated back in 1998 or 1999 when a lot of relative value players had been washed out of the markets. Did the Long Term Capital unwind create anomalous opportunities for the RV guys who stayed in business?

Gorton: No question about it—1998 was also a very good year for us because we made 10 percent while everybody else got hurt. We were a lot less leveraged in some of the RV things that blew out, and our ability to take macro positions saved us. For instance, when things really started to unravel, we bought as many short sterling and Eurodollar contracts as we were legally permitted. When the Fed eased by 75 basis points, our macro positions bailed us out of our RV losses.

Did you know Long Term Capital was unwinding their book or were your own RV positions the danger sign?

Gorton: We just saw things blowing out in general. Sterling asset swaps in particular were causing me a great deal of pain and I started wondering what was going on. Then we started hearing rumors that Long Term Capital and other funds were going bust. We had a bad sense prior to June that things could get ugly and we knew the financial system could not take a lot of stress, so we got into the front end of the United States and the United Kingdom very quickly.

Have you had any bad trades?

Standing: There have been a number of RV stresses that have been difficult. One was a simple, unexpected stretch after the United Kingdom raised rates on the back of an inaccurate average earnings figure. It turned out that the figure was calculated wrong, but it was too late for us when it came to how our positions fared in the market.

Another difficult time was market stress in the summer of 2003 when the U.S. Treasury market sold off hard. Yields went from 3 percent to 4.5 percent as the market attention shifted from deflation fears to inflation fears. There were some great opportunities after the transition, but we were caught wrong-footed during the shift. We were comfortable with the first leg of the sell-off but could not understand how the market could push rates up so quickly on the back of inflation fears so soon after the major deflation scare. That move caused our biggest drawdown and was a very difficult time. (*See Figure 15.2.*)

What lesson did you take from that?

Standing: Having gotten the first bit of the correction right in an RV sense, we allocated capital much too quickly in the early stages of cheapening. We did not want to miss what we thought was a great opportunity, but we did not factor in the positions in the market that had built up during the deflation fear–driven rally. When you see these pockets of volatility, it is hard to predict where it is going to end up, and we completely got it wrong.

David, what was your worst trade?

Gorton: This will sound awfully arrogant, but I have never held on to a trade to the point that it has become disastrous.

One trade I learned some lessons from was when I bought Greek T-bill floaters back in 1997. The Greeks were issuing five-year bonds which fixed quarterly against the Greek T-bill rate. It was a Greek T-bill floater but it did not pay the T-bill rate, but rather T-bills plus 100 basis points.

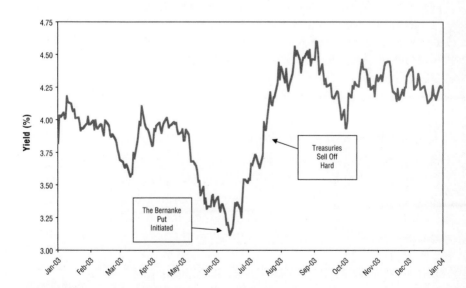

FIGURE 15.2   U.S. 10-Year Treasuries, 2003
Source: Bloomberg.

When I heard about this, I just sat there thinking, "Why on earth should I get T-bills plus 100? I will just buy these, short the T-bills, and collect the 100 basis points risk-free."

The only issue was that we could not repo the Greek T-bills, so we financed the Greek side in the forward market to make sure we were covered. At one fixing, I was trying to get the one-year forward done so that it would equate to a flat rate, which would mean I was locking the whole 100 basis points until the next fix.

The forward drachma market was illiquid and had a wide spread, so I could not get the hedge in exactly right. I could have had them at plus three basis points or something, but I was dicking around trying to get them in at flat. I decided to buy some cheap one-month and try for the one-year later. Then, on the day my one-month financing rolled off, short rates went from 7 percent to 100 percent as the Greeks tried to defend their currency from a speculative attack. I was forced to pay 100 percent interest to hold that money for two days and ended up losing all the profit on the trade.

What lesson did you learn from that trade?

Gorton: Don't be a dick for a tick! I could have locked in a 97 basis point risk-free profit but instead I held out for 100 basis points.

Nowadays, we are more than happy to pay to get trades done. We try to work with our sales coverage and the investment banks to get our transactions filled smoothly. We know they have to make a living so we do not like to put them in competition. If they respect our business and are happy to see the flow, they will not take too much out of us.

What happened next on the Greek trade?

Gorton: We held on to it, the market settled, we financed it out and made our money back. It turned out to be an outstanding trade. It was clearly mispriced by the Greeks and they actually stopped issuing the floaters. Essentially, they were issuing subsidies to their local banks by giving away 100 basis points for nothing. Once speculators caught on, they stopped.

Because they were transferring their citizen's tax to you?

Gorton: Exactly, but it was meant to go into their domestic banking system to shore it up prior to the euro entry.

Do you travel to check out a trade or to source ideas?

Gorton: Very rarely. We go to New York twice a year to meet with invest-ment bankers, strategists, and investors. Our investors are very nice but they do not really want to know what we do. They want to hear our big-picture view, not how we actually grind it out. Grinding out cash is bloody arcane rubbish.

What major themes are you telling your investors about these days?

Gorton: Right now, our biggest issue is that we do not really have any big, clear themes to build on. We are also having a bit of a shortage of great ideas. We are in quite an unusual period where long-term rates have been extraordinarily stable and volatility has declined commensurately.

The yield curve has flattened, which allows volatility to go even lower. We are expecting that trend to continue for a little while longer, but at this point it is extremely dangerous to try to eke out small gains from short vol or spread-tightening trades. We could milk 1 percent or a half percent per month for the next few months or so being short vol, which would probably work, but it has the danger of going horrifically wrong.

The interesting thing about the way VAR models work is that as the volatility in markets declines, your risk declines. To keep VAR levels stable, you have to do more and more of the same trade so that, in essence, the position is actually getting more and more dangerous.

As far as we are concerned, we are at a point now where we should not be playing. Our investors can expect subpar returns for the time being be-cause capital preservation comes first and foremost at times like these. Our style right now is like that of a wily old leopard: We are sitting, preserving energy and waiting for the opportunities to come to us.

Do you find it stressful having several billion dollars under management and no view?

Gorton: Yes. A big challenge for us as a business going forward is this low-vol environment. It is the worst thing for our style. It was great when we thought volatility was going down and we made money as it did, but now, with volatility at these levels, you risk losing an awful lot of investor money being short. That is what is driving our absence of any structural trades at the moment.

We might be in the process right now of pricing out risk premia in the bond markets. I don't know if it will be permanent, but it is rational that it gets priced out because for the last 20 years you have been paid to own bonds. Yield curves in general have been positive and in the absence of something better, you want to be long, because you get paid. The old banking adage "Lend long, borrow short" clearly works.

Tactical trading to the short side has had great wins here and there, but the reality is that good steady returns are made from being long. We want to be short interest rates right now because interest rates are clearly too low relative to nominal GDP. But we have been losing money in that trade, so we have to wait. Meanwhile, we have been long European bonds for a while, but we are now out of that trade because you would have to think that we are in a Japan-type situation to buy European bonds at 3 percent. In general, we don't have much risk on at the moment, so we are focusing on capital preservation.

CHAPTER 16

THE CURRENCY SPECIALIST

Anonymous[1]
Currency Fund Manager
London

The business of foreign exchange has evolved considerably since the introduction of the euro, which focused world economies on three principal currency zones. Simultaneously, many foreign exchange traders no longer want to be limited to just currency trades, which is logical considering that interest rates are embedded in foreign exchange trades held longer than one day.

The foreign exchange manager presented here has a rich background in interest rate trading, having started as a broker of interest rate products and then as a Eurobond market maker before moving into proprietary risk taking and then as fund management. He has held various jobs in and out of financial markets at many different institutions before landing his current role as a chief investment officer (CIO) at a several billion dollar hedge fund within the asset management unit of a bank. This manager's mandate now

---

[1]This trader works for a large international financial institution, one that deemed it controversial to reveal itself and its strategies inside the pages of a book on global macro trading. To protect the manager and the institution, this interview is presented anonymously.

includes currencies, interest rates, and their derivatives, but with a strict focus on liquidity.

When complimented about being a well-known star trader in the financial world, the manager seems unimpressed. "I was meant to be a rock star," he claims. He does not mean this in the metaphorical sense—he used to sing in a rock and roll band. His imposing stature applies to his suave physical demeanor as well as to his presence in the markets. And he is supremely confident. It is not difficult to imagine him holding court behind a high-end bar or strutting down a Paris runway—two of his jobs before trading.

The first time I met him, we had lunch in the Royal Exchange building in London, which was once home to the London International Financial Futures Exchange (LIFFE) open outcry trading floor. He entertained me with a collection of pet theories about the markets, the world, and life. He is always animated, waving his hands to articulate points, drawing diagrams, snapping his fingers, and portraying complicated financial concepts in the simplest terms. Although he exudes intelligence, he is the first to admit that his trading style comes from the school of hard knocks, having abandoned a formal university education after a year and having learned to trade at a time when bank traders and market makers took enormous risk in an aggressive, hypercompetitive head-to-head approach. His vision as to what trading is all about can be captured in this quote: "At the end of the day, if you have more discipline and bigger balls, you are probably going to win, because other people do not."

How did you get into macro trading?

I dropped out of college for personal reasons. After dropping out, I modeled a bit, which was hilariously good fun, and ran a very exclusive bar. Traders from The City would come into the bar and say, "What's a smart guy like you doing behind a bar?" One of them offered me a job as a money broker and I took it. They had me brokering floating rate notes when they first came out. I had no clue what they were, but it didn't matter, it was easy. Since then, I have worked at about seven or eight different shops, I can't really remember, but most of them were crap and didn't understand risk. Over time, I evolved my trading from purely interest rates to foreign exchange and a more global macro style.

How do you define global macro?

Global macro is trading in the asset classes that are driven by top-down analysis where you can't control any of the instruments for more than a two- to three-hour period because they are driven by the underlying economic environment and policy decisions.

Have global macro markets changed since you started?

Trading is just a series of single days, so I haven't really noticed, but I don't think the opportunity set has gotten any bigger or smaller in the real macro world where the variables aren't controlled by us.

How do you approach trading currencies in a global macro context?

To me, foreign exchange is not a true macro strategy. It's the tail of the distribution. There is only one true macro trade and that's the price of money. Everything else is a function of the price of money.

Central banks control the price of money and drive everything with their central bank rate. They use monetary policy to get supply and demand moving in the economy by encouraging people to move out along the risk curve. The risk curve, in essence, is the credit curve.

Of course fiscal policy is controlled by government, so we also keep that variable in mind when looking at the current and future prices of the assets we trade.

Meanwhile, monetary policy has high correlation among the G10, with the exception of Japan, because they're all driven by the same thing. There is really only one central bank and that's the U.S. Federal Reserve. The Fed sets the price of money.

In actual practice, the price of money is not the Fed's overnight rate but the interest rate that corporations use to evaluate investment opportunities. I would argue that's the 18-month to two-year interest rate. From there, you move out along the risk curve to government bonds, corporate bonds, and then equities. At the tail end, you have foreign exchange (FX) fanning out.

Foreign exchange is like the fan at the end of the credit curve. It's a function of how people are looking at those credits along the curve. For example, if the market decides that Brazil is a great credit, then other things being equal I'd expect the Brazilian real to rally because people have to go in and buy it if they want exposure to Brazil.

So, currencies are essentially beta on interest rate sentiment?

Yes. They are beta on interest rate and credit sentiment, or beta on beta. Foreign exchange is sentiment driven because it's a relative price between two countries. It reflects the relative sentiment of investors, reality and the perception of a bunch of different factors between two economies.

In managing my portfolio, I spend most of my time concentrating on the Fed because it is responsible for encouraging people to invest and move out the risk curve. It doesn't want everybody so scared that all they do is deposit their money in short rates. Economies don't expand in that scenario.

Consequently, we are very directional. At most, there are only three or four macro trades in the world at any one time. If there is only one, then we'll only have one trade on. Those three or four macro trades, apart from the cost of capital, are what the bond markets are doing, what the equity markets are doing, and what the dollar is doing.

The dollar in a broader sense only trades against three blocs—Europe, Asia, and Latin America—and rates/prices within those blocs correlate. It would be unusual to see the Chilean peso and Brazilian real moving in completely opposite directions, for example. The difficulty with foreign exchange is that there's no real anchor to FX policy. Who actually controls foreign exchange policy?

Foreign exchange is a very difficult tool to run policy with. The only large country that has used a foreign exchange policy in the last decade (who allegedly has a floating rate, i.e., not pegged) is Japan, which is why they don't correlate with the rest of the G10. Japan's monetary policy and fiscal policy are maxed out, so it's the only policy tool they have left to create any change in supply and demand conditions. Likewise, true global macro funds should make more money out of fixed income than foreign exchange, because fixed income is policy driven and foreign exchange is the anchorless tail thing.

Has the Fed gotten better at its job, thus reducing volatility as well as opportunities for global macro funds?

There aren't more or less opportunities because we still have those few macro calls to make. That won't change.

The Fed has created a new problem that it finds much harder to control, and that is the global business cycle. The global business cycle has created a new dynamic which has caused increased global correlations across asset classes. Arguably, it is now more difficult for the Fed to man-age the economy. It has become more like driving an oil tanker than a small dinghy, but it is still at the wheel. That's why I focus on the global price setter and the driver of global demand—the Fed—to make my few macro calls.

Where else do you get your information to make those few calls?

There's not that much information to get. The most important variables in global macro are the economic conditions and how central banks respond to those economic conditions.

To get that information, I read the paper, look at the data, watch what officials say, and try to read between the lines. From an actual trade point of view, it's price action that determines when and where to put on a trade.

Otherwise, there's a huge amount of noise in the world. Other people's opinions are irrelevant. I can't bear talking to salespeople because all they want to do is sell you something new, and things don't change enough to warrant that. I don't pick up the phone if I can avoid it.

What signals a great macro trade?

I'm looking for signs of a *gestalt shift* in markets, where all of a sudden, the market's view on something instantly changes. The Asia crisis was a great example, where overnight it went from the Asian miracle to a house built on sand. Both were wrong, by the way.

A gestalt shift usually comes after volatility gets pumped up because every-one is out there buying insurance. When people are buying options to protect positions, it means they have an underlying position they're nervous about.

The big trades in macro are when the market is going to reprice a view or shift to a whole different concept. I spend a lot of time looking at where market sentiment is in hopes of finding the next shift. I spend the rest of my time looking for the most efficient way of expressing what I think might happen.

Markets are just a compilation of information we know and informa-tion extrapolated from information we think we know. As such, the collec-tive knowledge of a group of people is always higher than the individual parts, even recognizing for experts. Price action tends to confirm that, and price action never lies.

Do you ever express your views through relative value (RV) trades or is it always directional?

I don't do relative value trades for two reasons: (1) Negative gamma is implicit in relative value trading because it works on regression to the mean; and (2) it is very labor intensive, which drives me nuts.

I came from a spread trading background so I very much understand all this carry stuff. It's not quite the greater fool theory, but you're always expecting somebody to value a spread a bit tighter than you did. That works until someone decides to sell. That's why you see RV funds with perfectly smooth returns of 1 percent per month for years, until all of a sudden there's a massive drawdown.

I have an absolute fear of negative gamma. My fear comes from having worked at brokers and bank trading rooms and knowing what these things go for wholesale. When you are sitting in a dealing room or trading floor, you have the ability to see wholesale prices. When you're sitting on this side of the desk, you can't.

It's the difference between trading futures from the pits versus from an office looking at computer screens. When you're looking at screens, you've got a one dimensional price. It goes from 5 to 6—that's all the information you've got. When you're standing in the pit and the price goes from 5 to 6, you can see who's buying it, how many they're buying, and who's behind that ready to buy more. The whole thing becomes very different depending on where you are sitting.

In RV land, as soon as you're positioned, you implicitly know that you've made the wrong price; otherwise the trade never would have happened. It's the whole winner's curse thing. When a position with negative gamma goes against you, it really goes against you and when you try to hedge, whatever you do is wrong. What is the point of putting yourself in that kind of situation?

I take it you're never short options?

Never. Again, negative gamma.

Liquidity, liquidity, liquidity is key in real macro trading. The hedge funds that blow up are always the one's who misestimate how much liquidity is in the marketplace. It's always the same thing, it's always liquidity.

Macro trading is 24/7 but you can't change your view that often, so

WINNER'S CURSE

Winner's curse is a concept applicable to bidding systems whereby the winning participant typically pays an overvalued price for the winning item. This problem is encountered during any auction process because bidders must estimate the true or final value of a desired good, including their own bid. Because of numerous factors, including emotions, incomplete information and others, estimating the intrinsic value of the product bid on can be difficult. In reality, the winning bid tends to exceed the intrinsic value because the highest overestimation made by any of the bidders will win the auction.

you might as well be in the liquid stuff with a directional position. If you look at central bank policy, it's unlikely that the Fed is going to raise rates, then cut, then raise again over the course of three meetings. It just doesn't work like that. Trends around Fed policy are not likely to change abruptly after a rate move in a new direction, because it's the first step in a long journey.

That's one of the reasons why I don't like yield curve trades. If I think the market is going to have a bearish flattening, I'm going to trade the end that moves the most, which would be the two-year note. It's easier for me to hedge, it's cleaner, and if I'm wrong, it's less of a problem.

When you sell two-year notes, do you buy put options, short the futures, or sell the cash bond?

Seventy percent of the time when we initiate the position, it's through options. Macro trading is all about timing. We all know stuff is going to move, but we're not exactly sure when. Options are the easiest way of controlling risk while affording a good return.

The right time to buy an option is when everyone is telling me that something is inevitable and the market is discounted to one extreme. I don't necessarily always go the other way, but I am less likely to get into the position if I share the same view. In general, the basic laws of macro trading are that when you're bullish you're long or flat, and when you're bearish you're short or flat.

When you say "everyone" is telling you, who is everyone? I thought you didn't pick up the phone.

My traders talk to sales guys and bank economists. I read the subject line of the *Bloomberg* messages I get, but most of it's rubbish anyway. Again, how many truly new pieces of data are there at any one time? Not very many.

Every time I hear people talk about China revaluing its currency, I tell them to shut up because it's just crap, absolute crap. Nobody knows, and the last person who is going to know is some sales guy at a bank. Opinions are like assholes—everybody's got one.

Do you systematically overpay for options like the empirical studies say?

Probably, but again the key to being long volatility is timing. The hardest thing in the world to articulate as a macro trader is timing. Why does a good sportsman always seem to have a little bit more time than other guys? I don't know, but they do. They always do.

Do you always have a position on?

Yes, because being flat is a very, very difficult position to run. You're wrong no matter what.

Let's take a step back and talk about market price action, which will help explain why I always have a position on. A market is a simple information-discounting mechanism. Price moves are mainly driven by government data that reflects the underlying economy. As a result, 75 percent of price movement happens only 10 to 15 percent of the time. The rest is nothing but noise within a range.

As a macro trader, I am trying to capture those occasional moves, and the best way I know to do that is by owning options, being long gamma and vega. The really cool thing about an option-based strategy like this is that my leverage becomes a function of my correct macro analysis. If I'm right in my macro call, I'm going to lever into it and if I am wrong, I am going to reduce leverage.

This is why Commodity Trading Advisors (CTAs) or black box trading systems work. I was always extremely skeptical of CTAs until I started trading macro and understood that the main drivers in macro are very different from what they may appear to be when trading relative value. At the end of the day, CTAs are not emotional and always involved in the markets. They are long risk premia. They catch these moves and add to their position quickly as it goes their way, and vice versa, giving them a payoff profile that is very similar to an option.

Do you get away from the markets a lot?

Yes. I hate to belabor this point, but information doesn't change that quickly, it just doesn't. I focus on the main drivers and forget the rest.

If everything is correlated and there's not that much information to get, how do you derive an edge?

A lot of strategies are cyclical, but global macro trading has the least amount of cyclicality to it. Macro doesn't rely on the economic cycle, whereas strategies like credit trading are clearly linked to the underlying economy. The way I approach macro, the global economic cycle has little correlation with my returns. I'm just trying to catch those few macro moves in the deep, liquid markets.

I don't get involved in illiquid, esoteric trades where, once they start to wobble, everyone's running for the exit. I don't ever want to be a forced seller. I understand the principle of high prices bring buyers and low prices bring sellers, and I don't want to be that guy.

My edge, I guess, is that when I see the forced sellers and forced buyers, I am able to take the other side, because I'm long gamma. I'm a buyer at low prices and a seller at high prices. My basic underlying strategy is to get long of gamma when I feel we're going to get movement due to an anticipated policy shift driven by new economic data.

So to me, this game is all about liquidity, liquidity, liquidity in the larger asset classes; making those few macro calls; and protecting risk by being long of gamma and long of vega. Clearly, if we read those few tea leaves wrong, we're not going to make any money.

Do you tell your investors to expect the occasional bad run?

Yes, of course we'll have drawdowns and bad runs. You can't make money without them.

Recently I had a drawdown and investors asked how my risk profile had changed. I told them it hadn't. If I've lost money, how on earth am I going to make it back if I cut my leverage? I can't. I know that sounds counterintuitive, but if I think I'm right and I'm managing my investment process and risk properly, I'll stay the course until the facts change. Just like Keynes, I, too, change my mind when the facts change. But recently, when

I was down, I didn't think the facts had changed and I hadn't hit my risk management stops, so I kept the same trades on.

One of the hardest things to do in trading is trade your way out of a hole. A well-known trader once said to me that the sign of a good trader is to recover from a drawdown with the same trade, and that's absolutely true.

How long does that theory hold, because Keynes also said, "Markets can stay irrational longer than you can stay solvent." At what point does your theory max out?

I look at the market over a five-month time horizon. At that point, there are enough data points to pass judgment. If my view of the macro drivers hasn't kicked in by that time, I would know that I'm analyzing the market wrong and get out. In the meantime, our internal drawdown constraints will limit how wrong I can be. Also, remember that I'm long gamma and vega.

It is important to recognize when you're wrong and when you're right. Recognizing when you're right is as hard for some people as recognizing when you're wrong. I find it comical to see people cut their profits and run their losses, but it happens all the time.

I personally don't find either particularly difficult because of how I structure my portfolio. I hate to keep hiding behind this positive gamma argument, but it really does take a lot of the crap emotional decisions away from you.

When you own an option that becomes very cheap or worthless, you don't sell it. You keep it in the back of a drawer and forget about it until the expiry date comes around, at which point you open the drawer and see if it's worth anything.

A great example of that was a trade we did in Argentina before its devaluation. After Brazil devalued its currency from 1 to 2 against the dollar, we looked at deep out-of-the-money put options on the Argentine peso and thought they were ridiculously cheap. We bought puts struck at 2 against the dollar when the peso was trading at 1 and threw them in the back of a drawer. They were cheap and got a lot cheaper, but when the peso devalued to 3 against the dollar, we made a killing. The guy we bought them from didn't hedge it and actually ended up getting fired after the devaluation. (*See Figure 16.1.*)

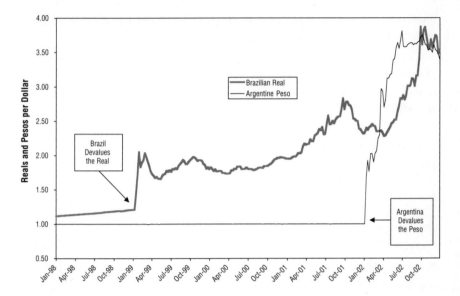

FIGURE 16.1 Brazilian Real and Argentine Peso, 1998–2002
Source: Bloomberg.

Was shorting the Argentine peso your favorite trade of all time?

No. I don't have a favorite trade of all time. My favorite trades are when I'm wrong and get out without losing too much money.

My worst trade ever occurred in 1998 when a very large, highly over-leveraged hedge fund was unwinding its portfolio. I was long a three-year into three-year forward receiver swaption, which was a bet on European and UK rates converging in the three-year, three-year forward part of the interest rate curve. I was betting that the United Kingdom would join Europe earlier than the market anticipated.

I put the trade on at a 150 basis point spread and it converged to 130 bps before this to-remain-unnamed hedge fund ran into trouble. They had it on in huge size, so as they started to unwind it and other similar trades, the spread blew out to around 220 bps. I was forced to get out of the position due to our 5 percent monthly loss rule.

It was my worst trade because I miscalculated both how big the rest of the market had it on, particularly the high-profile hedge fund, and how wide the spread could get when it started going wrong. It was a complete function of misjudging liquidity in the market. Again, I cannot emphasize enough the importance of liquidity. It is liquidity where most traders mis- price assets relative to the returns they expect.

After that experience, my strategy for trading relative value positions changed very quickly: I don't! All RV trades have directionality in them, no matter what people say. The directionality in this trade was that the liq- uidity going in was a lot deeper than the liquidity getting out.

Did you know the trade was crowded when you put it on?

I did know it was a popular trade. It was a policy-driven trade and the market was talking about it a lot. Again, the lesson here is when everyone is saying something is inevitable, think twice.

No one owns or controls a macro trade, because it is impossible. If you can control them, then it means you have become the market, and when you become the market, you've got a bit of a problem. There are several examples of very good, smart macro traders who have fallen foul of this rule. When you own 25 percent of a stock, you cease to be a macro trader and become an owner. In the fall of 1998, one hedge fund owned its mar- kets and it became a problem.

I have this theory on liquidity, relative value, and markets that I call my "frozen ice theory." It also highlights the dangers of negative gamma— again! The frozen ice theory goes like this: When a lake freezes, it's thicker at the sides than the middle, right?

Go back to 1995 when the Japanese yen was trading at an all-time low of 80 to the dollar. Everyone was blaming everything that was wrong in the world on the yen's strength. The economy in Japan was sliding, they had repatriated all their money, politicians were protesting the level— bloody, bloody blah. It was clear to everyone that the dollar/yen exchange rate was the wrong price at 80.

Eventually, traders started buying dollar/yen in anticipation of yen weakness. Smart trade, right trade. In the frozen ice theory, this occurs at the sides of the lake where the ice is thickest. The trade is solid and the theory behind it is sound.

Dollar/yen started to go up as expected and the people involved cashed in their profits, but they took their profits too early. As dollar/yen contin- ued to rally, they were left watching their macro call run away from them without position. By now dollar/yen has gone from 80 to 100 and it looks to be on its way to 120, but everyone took profit when it was in the 90s.

Traders have a very hard time buying something at a greater value than what they just took profit on, so they look for a proxy, or relative value. They buy dollar/Thai and go through the same process. Then it's dollar/Malay, dollar/Korea, dollar/Philippine peso, and so on.

Next thing you know, everyone and their grandmother is long dollar/Taiwan, dollar/rupee, and dollar/rubbish, yet they don't remember why they have dollar/Asia on in the first place. Nobody is long dollar/yen anymore and it's at 135.

Everyone has rotated out toward the middle of the lake where the ice is thinnest. In essence, they've all moved out the spectrum of, guess what, our old friends: liquidity and credit. Suddenly, dollar/yen (the liquid stuff) starts to reverse. Game over. Everyone stops, looks around, and finally notices everyone is surrounded by people with the same illiquid stuff on the thin ice. People start trying to get out and asking for prices in size. Yeah, right. How about down here, buddy? No, off that, actually how about down here? And so on and so on.

The weaker credits always have the least liquidity and the so-called highest returns. All the crap rallies at the end of a bull market, which is how you know it's near the end. When triple rubbish like winganda prayer.com is suddenly worth more than great, long-standing companies, you have to stop and question things.

It happens time and time and time again in the markets. Everybody's standing there in the middle of the thin ice with pretty much the same position, having forgotten why they put the trade on in the first place. The reason they've forgotten is because they don't have the original trade on anymore because they got out too early. They're in, they're out. They missed the main move so they buy something else, and then something else and something else. We've all done it. Everybody does it. Everybody runs a vicarious relative value book in how they trade. The yen in the second half of the 1990s was a classic case. (*See Figure 16.2.*)

It's always important to look back at why you did something. If you don't, you start doing what economists do, which is raise a price target after it gets hit.

This thin ice argument works when you look at funds of hedge funds as well. Institutional hedge fund investors often allocate to a hedge fund only after it has had a solid run, when performance is peaking. Investors who got in at the beginning can weather a drawdown because they've made some money, but institutional investors usually aren't there at the beginning. They get exposure late in the game and wind up getting hurt.

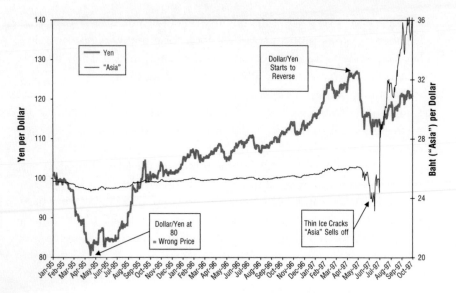

FIGURE 16.2   Dollar/Yen and Dollar/"Asia," 1995–1997
Source: Bloomberg.

How should investors go about allocating to hedge funds?

The way to pick a hedge fund is to look deeply at how the team is structured, how they function together, and how well they handle and decipher new information. The team's lack of collectivity is very important as there should only be one or two people managing the majority of the risk.

The problem with the fund of funds business is that it's all about not making a decision. Allocation decisions are made collectively so that no one is culpable. I guess that's part of human nature. At the end of the day, after they go through all their sophisticated processes, the investment committee may end up arbitrarily picking a guy who has a few billion dollars under management, based on the rationale that he must be good or else he wouldn't have a few billion dollars under management, as opposed to asking if it is the right strategy, if the space is crowded, or if the macro environment is about to create a different dynamic.

There are all these supposed experts and PhDs working in the fund of funds business, but you have to ask, if they're that smart, why aren't they running a hedge fund? When I meet a recognized expert in the hedge fund industry, I almost always know what he's going to say next.

Have you done a good job picking traders to work for you?

It's incredibly difficult to spot a good macro trader. To be a good macro trader, you have to see future value, as opposed to present value. A lot of today's traders know the price of everything but the value of nothing. They grew up in a world of derivatives and financial engineering as opposed to trading. There are nine ways to skin a cat when it comes to financial engineering, but there's no silver bullet when it comes to investing.

At what point in your career did you know you were good at trading?

Pretty much the first week I started. I just had a knack for it. It's like golf—either you get it or you don't. In golf, when you're in the deep rough 250 yards out from the green and pull out a bloody 3-iron, you ain't playing the game properly. You are never, ever, ever gonna hit the green unless you're Tiger Woods, and even he's unlikely to. You need to pull out your 9-iron and play it safe. In trading, like golf, it's how you play the bad shots that really matters. How you play the really crap shots is the difference between the good guys and bad guys. When the shit's hitting the fan, you don't pull out a 1-iron. You just don't—you play defense.

Do you have any favorite market books you recommend to your traders?

Haven't got any. They're all obvious rubbish, full of stupid things that probably don't work anymore. The best experience a young trader can have is to know what it's really like to have on the wrong position and not be able to get out. There is nothing you can read to learn that.

A good friend of mine, who is a very smart salesman, once financed a bullish call on Bunds by shorting the puts. Boy did he ever squeal when the market fell two points as his position got bigger and bigger the more it fell!

At the end of the day, if you have more discipline and bigger balls, you're probably going to win because other people don't. A great example of bigger balls is from an experience I had when running the trading desk at a bank. I was helping one of our market makers get out of a position and the thing we were trading was priced at 99. I phoned up one of the big banks and asked for a price. The guy really marked the thing down to 96–97, but I said, "Fine, yours."

He then asked me my price, so I made him a market of 85 bid, 86 offered, in any size.

He said, "Excuse me?"

I said, "85, 86, what do you want to do? Any size."

"Nothing done," he said.

Now, if that were me, I would have bought as much as possible because you just know it's the wrong price. The problem for him was that he felt I knew something and because of that feeling, he completely replaced his "pricing model" with "this other guy's opinion is correct." So much for experts.

What's your opinion of the world right now?

My core view is that the globe is actually okay. We're having a bit of a love-in in the Middle East right now and that's important. Geopolitics is a big driver in our markets and they're pretty stable at the moment.

You sound surprised you think the world is okay. Is that because you are normally bearish like most global macro guys?

Sometimes when I walk out on the street and look around, I get so bearish that I think about buying a bloody castle in Scotland and moving up there with a couple of loaded shotguns and a truckload of canned foods.

When you look at the whole world and see what it's built on, it's not sustainable. It is totally, clearly not sustainable. The biggest thing that scares me is that we are about four meals away from total anarchy. I don't know how much food you have in your house, but if there is a run on the food supply with nothing available at supermarkets or restaurants, we are in deep trouble. Anarchy on the streets. I think about that often!

CONCLUSION

In the long run, we're all dead.

—John Maynard Keynes

APPENDIX A

WHY GLOBAL MACRO IS THE WAY TO GO

By Dr. Lee R. Thomas III

The global macro approach to investing allows for diversification across markets, products, geographies, time frames, strategies, and skills. It is often said that diversification is the only "free lunch" in finance. To see why, we'll first examine a hedge fund manager using a single big-bet approach and then move on to assess the mathematical impact of a multibet diversified portfolio approach.

THE BIG BET APPROACH

Suppose a hedge fund manager makes a single big bet each year and that the manager has told investors that the fund would target annualized returns of 10 percent. Let's also suppose that the manager has better-than-average skill such that the probability of getting that one big bet right is 60 percent. Why 60 percent? Repeated enough times, throwing darts at a page of stock quotes can be expected to pick winning stocks about 50 percent of the time. A hedge fund manager who makes money less than half the time will quickly lose investors, while a manager who makes money 60 percent of the time will be well inside the upper half of the league tables. While 60 percent may sound low, the nature of *nearly* efficient markets is such that the margin between winning and losing is very small and is often resolved only by chance. Experience quickly reaffirms that markets are difficult. Winning bets are not easy to come by because market prices reflect the collective wisdom of scores of skillful participants.

Back to the single big bet: If it is a winner 60 percent of the time, that means it will be a loser 40 percent of the time. Thus, in order to meet the promised average annual return target of 10 percent, the bet has to be sized such that it returns 50 percent when it is right and loses 50 percent when wrong. When it succeeds, it produces a 50 percent return 60 percent of the time and when it is wrong, it loses 50 percent 40 percent of the time. If repeated year in and year out, the expected average gain of 30 percent (0.50 × 0.60) minus the expected average loss of 20 percent (0.50 × 0.40) would produce an average annual return of 10 percent. (*See Figure A.1.*)

Big Bet Performance Analysis

Hedge fund managers are often judged by their Sharpe ratios, which are calculated as the fund's return minus the risk-free rate divided by the volatility of returns. The Sharpe ratio is also known as the reward-to-volatility ratio and provides a sense of the quality of the managers' returns per unit of risk. It allows for some element of comparison across managers. Hedge funds often strive for a Sharpe ratio of at least 1.0 such that their

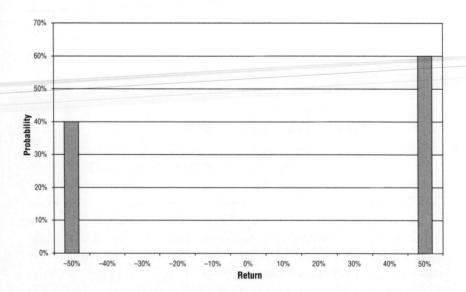

FIGURE A.1   Hypothetical Big Bet Portfolio

performance is commensurate with the amount of risk assumed. Hedge funds that produce a Sharpe ratio well over 1.0 attract investor interest while those with a Sharpe ratio well below 1.0 do not.

In the example of the single big bet, with a volatility of approximately 50 percent, the strategy delivers a Sharpe ratio of 0.1 assuming a risk-free rate of 5 percent $[(10 - 5)/50 = 0.1]$. While investors would probably be pleased with a 50 percent return in the good years, it is unlikely that they would tolerate the negative 50 percent years and remain invested long enough to witness a 10 percent average annual return. In sum, a hedge fund manager taking the big-bet approach may prove lucky for a spell, but that luck would eventually run out in the longer term and the manager would be forced out of business.

To improve the Sharpe ratio, a manager can try to improve the probability of getting that single big bet right, but that is difficult in nearly efficient markets. A manager can also focus on making more from winning trades than is lost on losing trades but again, over time, nearly efficient markets will prove such an approach difficult. Another approach to producing better Sharpe ratios with the same level of skill is to diversify.

THE MULTIBET PORTFOLIO APPROACH

Assuming the hedge fund manager's stated goal to investors remains to produce a 10 percent average annual return, the same better-than-average manager can produce a superior Sharpe ratio by increasing the number of bets per year. *The key is that the bets must be independent (i.e., uncorrelated).* If the manager increases the number of bets from one to just five, the average position size can be reduced from 50 percent to 10 percent and still meet the annual return targets promised to investors.

With an average bet size of 10 percent, the hedge fund manager can still deliver a 50 percent up year if the stars align and all five bets prove to be winners. The probability of returns being 50 percent is about 8 percent $(0.60^5 = 0.0776)$. Meanwhile, the probability of losing 50 percent in an extremely unfortunate year is only about 1 percent $(0.40^5 = 0.0102)$. As you can see, a 1 percent chance of losing half your money under the multibet approach compares favorably to a 40 percent chance of the same result under the big bet approach.

After running a scenario analysis of the five-bet strategy, a return distribution shows a classic normal distribution slightly skewed to the positive side of

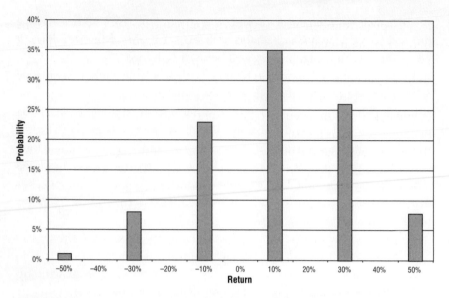

FIGURE A.2   Hypothetical Five Bet Portfolio

the return spectrum. In most scenarios, however, performance tends to cluster around the 10 percent return investors were told to expect. (*See Figure A.2.*)

Multibet Performance Analysis

Checking the performance of the multibet approach, we find the strategy had a volatility of about 20 percent, resulting in a Sharpe ratio of 0.25. While this figure is not particularly impressive, it represents a drastic improvement to the 0.1 Sharpe ratio produced by the single big bet approach. Both the big bet strategy and the multibet strategy produced average annual returns of 10 percent, but the multibet approach produced much less volatility and thus a higher Sharpe ratio. In sum, the smoother ride of the diversified portfolio might have compelled investors to stick around.

HOW TO PRODUCE SUPERIOR RISK-ADJUSTED RETURNS

By simply increasing the number of independent bets from one to five per year, the same better-than-average hedge fund manager increased the quality of returns considerably. Likewise, by continuing to find and increase the number of high-quality independent bets per year, a manager can raise a fund's Sharpe ratio dramatically and push it toward the magical 1.0 through the reduction of volatility.

The difficulty in this approach is that the bets must be both better-than-average and independent. For example, a hedge fund manager might be long equities in Thailand and Indonesia, considering these to be two independent bets. But the nature of these markets at the moment is such that they have a high degree of correlation. As such, the two trades should be considered a single bet—long Southeast Asian equities. Because finding high-quality, uncorrelated trades is not easy, the ability to find multiple better-than-average independent bets is what separates a star hedge fund manager from the rest of the herd. To become a star, the notion of diversification must be pushed to an extreme.

Diversification in this sense goes far beyond traditional notions of the term. It means diversifying in many different ways, and the flexibility to do so is particularly evident within the global macro style of investing. Global macro managers have the breadth of mandate to look for inefficiencies and opportunities across the spectrum of products, geographic regions, and strategies. Here we'll briefly examine why global macro is an optimal strategy for building a diversified portfolio.

Asset Classes and Products

The easiest way for a global macro hedge fund manager to find diversified, independent bets is to trade different asset classes and different investment products within those asset classes. Global macro managers monitor interest rates, equities, currencies, commodities, and real estate, and within each of these categories, managers consider a range of products. Whether it be cash, physical commodities, futures, derivatives, or direct investment, the key is to not limit choice. Better-than-average bets are a rarity and can occur in some products but not others for various fundamental or technical reasons. As such, global macro managers need to watch all asset classes and products all the time with an eye out for such inefficiencies. The mandate of global macro hedge funds affords the latitude to allocate capital to any asset class or product, allowing global macro managers the freedom to exploit a particular inefficiency in the most effective manner.

Geography

Global macro hedge fund managers also achieve diversification by investing anywhere geographically. By doubling the number of countries a manager can invest in, the number of independent investment opportunities available more than doubles. There are innumerable independent bets that can be made within countries, across countries, within regions, and across regions. Because the number of opportunities and potential inefficiencies is so vast, it takes significant time and effort to monitor them all in a meaningful manner. But such a broad selection provides significant opportunities to global macro managers seeking multiple uncorrelated, better-than-average bets.

Strategies

Most hedge funds stick to one particular investment strategy. Increased specialization is a trend that has been developing for years in the money management world, allowing investors to better understand exactly what managers are doing and permitting managers to attract capital through differentiation. Diversion from a stated investing style is a penalty known within the business as *style drift*. Global macro managers, in contrast, are able and encouraged to move in and out of various investment disciplines as warranted by the macroeconomic climate. Global macro hedge funds often hire traders, analysts, and teams with a wide array of styles and skill sets in search of independent ideas. Fundamental analysis, technical analysis, relative value, arbitrage, top-down, bottom-up, quantitative analysis, and long/short are just some of the skills and styles open to global macro managers. The key is for chief investment officers to have at least a basic understanding of all strategies and skills such that they can accumulate, synthesize, and translate the recommendations into themes and trades employable within the overall portfolio.

CONCLUSION

In sum, while diversification may not be a good way to make headlines, it is a very effective way to make money. Although there will always be a hotshot hedge fund manager who produces attractive results for a period of time through a focused portfolio approach, the key to consistent performance over time is diversifying smart bets. Global macro's mandate affords the latitude to achieve such diversification. For consistent superior risk-adjusted returns, global macro is the way to go.

Dr. Lee R. Thomas III is the chief investment officer of Alpha Vision Capital and the Vision Fund Group, a suite of global macro absolute return products offered by Allianz Global Investors. Prior to Vision, Dr. Thomas was managing director and the chief global strategist at Pacific Investment Management Company (PIMCO). Prior to PIMCO, Thomas worked for Investcorp, Chase, Citibank, and Goldman Sachs. Dr. Thomas holds a bachelor's degree and a PhD in economics from Tulane University.

APPENDIX B

A NOTE TO INVESTORS ABOUT GLOBAL MACRO

Dr. Lee R. Thomas III's eloquent presentation in Appendix A helps detail some of the mathematics driving the evolution of global macro to more of a global micro style. Although he makes it sound easy, in truth, the global micro approach to investing, which requires multiple better-than-average, independent bets, is extremely difficult to put into practice. My interviews with global macro managers hammered home the recurring theme of the growing shortage of opportunities in today's markets, a trend that seems to be affecting all investment strategies.

In the modern globalized interconnected world, uncorrelated markets seem difficult to come by. Likewise, yield curves are flat and volatilities across various markets are at all-time lows, further reducing investment opportunities. But, as Marko Dimitrijević stated in his interview, periods of stability and low volatility tend to be a temporary phenomenon. Indeed, historically, long periods of stability are often followed by extreme dislocations as leveraged positions built up during the "safe" environment cause significant bottlenecks when there is a sudden shift in the investment climate and a rush for the exit.

Major imbalances across the globe are building up in many areas today. Central bankers, politicians, and other policy makers are beginning to get concerned that things might be getting dangerously out of line. Housing bubbles, divergent and extreme deficits and surpluses, and unstable currency regimes are compounded by other exogenous uncertainties such as terrorism and natural disasters. But with uncertainty comes opportunity.

Historically, allocations to global macro managers have been reduced during such stable periods. However, these have often proven to be the best times to be invested in global macro. Today may be an ideal time to gain exposure to global macro managers, before the large imbalances unwind, the housing bubble pops, equities finally revert to their historical mean, the U.S. deficit becomes a real problem, existing currency regimes come unglued, global markets become uncorrelated, and the new Federal Reserve chairman, Ben Bernanke, lifts the Greenspan put. These are dream scenarios for global macro managers, who can span the globe seamlessly, reallocating risk on the fly to where the opportunities are.

To reiterate, it is difficult to precisely define the global macro strategy because these elements of style drift and flexibility allow managers enhanced dexterity in times of crisis. But the ability to position themselves for outsized profits during such market inflection points is one reason why global macro managers should be included in the portfolios of all investors and asset allocators. Global macro has historically performed well, especially so during times of turmoil when other strategies and markets are doing poorly. As such, the addition of global macro hedge funds to any portfolio should serve as a hedge and a diversification tool, thus reducing risk.

Given their idiosyncratic nature and open mandate, individual macro funds can offer a wide variety of returns. In 2005, for example, the returns for global macro hedge funds ranged from +57 percent to –8 percent. Thus, diversification among global macro managers becomes paramount.

Dr. Thomas's diversified approach to global macro/global micro trading is roughly the same approach investors should use when allocating capital to global macro hedge funds. While some of the larger multistrategy macro fund managers have the breadth and depth to cover all markets, other managers have certain skill sets; utilize different approaches; and focus on different products, regions, and time frames that often lead to uncorrelated results. At the same time, investors should focus on managers who exhibit the skills required to produce strong returns over time and worry less about a manager's volatility characteristics. By combining uncorrelated global macro managers in a portfolio context, investors are able to significantly reduce volatility in their own portfolios.

To conclude, global macro offers opportunities for almost any portfolio, and its facility in times of turmoil make it look particularly attractive in today's uncertain world. As Christian Siva-Jothy notes in his interview, "It's the dichotomy of this business that we thrive on dislocation and economic upsets. Macro traders always do better when the world economy is tanking. It's a great hedge, in a way."

Hopefully, the interviews with global macro managers in this book have helped deepen your understanding of what today's global macro managers actually do, allowing you to make more informed, educated, and profitable investment decisions.

Acknowledgments

A few years ago, I promised myself that the next time I began to utter the phrase, "They should have . . . ," I would pause and consider doing the project myself if it was compelling enough. When "They should have a book about global macro hedge funds," crossed my mind, I scribbled some notes and started the process that became this book.

As this book grew from idea to initial interviews to a much broader undertaking than first anticipated, there was a surprisingly large number of individuals who offered assistance, guidance, or merely critical advice. While this list is by no means exhaustive, I hope that it goes some way in expressing the immeasurable gratitude I have to all those who in some way contributed to this project.

I would first like to thank all of the managers interviewed for spending precious time downloading their thoughts and perspectives into my recording device. Most of these participants have nothing to gain from this project, their funds having been closed to new investors for some time. With mainstream media attention often focusing on misleading aspects of the hedge fund business, the managers themselves agreed with me that it was time to set the record straight. These are their words, their edits, their book, and I feel privileged to have been able to facilitate such an undertaking.

The managers featured in this book do not comprise an exhaustive list of the top global macro fund managers today but rather are a collection of successful managers who I feel accurately portray the various intricacies of the global macro universe. As such, the omission of any manager should not be construed as having any meaning whatsoever.

While each of these managers has advanced my understanding of the business in very tangible ways, one stands out as someone who took a personal interest in my professional development from the very first time we spoke: Jim Leitner. For such a prolific net taker from the markets, Jim has

been a net giver in so many other ways, having been a patient and generous client to me when at Deutsche Bank; having been the first to suggest I
contact my future business partner, Andres; having taken an advisory role
to help guide the growth of Drobny Global Advisors; and having stood
firmly as a mentor and friend in a business where both are extremely rare.
Jim was the first manager interviewed for this book, and he has taken great
interest in the project from idea through to completion.

I would also like to thank a host of people who helped arrange inter-
views, provided background information, or assisted in some way on this
project. In alphabetical order: Michael Barry, Sean Bill, John Brady, Seb
Calabro, Jason Capello, Sandra d'Italia, Niall Ferguson, Miguel Forbes,
Bruce Gibney, Jane "£3" Hambling, Ralph Ho, Brian Mathis, Ben Mayer,
Mark McLornan, Tim Mistele, Jason Mraz, Yasmin Ocakli, Michael Ohr,
Josh Rosenberg, Peter Sasaki, Barbara Strauch, Gary Sutton, Eric Vincent,
Sol Waksman, Diana Way, and Helmut Weymar.

In terms of making this book look and feel the way it does, there were
several people who got their hands dirty by reading and editing various interviews and drafts. I would like to give special thanks to Dave Berry,
Brian Cordischi, Robin Davies, Andres Drobny, Don Drobny, Martin Kenner, Zach Kenner, Manu Kumar, Patrik Safvenblad, Lee Thomas, Walter
Thomas, Pamela van Giessen, and the people at John Wiley & Sons. I'd like
to extend a huge thank-you to my editor on this project, John Bonaccolta,
who dropped everything at a moment's notice to take on this task and
without whom this would not have been possible.

I am also grateful to the Drobny Global Advisors community, with whom
we have embarked on a truly unique business model of interactive research
and conferences that would not be possible without their input and energy.
Along these lines, it goes without saying that I extend the warmest possible
thank-you to my business partner and friend, magician and market maestro,
a man who is sometimes difficult and all the time brilliant, Dr. Andres
Drobny, who has made this a wild, fascinating, and fun journey.

Others I would like to thank for being great supporters of the business
since its infancy and of me throughout my career: Kenan Altunis, Zar Am-
rolia, Barry Bausano, Kieran Cavanna, Marc Cohen, Graham Duncan, Peter Early, Christian Exshaw, Adrian Fairbourn, Kevin Giblin, Chris
Gorman, Steve Gregornik, Rashid Hoosenally, Bill Lawton, Kevin Lecocq,
Andrew Marsh, Joe Nicholas, David O'Connor, Christian Pandolfino, Cliff
Papish, Mike Reveley, Tim Rustow, Greg Skibiski, Chris Smith, Steve

Solomon, Mark Strome, Yai Sukonthabhund, James Tar, Jim Turley, Steve Turner, and Bobby Vedral.

I would also like to thank my parents, Don and Susie, my sister Paige, and my extended family in Maui, Iowa, and Wales for being the greatest supporters. Finally, last but certainly not least, I would like to thank my wife, Clare, for being my biggest fan as well as putting up with me for more than the year it has taken to realize this (admittedly wildly underestimated) undertaking.

Steven Drobny
Manhattan Beach, California
January 2006

BIBLIOGRAPHY

For additional information, go to www.insidethehouseofmoney.com or send any questions to book@drobny.com.

Adamson, Loch. "The Money Machine for Hard Times." *Worth*, October 2002.

Asgharian, M., F. Diz, G. Gregoriou, and F. Rouah. "The Global Macro Hedge Fund Cemetery." *Journal of Derivative Accounting*, 2004.

BBC News, "Hedge Fund Man for MPC," April 26, 1999.

Beams, Nick. "Russian Crisis Shakes Global Markets." *ICFI*, August 25, 1998.

Brown, Heidi, and John H. Christy. "Growing Pains." *Forbes*, June 11, 2001.

Burton, Katherine. "Paul Tudor Jones, Saying 'Adapt or Die,' Invests More." *Bloomberg Markets*, May 3, 2004.

Calabro, Seb, and Thomas Dobler. "Macro and Managed Futures: What Can They Add to Your Portfolio?" *Goldman Sachs Conference Call Series*, November 17, 2003.

Caldwell, Ted, and Tom Kirkpatrick. *A Primer on Hedge Funds*. Lookout Mountain, TN: Lookout Mountain Capital, Inc., 1995.

Cecchetti, S.G., H. Genberg, J. Lipsky, and S. Wadhwani. "Asset Prices and Central Bank Policy." *Geneva Reports on the World Economy*, Vol. 2. London, U.K.: International Centre for Monetary and Banking Studies and Centre for Economic Policy Research, July 6, 2000.

Chancellor, Edward. "Hedge Funds Today: So Much Money, So Little Talent." *Wall Street Journal*, August 24, 2005.

CNNfn, "One More Soros Farewell," June 9, 2000.

Connor, Gregory, and Mason Woo. *An Introduction to Hedge Funds*. London: London School of Economics, 2003.

Cottier, Philipp. "The Origin of Hedge Funds." *Hedge Funds and Managed Futures* Bern: P. Haupt, 1997.

Coy, Peter, and Suzanne Woolley. "The Failed Wizards of Wall Street." *BusinessWeek*, September 21, 1998.

Craig, Susanne. "Goldman to Lose Two Traders." *Wall Street Journal*, September 24, 2004.

Dennis, Richard. "The Slower Fool Theory." *New Perspectives Quarterly*, Fall 1987.

Desai, Pratima. "Average Hedge Fund Leverage Falls Since LTCM Era." *Reuters*, March 6, 2005.

Dunbar, Nicholas. *Inventing Money: The Story of Long-Term Capital Management and the Legends Behind It*. New York: John Wiley & Sons, 2001.

Dunn, John E. III. "The Hedge Fund Life Cycle Concept—Those Feisty Adolescents Still Run Fastest." *Eurekahedge*, October 5, 2005.

Eichengreen, Barry, and Donald Mathieson. "Hedge Funds: What Do We Really Know?" *International Monetary Fund*, September 1999.

Endlich, Lisa. *Goldman Sachs: The Culture of Success*. New York: Touchstone, 2000.

Fry, Eric J. "1994 Revisited." *The Rude Awakening*, March 24, 2005.

Gerwitz, Carl. "As Currency Crisis Looms Before Maastricht Summit: Traders Rush to Buy Marks." *International Herald Tribune*, November 23, 1991.

Ghaleb-Harter, Tanya. "The Case For Global Macro." *DB Absolute Return Strategies Research*, December 31, 2003.

Greenspan, Alan. "Private-sector refinancing of the large hedge fund, Long Term Capital Management." Testimony before Committee on Banking and Financial Services, U.S. House of Representatives, October 1, 1998.

Gross, Martin J. "Hedge Funds Today: Seven Myths." *Wall Street Journal*, July 7, 2005.

Grossman, Sanford J. "Hedge Funds Today: Talent Required." *Wall Street Journal*, September 29, 2005.

Hedge Fund Research, Inc., "HFR Q3 2005 Industry Report," October 20, 2005.

Hibbard, Justin. "Big Bucks From Bubble Fears." *BusinessWeek*, November 8, 2004.

Hosking, Patrick. "News Analysis: History Shows Betting the Bank is a Sweet Delusion." *Financial News*, September 6, 2004.

Hsieh, David A. "Hedge Fund Risk Disclosure and Transparency." SEC Hedge Fund Roundtable, Duke University, May 14–15, 2003.

Huttman, Michael, and Mark Astley. "Why Macro Investing Is Back. . . ." *AIMA Newsletter*, June 2002.

Ineichen, Alexander M. *Absolute Returns*, 1st ed. New York: John Wiley & Sons, 2002.

Jereski, Laura. "Robertson's Tiger Hedge Funds Maul Rivals, Returning 63% Before Fees, Mainly Since June." *Wall Street Journal*, December 19, 1997.

Keegan, William. "Black Wednesday Gets a Whitewash." *The Observer*, February 13, 2005.

Keynes, John Maynard. *The General Theory of Employment, Interest, and Money*. New York: First Harvest/Harcourt Inc., June 1965.

Kolman, Joe. "LTCM Speaks." *Derivative Strategy*, April 1999.

Koshauji, Atul. "Dr. Sushil Wadhwani Reveals His Secret of Success." *Jain Spirit*.

Lewis, Michael. "For Love of Money: Why Central Bankers and Speculators Need Each Other." *Foreign Affairs*, March/April 1995.

———. "How the Eggheads Cracked." *New York Times*, January 24, 1999.

———. *Liar's Poker*. London: Coronet, 1990.

Liu, Henry C. K. "Part 2: The European Experience." *Asia Times*, November 8, 2002.

Lowenstein, Roger. *When Genius Failed: The Rise and Fall of Long-Term Capital Management*. New York: Random House Trade Paperbacks, October 9, 2001.

Martin, Mitchell. "Soros Shuffles Management as Big Funds Struggle." *International Herald Tribune*, April 29, 2000.

Max, Kevin, and Brett D. Fromson. "Multibillionaire Speculator Soros Exiting Risk Business." www.TheStreet.com, April 28, 2000.

Moggridge, Donald E. *Keynes*. London, UK: Fontana Modern Masters, 1976.

Morgan Stanley—U.S. and the Americas Investment Research. "In Praise of Hedge Fund Volatility." November 15, 2004.

Nicholas, Joseph G. *Investing in Hedge Funds*. Princeton: Bloomberg Press, 2005.

Nocera, Joseph. "The Quantitative, Data-Based, Risk-Massaging Road to Riches." *New York Times Magazine*, June 5, 2005.

O'Keefe, Brian. "It's the End of the World as We Know It, and He Feels Fine." *Fortune*, December 13, 2004.

Owen, James P. *The Prudent Investor's Guide to Hedge Funds: Profiting from Uncertainty and Volatility*. New York: John Wiley & Sons, 2000.

Ozzard, Janet. "The Money Man." *W*, September 1, 2000.

Pacelle, Mitchell. "Soros' Quantum Embraces Technology, Feels Squeeze." *Wall Street Journal*, Jan. 6, 2000.

Parikh, Chetan. "The Advent of Hedge Funds." *Capital Ideas*, November 17, 2004.

Paton, Maynard. "Beating the Bear Market." *The Motley Fool*, July 29, 2002.

Peltz, Lois. *The New Investment Superstars*. New York: John Wiley & Sons, Inc., 2001.

Reier, Sharon. "Once Heroic, Now Humbled, Global Hedge Funds Seek Safer Turf." *International Herald Tribune*, December 2, 2000.

Richards, Patsy. "Inflation: The Value of the Pound 1750–2001." *House of Commons Library Research Paper* 02/44, July 11, 2002.

Rosenblum, Irwin. *Up, Down, Up, Down, Up*. Philadelphia: Xlibris Corporation, October 2003.

Säfvenblad, Patrik. "Global Macro and Managed Futures Strategies." *RPM Risk and Portfolio Management AB*, October 1, 2003.

Samuelson, Robert J. "The Risk Manager." *Washington Post*, September 3, 2005.

Savitz, Eric J. "Game Theory." *Barron's*, March 1, 2004.

Skidelsky, Robert. "Commanding Heights," interview by, PBS, July 18, 2000.

Skidelsky, Robert. *John Maynard Keynes: Hopes Betrayed 1883–1920*. New York: Penguin Books, January 1994.

———. *John Maynard Keynes: Fighting for Freedom, 1937–1946*. New York: Penguin, 2003.

Soros, George. *The Alchemy of Finance: Reading the Mind of the Market*. New York: John Wiley & Sons, April, 1994.

———. *Letter to shareholders from George Soros, April 28, 2000*.

Strachman, Daniel A. *Julian Robertson: A Tiger in the Land of Bulls and Bears*. New York: John Wiley & Sons, August 20, 2004.

Sunday Business, London, England. "Soros Old Boys Ride Again." October 1, 2000.

Train, John. *Money Masters of Our Time*. New York: HarperCollins, 2003.

Vickers, Marcia, Debra Sparks, and Heather Timmons. "Hedge Funds Are Hot Again." *BusinessWeek*, February 26, 2001.

Wright, Ben. "Betting on the Bank." *The Business*, September 26, 2004.

Woodward, Bob. *Maestro: Greenspan's Fed and the American Boom*. New York: Simon & Schuster, 2000.

Zuckerman, Gregory. "Wall Street Avoiding Risk? Ha! Bets Are Getting Bigger." *Wall Street Journal*, March 12, 2003.

Zuckerman, Gregory, and Susanne Craig. "To Weather Rocky Period, Goldman Makes Riskier Bets—Investors Worry as Traders Make Brash Bets Using Firm's Own Cash." *Wall Street Journal*, December 17, 2002.

INDEX